D0539930

INSIGHT GUIDE

NAMIBIA

Discovery
CHANNEL

APA PUBLICATIONS
Part of the Langenscheidt Publishing Group

ABOUT THIS BOOK

Editorial

Project Editor
Richard Carmichael
Managing Editor
Lesley Gordon
Editorial Director
Brian Bell

Distribution

UK & Ireland
GeoCenter International Ltd
Meridian House, Churchill Way West
Basingstoke, Hants RG21 6YR
Fax: (44) 1256 817988

United States
Langenscheidt Publishers, Inc.
36–36 33rd Street 4th Floor
Long Island City, New York 11106
Fax: 1 (718) 784 0640

Australia
Universal Publishers
1 Waterloo Road
Macquarie Park, NSW 2113
Fax: (61) 2 9888 9074

New Zealand
Hema Maps New Zealand Ltd (HNZ)
Unit D, 24 Ra ORA Drive
East Tamaki, Auckland
Fax: (64) 9 273 6479

Worldwide
**Apa Publications GmbH & Co.
Verlag KG (Singapore branch)**
38 Joo Koon Road, Singapore 628990
Tel: (65) 6865 1600. Fax: (65) 6861 6438

Printing

Insight Print Services (Pte) Ltd
38 Joo Koon Road, Singapore 628990
Tel: (65) 6865-1600. Fax: (65) 6861-6438

©2006 Apa Publications GmbH & Co.
Verlag KG (Singapore branch)
All Rights Reserved
First Edition 1994
Second Edition 2000
Updated 2006

The first Insight Guide pioneered
the use of creative full-colour photography in travel guides in 1970.
Since then, we have expanded our
range to cater for our readers' need
not only for reliable information about
their chosen destination but also for
a real understanding of the culture
and workings of that destination.
Now, when the internet can supply
inexhaustible (but not always reliable)
facts, our books marry text and pictures to provide those much more
elusive qualities: knowledge and dis-
cernment. To achieve this, they rely
heavily on the authority of locally
based writers and photographers.

How to use this book

This fully updated edition of *Insight
Guide: Namibia* is carefully struc-
tured to convey an understanding of
Namibia and its culture as well as

to guide readers through its sights
and activities:

◆ The **Features** section, indicated
by a yellow bar at the top of each
page, covers the history and culture
of the country in a series of infor-
mative essays.
◆ The **Places** section, indicated by
a blue bar, is a complete guide to all
the sights and attractions worth visiting. Places of interest are coordinated by number with the maps.
◆ The **Travel Tips** listings, with an
orange bar, provide a point of reference for useful information on
travel, hotels, restaurants, shops
and much more. A handy index is on
the back flap, which is also a book-
mark.

The contributors

This new version of *Insight Guide:
Namibia* was updated by **Philip**

essay on Eating Out and Entertainment. **Claire Foottit**, a British travel journalist with a passion for southern Africa, contributed the features on The Safari Experience and Active Pursuits. **Michael Woods** expanded the wildlife section (The Predators, Grazers and Browsers, Namibia's Birds, Amphibians and Reptiles, and Plant Life). He also revised the chapters on Etosha National Park, The Caprivi, The Skeleton Coast, The Namib and Southern Namibia. London-based editor **Jeffery Pike** assisted with the editing of the Features section.

Dr Beatrice Sandelowsky, an archaeologist and curator of the Reheboth Museum, wrote about Namibia's early history. **Dr Hans Jenny** contributed the chapters on the German colonial period, while the task of chronicling the years before independence fell to **Eberhard Hoffman**, a former journalist who subsequently worked with Namibia's Department of Information. **Sean Cleary**, director of the Johannesburg-based Institute of Strategic Concepts, described "The Economic Balancing Act".

Amy Schoeman, **Brian Jones**, **Marie Osgood** and **Willie** and **Sandra Olivier** were each responsible for different chapters in the Places section, while **Sigrid Nilssen**, **Mary Seely**, **Professor Erik Holm**, **Wulf Haacke** and **Willie Gless** were among the large team of writers who contributed further material. **Fiona Cook** proofread this edition of *Insight Guide: Namibia* and **Caroline Wilding** indexed it.

This updated version was edited by **Richard Carmichael** at Insight Guides' London office.

Briggs, a travel writer based in Johannesburg, South Africa. The author of 10 travel guides to African destinations, including South Africa, Tanzania, Uganda, Kenya, Ethiopia, Malawi, Mozambique, Ghana and Senegal, Briggs contributes regularly to a number of leading wildlife periodicals in South Africa and in the UK.

The current edition builds on the excellent foundations created by the editors and writers of previous editions of the book, most notably **Melissa de Villiers**, who introduced several new chapters covering wildlife, active pursuits and entertainment for the visitor and **Johannes Haape**, editor of the original *Insight Guide: Namibia*.

Kurt Schlenther, a Windhoek-based tour operator and former lecturer on tourism and travel at the Polytechnic of Namibia, wrote the

Map Legend

▬ ▬ ▪ ▪	International Boundary
▬ ▬ ▬ ▬	Province Boundary
⊖	Border Crossing
▬ ▪ ▬	National Park/Reserve
✈ ✈	Airport: International/Regional
🚌	Bus Station
❶	Tourist Information
✉	Post Office
✝ ✝	Church/Ruins
✝	Monastery
☾	Mosque
✡	Synagogue
⌂ ⌂	Castle/Ruins
∴	Archaeological Site
∩	Cave
↑	Statue/Monument
★	Place of Interest

The main places of interest in the Places section are coordinated by number with a full-colour map (e.g. ❶), and a symbol at the top of every right-hand page tells you where to find the map.

INSIGHT GUIDE
Namibia

CONTENTS

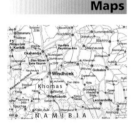

Aerial view of the
sand dunes in
NamibRand
Nature Reserve

Insight on ...

Information panels

Travel Tips

Places

UNITED COLOURS

Namibia survived the transition to independence with comparative ease. Why did it succeed where others failed?

What can explain the harmony that prevails in Namibia today, given that the population consists of at least 11 major ethnic groupings and an even greater variety of languages? The reason may be that although the Namibians have endured the worst of all worlds – a century of ruthless colonialism, decades of apartheid and a bitter struggle for independence – the majority of ordinary people nevertheless always stood together, working and suffering as one, mingling on farms and in small towns, sharing the bitter and the sweet.

The Europeans conquered Africa with their languages, religions, education, technology and agricultural know-how – with everything, in other words, that made Europe great. But a barrier of deep mistrust always remained between the indigenous inhabitants and their conquerors, with one side fearful of demographic numbers, the other of exploitation and deceit.

As one might expect, 23 years of occupation by apartheid South Africa singularly failed to resolve the situation – yet nevertheless the independence struggles of the 1970s and 1980s somehow managed to bring white and black Namibians together. It was as if they realised that by staying apart, they risked becoming one another's greatest enemies. Genuine mutual friendship, on the other hand, could guarantee peace and security for all.

Once this had been recognised, the barriers began to break down. White Namibians – originally Europeans, but long since people of Africa – managed to overcome their fears of the "black peril", and black and brown people their mistrust of the "white peril". The area in between was no longer uncharted territory.

In 1989, the powerful political organisation known as SWAPO took the decision to get involved in the independence negotiations (with most of its leaders in exile abroad, it had initially stayed aloof). Now at last the Namibians could get on with the complex process of drafting a new democratic constitution, and finally declaring themselves independent in 1994.

This very comprehensive process of reconciliation – or, rather mutual safeguarding – is ongoing. Today the country possesses a constitutional and political system based on sound democratic principles, with great regard for the origins, language, culture, religion and political convictions of all its peoples. A *bonhomie* has taken root among the people of Namibia; you'll find it readily communicated to visitors, too. ❏

PRECEDING PAGES: the haunting and evocative Skeleton Coast; the Namib is one of the oldest deserts on earth; life and death in the desert sands; under African skies. **LEFT:** like its lions (this one has grown used to the rigours of the desert), Namibia has managed to adapt to new conditions since independence in 1994.

Decisive Dates

12 million BC A hominid (an ape-like creature) known as *Otavipithecus namibiensis* occupies Namibia.

25,000 BC Namibia is inhabited by the San, hunter-gatherers who use stone tools, hunt with bows and arrows, and cover the rocks at Twyfelfontein (and elsewhere) with their art.

500 BC–AD 500 Khoi-Khoi (or Nama) migrants arrive from Botswana, bringing pastoral practices and metal-working skills. Namibia enters the Iron Age.

c900 A Khoi-San group of pastoralists, the Damara, establish themselves in northwestern Namibia.

DISCOVERY AND EXPLORATION

1485 The Portuguese explorer Diego Cão erects a stone cross at Cape Cross on the Skeleton Coast.

1488 Bartholomeu Diaz, following in Cão's footsteps, puts up a second cross at Lüderitz Bay. For the next three centuries, apart from exploration from the San and some overland expeditions in the south, the country remains largely uncharted by Europeans.

1500s The Herero (Bantu migrants from East Africa) arrive in Namibia, settling in the Kaokoveld.

Late 1700s American, British and French whalers begin to make use of the harbours at Walvis Bay and Lüderitz.

1802 Establishment of the London Mission Society along the Orange River, and the beginnings of intense military activity among Namibia's indigenous peoples.

1820s Khoi-San groups such as the Oorlam Nama and the Basters migrate from the Cape into Namibia.

1862–70 The Nama-Herero wars.

1876 South African Boers trek away from the Cape Colony and cross northeastern Namibia.

THE COLONIAL ERA

1878 Britain – who also has control over the Cape colony – annexes the port of Walvis Bay.

1884 Germany claims Namibia as a colony (known as German South West Africa) at the Congress of Berlin. Walvis Bay remains British.

1889 German troops arrive and clear the indigenous Namibians off much of their land.

1890s German settlers take over the land for farming.

1904–06 Widespread Herero and Nama uprisings against German colonial rule, in which over 80,000 people are killed. The indigenous peoples are defeated and their lands systematically expropriated by the colonial administration.

1915 During World War I, South Africa invades Namibia and forces the Germans to surrender. The country is placed under South African military rule.

1920 Under League of Nations mandate, Namibia is to be administered by South Africa on behalf of Britain.

1922 South Africa establishes "reserves" for black Namibians and distributes more land to South African and German settlers. Uprisings by Namibians are violently crushed.

1939 World War II is declared. South African troops are sent to Namibia to prevent pro-Nazi German coup. Many black Namibians serve with the South African forces fighting Nazism.

1946 South Africa refuses to hand over its mandate to the United Nations, claiming it does not recognise the UN as the successor to the League of Nations.

TOWARDS INDEPENDENCE

1960 The South West Africa People's Organisation (SWAPO) is founded under leadership of Sam Nujoma.

1961 Legal action begins at the International Court of Justice to end South Africa's mandate over Namibia.

1964 South Africa consolidates its apartheid policies in Namibia. The Odendaal Commission recommends that 10 ethnic "homelands" are established.

1966 The International Court of Justice refuses to issue a judgement on Namibia. SWAPO undertakes its first military action, thus launching the 'liberation war'. The UN finally ends South Africa's mandate, but South Africa refuses to withdraw.

1967 The UN Council for Namibia (UNCN) is established to administer the country until independence. South Africa refuses UNCN access to Namibia.

1971 The International Court of Justice declares that South Africa's presence in Namibia is illegal.

1973 The UN recognises SWAPO as the "sole authentic representation of the Namibian people".

1975 Angola grants SWAPO new military bases.

1976 UN Security Council adopts Resolution 385 calling for elections in Namibia organised by the UN.

1977 South Africa refuses to allow implementation of Resolution 385. The West forms a "Contact Group" on Namibia to negotiate with South Africa as an alternative to sanctions. South Africa appoints an Administrator General for Namibia and re-annexes Walvis Bay.

1978 Attack by the South African Defence Force (SADF) kills 800 Namibian refugees in a raid on Kassinga in Angola. Western proposals for elections in Namibia accepted by SWAPO and adopted by the UN as Resolution 435. South Africa rejects election proposals and refuses to allow Resolution 435 to be implemented.

1979–80 South Africa sets up an "internal government" in Namibia.

MODERN NAMIBIA

1981 Ronald Reagan's new administration in the US makes the implementation of Resolution 435 conditional upon Cubans leaving Angola.

1983 Namibia's "internal government" collapses. The South African Administrator General resumes direct rule. A Multi-Party Conference (MPC) meets in Namibia to prepare for the new South African-supported "internal government".

1984 South Africa and SWAPO meet in Lusaka and Cape Verde. South Africa's insistence on "Cuban Linkage" finally undermines any progress.

1985 The MPC's internal government, the "Transitional Government of National Unity", is installed in Windhoek. The UN's Resolution 566 condemns South Africa as a result. The SADF increases its military involvement in Angola.

1987 UN Resolution 601 calls for implementation of Resolution 435. Heavy fighting involving the SADF continues in Angola.

1988 US-mediated negotiations take place between Angola, South Africa and Cuba about South African withdrawal from Angola and Namibia and the imple-

mentation of Resolution 435. SWAPO is excluded from the talks. No settlement is reached.

1989 A formal cessation of hostilities is declared on 1 April. In November, elections to the Constituent Assembly (which will draft the country's first constitution) are held, supervised by UNTAG. SWAPO win 57 percent of the vote and 41 of the 72 seats.

1990 On 21 March the Namibian flag replaces South Africa's; independence is finally won.

1994 Walvis Bay is ceded to Namibia on 28 February. The general elections see SWAPO returned to power.

1995–99 Peace and stability mean that a fledgling tourist industry develops in Namibia.

2000 Civil war continues in Angola. Nujoma allows

Angolan government troops to attack rebel forces from Namibian soil, bringing reprisals by Angolan guerillas.

2002 New prime minister, Theo-Ben Gurirab, says land reform is a priority. Ceasefire in Angola encourages economic development in Northern Namibia.

2004 New road bridge across Zambezi river to Zambia gives hope for increase in trade. Germany makes an official apology to the Herero people for the killings of the colonial era but rules out compensation.

2005 Hifikepunye Pohamba (SWAPO) wins presidential elections and begins a land-reform programme. Mass graves are found near a former South African military base in the north.

2006 The birth of Angelina Jolie and Brad Pitt's baby in Swakopmund in May is a boon to Namibian tourism. ❑

PRECEDING PAGES: open-air gallery at Twyfelfontein, one of the richest rock art sites in the world.

LEFT: chiselling for evidence – Namibia has rich pickings for palaeontologists.

RIGHT: young Namibian proudly bearing instructions for first-time voters in the historic 1990 elections.

BEGINNINGS

Palaeontologists looking for evidence of the origins of modern man
have found much to interest them in Namibia's ancient sites

Scientists now agree with some confidence that Africa was indeed the cradle of mankind. Palaeontological evidence indicates that it was here, on the African continent, that the earliest known varieties of human beings emerged, before migrating northwards into Europe and Asia. Physical anthropologists call them hominids, meaning that they were more than apes but less than humans. Different types of hominid had different characteristics. The *Australopithecus* (an "upright-walking small-brained creature") co-existed in southern Africa with the more sophisticated *Homo habilis* for more than a million years before finally biting the dust – surely a worthy theme for a high-tech, big-budget movie.

In 1991, a thrilling discovery was made by an American-French team of palaeontologists in the Otavi Mountains to the north of Windhoek. The scientists found the fossilised jawbone of an anthropoid from the Middle Miocene period – that is, dating back between 12 and 15 million years. The first discovery of its kind south of Kenya, it was named *Otavipithecus namibiensis*, or Otjiseva Man.

Relics of early man

Remnants of our own direct ancestor, *Homo sapiens*, have been found widely distributed throughout southern Africa. African variants of *Homo sapiens* display genetic markers that are called Negroid – as opposed to the Mongoloid and Caucasoid variants found elsewhere. Crudely stated, this implies that black people have been living in southern Africa for about 100,000 years.

Within the Negroid genetic constellation, however, different groups developed in relative isolation from each other. One sub-group which we particularly need to notice must have lived in relative isolation in the southwestern corner of the continent for about 40,000 years. These were the so-called Khoisan peoples, who once inhabited substantial parts of what is now Namibia, South Africa and Botswana.

Hand axes, cleavers, pebble choppers and other tools dating from the Early and Middle Stone Age (between 25,000 to 27,000 years ago) have been found at sites throughout the territory – even in the heart of the Namib

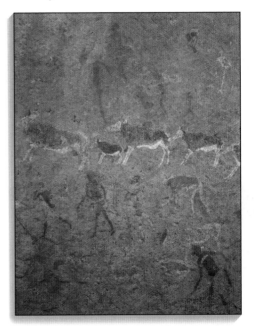

Desert, which indicate that major climatic changes must have occurred there in the not too distant past. Most of the relics have been found along seasonal riverbeds and coastline, and around natural springs. One interesting find was in present-day Windhoek, which tells us that these Early and Middle Stone Age people were hunting elephant and other big game in what is now the heart of the capital.

It's estimated that small bands of these hunter-gatherers wandered from one hunting ground to another, following the seasonal migrations of game. Painted and engraved stone slabs depicting their domestic life and religious rites have been found in abundance all over Namibia –

LEFT: modern San hunter tapping underground water.
RIGHT: the "White Lady" rock frieze near Twyfelfontein.

most significantly in Damaraland, and in the Huns mountains to the south of the country.

The Khoisan were shorter and had lighter-coloured skin than most other Africans, their language contained clicking sounds and other unusual consonants, and they knew nothing of agriculture or iron-working.

Then, about 2,600 years ago, one group of Khoisan living in northern Botswana were initiated into cattle-keeping by other Africans. Being herders rather than hunters, they multi-

A QUESTION OF NAMES

The hunter-gather tribes each had their own names but were referred to collectively as 'San' or 'Bushmen'. Neither term is satisfactory but, in lieu of an alternative, both are still used.

and South Africa. But during the apartheid era, this word "Bantu" was so abused by the South African administration in Namibia that it is no longer socially acceptable there, in any context.

Settling in the northeast (the present-day Caprivi and Kavango regions), the north-central (Ovamboland) and the northwest (Kaokoland), these Africans brought with them pastoral practices as well as pottery and metal-working skills – but as they moved in, the indigenous San groupings were pushed steadily southwards.

The apartheid picture

Yet a very different picture of the origins of Namibia's peoples was painted during South Africa's long occupation of Namibia in the 20th century. Apartheid theorists were fond of describing the southwestern corner of the African continent as an empty land, peopled solely by immigrants. Apartheid maps showed fat black arrows depicting waves of Africans migrating into the region from the far north, while much thinner white arrows discreetly indicated the European incursions from the south. The intention, of course, was to give the impression that Namibians both white and black, equally, were intruders of alien origin, and that the white minority had the same moral right to the land as the black majority.

For similar reasons, apartheid theorists went to great lengths to emphasise what they saw as the cultural differences between different kinds of Africans. Black Africans were alleged to belong to "tribes" that were culturally mono-lithic and mutually incompatible. These could not be trusted to live in peace, and had to be sharply segregated from each other. Apartheid theory also sought to disaggregate this African majority into much smaller components so that the white minority no longer seemed like a white minority, but more like one tribe among many other tribes.

Such theories are rarely met within Namibia today, but unfortunately the underlying stereotypes still persist to a surprising degree. ❑

plied and dispersed very rapidly. They called themselves *Khoikhoi* – "men of men" – or Nama people, and they called the remaining hunter-gatherers *San*.

Migrations from the north

By the beginning of the 9th century, groups of Bantu-speaking people from central Africa started migrating into Namibia. Taller, darker-skinned and more technologically sophisticated than the Khoisan-speaking peoples, they spoke languages that clearly indicate their cultural links with the rest of Sub-Saharan Africa. Internationally, these are known as Bantu languages, a perfectly respectable term outside Namibia

LEFT: San (Bushmen) hunter with warthog trophy.
RIGHT: Namibia's earliest settlers had to be tough to survive the country's arid climate and conditions.

EARLY EXPLORERS

*Although the Portuguese first set foot on Namibian soil as far back as 1486,
nearly four centuries were to pass before European expansionism really took root*

The first European to step onto Namibian soil was the Portuguese explorer Diego Cão, who reached the Skeleton Coast in 1486 and put up a stone cross at Cape Cross to prove it. He was followed in 1488 by another explorer, his fellow-countryman Bartholomeu Diaz, who erected his own cross at Angra

ORIGINAL MAP
OF
GREAT NAMAQUALAND
AND
DAMARALAND

Pequena (which is now known as Lüderitz).

Prior to this, Namibia's forbidding climate and inhospitable terrain had always shielded the land from European expansionism. Only in the 15th century, as trade with the East took off, did European ships begin to search for a new sea route to India via the Cape of Good Hope – which meant sailing along the Namibian coast as well.

Yet for both explorers and traders, the very notion of settling on a coastline that offered neither food nor water for sustenance – nor slaves and ivory for trade – was a complete waste of time. As the captain of a passing Dutch vessel, the *Bode*, noted at the time: "Here for

nothing in the world is there even the smallest gain for our masters... there is only sand, rock, and storm."

Towards the end of the 18th century, however, the ports of Lüderitz and Walvis Bay began to be visited more frequently by whalers and seal-catchers from France, Britain and America, and by passing Indian trade. The areas around these harbours, meanwhile, began to be harvested for guano.

The Oorlam invasions

With war on the horizon in Europe, in 1793 the Dutch government claimed Walvis Bay (the only decent deepwater port along the coast) and Angra Pequena, as well as Halifax Island off the coast. When the British annexed the Cape Colony two years later they, too, hoisted their flag along the Namibian shore – although it was not until 1878 that they annexed Walvis Bay and its environs (approximately 1,165 square km/450 square miles) for themselves as well.

Even at this stage, however, scarcely anything was known about the Namibian interior, although the discovery of the Orange River in 1760 did open up the territory somewhat to traders, hunters and missionaries.

At the turn of the 18th century, southern Namibia was thrown into something of a turmoil with the arrival of large numbers of Oorlam people, roving bands of dispossessed Khoisan fleeing Dutch persecution in the Cape. Although the Oorlams were of the same origins as the Nama pastoralists already settled in southern Namibia (and spoke a similar language), many had guns and horses, giving them both mobility and a technological edge. Some were outlaws, while others had broken away from scattered Nama settlements en route to take their chances with the Oorlams as they traded, thieved and hunted their way north.

Thanks to their commando-style military structures, which they'd copied from the Boer frontiersmen, the South Africans quickly subdued the indigenous Namibians and their bows and arrows. Soon the Oorlams – led by a paramount chief named Jonker Afrikaner – had subjugated the Namas and Damaras in the south and reduced the Herero clans in the east and centre-north to mere vassal status.

Nevertheless, the locals fought back. Ongoing skirmishes amounting almost to low-level warfare raged throughout the region for the next 70 years, as Oorlam commandos continued to raid the cattle of local clans, and pillage their settlements. The inexhaustible demand for commodities to trade for arms also led to the wholesale slaughter of game stocks, especially elephant and ostriches.

Traders and missionaries

Temporary calm was brought to this unhappy situation in 1840, when Jonker Afrikaner struck a peace deal with Paramount Chief Oaseb of the Nama. Southern Namibia was effectively split between the Nama and a range of Oorlam groups, while the Oorlams obtained the rights to the land between the Swakop and the Kuiseb rivers in the centre of the country. Jonker Afrikaner was also given rights over the people living north of the Kuiseb. In practice, this meant that the Oorlams formed a buffer zone between the Nama in the south, and the Hereros further north in Kaokoland – although the latter had been steadily moving south themselves ever since the middle of the 18th century.

Nonetheless, the disruption of indigenous community life continued, thanks to the reduction of cattle stock through warfare and drought and the destruction of water reserves. The resulting discontent deepened opposition to Jonker Afrikaner's rule, and forged a broad alliance between Hereros, rival Nama clans, traders and missionaries. Yet Afrikaner's central Namibian 'empire' continued even after his death in 1861, when his eldest son and heir, Christian, inherited the reins of power,

By this time, traders and hunters on the lookout for valuable commodities such as ostrich feathers and ivory had begun venturing deep into the Namibian interior. One of the most important figures was a certain Charles John

Andersson, who – with the help of a band of hunters acting as a sort of armed guard in this lawless territory – established a trading post at Otjimbingwe and started to explore new trade routes further north and east. It was his men who in 1863 shot and killed Christian Afrikaner, who had rashly mounted a raid on Otjimbingwe.

In the traders' wake came various missionaries – in particular the London Mission Society, Wesleyan Methodists, and Rhenish and Finnish Lutherans – who estab-

lished small stations throughout the south and central regions. They were able to extend their influence reasonably easily during the 1870s, a relatively calm decade thanks to a treaty signed in 1870 by the Herero chief, Kamherero and Christian's successor, Jan Jonker Afrikaner. But by the 1880s fighting had once again broken out between the various Nama groups, the Hereros and the Basters – new arrivals from the Cape who had settled in the Reheboth area. All these groups had by now also started to trade extensively with the Europeans.

It was into this cauldron – pre-colonised by European technology and firepower, as well as Christianity – that Germany now stepped. ❑

> **SOUTHERN STRIFE**
>
> Namibia's northernmost peoples – the Ovambo and the Kavango – remained relatively isolated from the troubles down south during the Oorlam invasions.

LEFT: this map – dated 1894 – shows just how uncharted the Namibian territory still was.
RIGHT: the mighty Herero chief, Maherero.

ENTER THE GERMANS

Having acquired Namibia relatively late in the "Scramble for Africa", Germany
set about subduing the Namibians with a series of ruthless military campaigns

The Germans were relative latecomers to the great "Scramble for Africa" which in the late 19th century found the British, the French, the Portuguese and the Belgians racing to carve up the continent between them. Although during the 1870s the German missionaries stationed in Namibia sent repeated requests to their government for military backup to help establish law and order in the war-torn southern and central regions, their appeals met with little response; a colonial policy was at this stage simply not part of Germany's overall plan.

It was only in 1884 – after much internal wrangling and debate – that the German government under Chancellor Otto van Bismarck decided to abandon its anti-colonial policy and enter the fray. As far as Namibia was concerned, colonisation was greatly aided by an enterprising trader from Bremen called Adolf Lüderitz, who had the previous year bought several coastal territories (including the port of Angra Pequena) from a local Nama chieftain. At the time of the sale, he had asked for German protection, and in 1884 he got it. In April of that year, two German gunboats arrived in Angra Pequena – now known as Lüderitz – and the German flag was officially raised over Namibian soil.

A protectorate proclaimed

Although Bismarck proclaimed the Lüderitz area a protectorate of the German Reich on 24 April 1884, the purchase was not without its negative aspects. This was a desert region, after all, and its economic outlook looked bleak.

It was a gamble that paid off, however, for the dunes of the Namib Desert concealed a fortune. Diamonds were discovered in the region some 24 years later, although Lüderitz himself was destined never to reap any rewards

PRECEDING PAGES: camels were more practical than horses for some *Schutztruppe* divisions.
LEFT: Major Theodor von Leutwein.
RIGHT: Adolf Lüderitz, trader and pioneer.

from this windfall; his life ended tragically early in a mysterious accident at sea. In October 1886 he embarked on an expedition overland from Angra Pequena south to the Orange River, and back up the coast again by boat. On 22 October, he and his crew set off from South Africa's Alexander Bay bound for Angra

Pequena – but the vessel never reached its destination, and the entire crew perished.

Before the discovery of the Namib diamond fields, however, Bismarck planned to turn over this new overseas territory to private investors. As a result, only three officials were sent out to administer the brand-new colony of South West Africa. With the flourishing little trading post of Otjimbingwe for a base, the colonial staff's efficiency was proportional to its size; although the Imperial Commissioner Dr Heinrich Göring managed to get the powerful Herero chief Maharero to sign a "protection treaty" with Germany, he failed to build any sort of relationship with the equally powerful

Witbooi Namas, who occupied a large tranche of land south of Windhoek. He also failed utterly in his attempts to impose a prohibition on the locals' importation of weapons and ammunition. As a result, unrest between the indigenous clans continued to rage; from time to time, the Commissioner was even compelled to seek shelter from them in the British enclave of Walvis Bay.

A time of consolidation

By 1889, Berlin was forced to recognise that an absentee policy in Namibia was doomed to failure. In an attempt to develop the colony's

infrastructure, the first 21 German soldiers (*Schutztruppe*) were sent out to Namibia that same year and ordered to erect a fortress at Windhoek; two years later, a makeshift landing stage was set up in Swakopmund. In the wake of the soldiers came the first trickle of settlers to Windhoek.

Then, on 1 January 1894, a man who was to decisively shape Namibia's destiny stepped ashore at Swakopmund. Not only did Major Theodor von Leutwein succeed in forming a 10-year alliance with the rebellious Nama chief Hendrik Witbooi, along with numerous smaller Baster and Nama groupings – he also conducted intensive negotiations with the Herero's paramount chief, Samuel Maharero. As a result of von Leutwein's diplomacy, a truce was, for a time, effected between the Hereros and their old enemies, the Nama.

In the southern and central regions, the turn of the 19th century saw a steady dwindling of power on the part of the indigenous peoples in favour of the colonial government. Newly arrived settlers, for example, bought up land from both the Hereros and the Nama, who for their part bought large amounts of Western goods on credit and became heavily indebted.

This was not an auspicious situation for a lengthy peace, however diplomatically and strategically von Leutwein tried to proceed, and inevitably, tensions mounted; on 12 January 1904, Maherero ordered a Herero uprising against the German settlers which took the colonial forces completely by surprise. No fewer than 123 settlers were killed on their farms with *kirries* (wooden clubs); their homes were plundered and burned, their cattle driven away. Only women and children were spared. As a result, reinforcements were urgently summoned from Berlin.

The Hereros defeated

With German opinion at home demanding that the government "bring the rebels to their senses", Berlin's response was to replace von Leutwein with a certain General Lothar von Trotha, who had already served in East Africa and garnered a reputation for ruthlessness. With him came an entire division of reinforcement troops, including heavy artillery.

It did not take long to break the Herero's resistance, although they fought hard. By the beginning of August 1904, their warriors –

A SERIOUS LACK OF RESOURCES

Major von Lutwein's efforts to establish some sort of order over the fledgling colony were seriously hampered by a lack of resources. A mere four companies and one artillery battalion were simply not enough to make the German presence felt in this enormous territory – particularly in the northernmost regions of Kaokoland, Ovamboland and the Okavango. Kurt Schwabe, a Schutztruppe member who later published his memoirs, described the situation thus: "The German government had for years no relation to the Ovambo, who were, on the map, German vassals, but who were neither themselves aware of this fact, nor would have acknowledged it if they had known it."

along with their wives, children and cattle – had been pushed back and confined to a stronghold at Waterberg. By 11 August, the tide had turned in the Germans' favour, although not decisively; they lacked the strength to force the enemy's complete capitulation. As a result, following this victory, von Trotha issued his notorious "extermination order", which forced thousands of the surviving Hereros to flee the country. Most headed east into the Omaheke sandveld and from there to Botswana, burning the bush behind them as they went.

Von Trotha's implacable "all-or-nothing" campaign against the Hereros had succeeded –

An economic flurry

The six years of German rule before World War I saw the colony thrive. Not only was there an influx of settlers – who were granted large tranches of the most fertile land – but the railway system was expanded and the towns grew. In 1908, a railway inspector named August Stauch discovered one of the world's richest diamond deposits in the Namib, which formed the basis for an economic boom in the south. Meanwhile, the development of the Tsumeb mines – yielding copper, zinc and lead – brought about prosperity in the north.

Black Namibians, on the other hand, were

although it was heavily criticised by the British, in particular, who called it genocide. It also spurred the Nama people into outright revolt; for the next three years, most of the local clans joined forces to wage what was in effect a guerilla war against the *Schutztruppe* from their strongholds in the barren Kalahari. In 1907, however, the powerful Nama leader Hendrik Witbooi was killed, and after that the remaining leaders sued for peace. Namibia was finally under colonial control.

LEFT: at the turn of the 19th century, German settlers to Namibia were rewarded with the most fertile land. **ABOVE:** early settlers arrive.

increasingly restricted to "native areas" – usually infertile land that was difficult to farm – and exploited as a source of cheap labour.

By this time, the country's borders had been more clearly defined in a series of territorial deals struck by the colonial powers. In 1890, for example, Britain ceded South West Africa a long, emaciated corridor of land, giving it access to the Zambezi. It was named the Caprivi Strip, after the German chancellor.

All this changed with the outbreak of war in 1914. South Africa entered the war on the side of the Allies, attacking German troops with overwhelming force; the Germans surrendered at Khorab near Otavi on 9 July 1915. ❏

A GLITTERING PRIZE BENEATH THE SANDS

Thanks to its astonishing wealth of semi-precious stones, Namibia's a happy hunting ground for mineralogists and souvenir-hunters alike

Not only is Namibia home to one of the richest alluvial diamond fields in the world, it's also endowed with large quantities of high-grade semi-precious stones. The first **topaz** was discovered at the end of the 19th century near Spitzkoppe in northwestern Namibia, an area rich in the translucent, brilliant crystals known as silver topaz; there have been record finds here of crystals up to 15 cm (6 inches) long and 12 cm (5 inches) wide. The mineral **beryl** also occurs in abundance, from the blue variety (aquamarine) to the pink beryl (morganite) and the yellow, known as heliodor. The much-prized green beryl, however – more commonly known as emerald – doesn't occur in Namibia. Most valuable of all, though, is the **tourmaline**, mined in numerous small quarries around Karibib, Usakos and the Spitzkoppe. This crystal often has a red core with a green "skin"; cut into slices and then polished, it is easy to see how it came by its nickname of "watermelon tourmaline".

UNIQUE MINERALS

Yet it is the country's exceptional ore deposits containing rare and often unique minerals which are of most interest to mineralogists. The Ysterpütz farm in the southerly Karasburg district, for example, is home to substantial deposits of the rare gemstone known as **'blue lace' agate**. **Pollucite**, an extremely rare caesium mineral, is mined south of Karibib. The best-known deposit of all, however, is in the Tsumeb Mine in the north-central region, where the Tsumeb Corporation mines a pipe which has produced some 217 different minerals and gemstones – 40 of which are unique to Namibia.

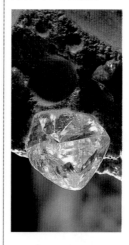

▷ **LOVELY MANORS**
Built in grand Art Nouveau style by a German diamond magnate, Goerke House is one of several diamond-rush houses to grace the little coastal town of Lüderitz

△ **DIAMOND GEYSERS**
Namibia's diamonds are found in deposits or 'pipes' of volcanic material called kimberlite, which were forced up to the earth's surface in ancient eruptions.

◁ **ROCK ART**
Numerous varieties of quartz are found in Namibia. This chunk contains malachite, which is often carved into ornaments and jewellery.

▽ **RICH PICKINGS**
Worker vacuuming the exposed bedrock for diamonds in southern Namibia's *Sperrgebiet* (Forbidden Territory) area.

NAMIBIA'S DIAMOND RUSH

In 1908 a mixed-race worker called Zacharias Lewala – part of a team hired to clear desert sand off the newly built railway line near Grasplatz – found a small, unusual stone stuck to his oiled shovel. Lewala turned the crystal over to his boss, German railway inspector August Stauch, who, fortunately for him if not for Lewala, had already applied for a prospector's claim for "minerals of all kinds" – just in case. The stone turned out to be a diamond, precipitating a major case of diamond fever in German South West Africa. Sailors left their ships, salesmen their shops, men their wives – all to try their luck in the Namib sands. The town of Lüderitz expanded rapidly. Fine stone houses designed in the German Art Nouveau style replaced the village's corrugated-iron huts. A school and electricity plant were built, and streetlights installed. Churches sprang up. A stock exchange was founded. After the First World War, the mining rights went to the powerful mining-house, the Anglo-American Corporation, and a new company was formed: the Consolidated Diamond Mines, known today as NAMDEB.

▽ NO TRESPASSERS
Aerial view of the diamond-mining area known as Sperrgebiet, on the Skeleton Coast. Strict security measures are enforced here.

△ STONE ROSES
Around 300 tons of rose quartz is produced in Namibia every year, although the quality varies considerably.

▷ SHINING EXAMPLE
Beautifully cut pieces like this aquamarine can be found on the local jewellery market, especially in Windhoek.

THE PATH TO INDEPENDENCE

It would take more than 70 years of bitter struggle to transform Namibia

from colonial protectorate to mandate and, finally, to independent state

Imperial Germany's role as a colonial power on the international stage was short-lived. German South West Africa came to an end when the government surrendered to the South Africans at Khorab in 1915. The territory was placed under military rule for the duration of World War I.

Louis Botha, the South African premier and commander-in-chief of the Union troops, could make no answer to the capitulating Imperial governor, Dr Theodor Seitz, when the latter said that South West Africa's fate would not be determined there, but by the course of the war in Europe. History vindicated Seitz's prophecy. The Treaty of Versailles, signed on 26 June 1919, Germany had to renounce all its colonial holdings abroad.

"The German colonies in the Pacific and Africa are inhabited by barbarians," wrote South Africa's prime minister Jan Christiaan Smuts in 1918. "They are incapable of ruling themselves, and it would furthermore be impractical to attempt to implement the idea of self-government in the European sense." Smuts's suggestion was that South West Africa should be incorporated into South Africa – although in the end the victorious Allies agreed to restrict themselves to an administrative and supervisory role as far as Germany's former colonies were concerned.

As a result, South Africa was awarded responsibility for the country, but only as a League of Nations "trust territory". Nevertheless, this meant that, for the following 75 years, Pretoria's influence would extend all the way north as far as the southern border of Angola.

A new administration

In a show of strength by South Africa, a number of German "undesirables" (officials, defence force personnel and police) were turfed out of South West Africa immediately after the

LEFT: the road to independence was long and hard.
RIGHT: black aspirations were soundly dashed by the new South African administration.

Armistice on 11 November 1918. Some 1,400 nationals returned to Germany voluntarily, while 6,374 were deported – nearly half of the territory's German population. The German diamond concession was given to Consolidated Diamond Mines, which later became the world-famous De Beers.

The mandate government

The agreement formulated by the Allies, according to which South West Africa was made an "integral part" of South Africa, was formally ratified by the League of Nations on 17 December 1920. The ambiguities implied by this phrase "integral part" were to prove a major stumbling block in the administration of the territory over the next few decades; a vital definition was left too open to interpretation.

South Africa's responsibilities were outlined in this sentence: "The mandatory shall promote to the utmost the material and moral well-being and the social progress of the inhabitants of the territory subject to the present mandate." In the years that followed, the formulation became more specific: the territory should, under the protection of South Africa, be guided towards independence.

Beyond merely administering the country, the South African government concerned itself with continuing the white-settlement policy which had been initiated by the previous German administration. In a clear bid to increase the Boer population, it gradually parcelled out more and more of the land to "poor white" settler families from South Africa, rather than to Germans. Between 1915 and 1920, 6 million hectares (15 million acres) of land were given to South Africans. In the years 1928–29, another large chunk of the territory was distributed during the repopulation of Boers who had been living in Angola, while the third, and last, phase of white settlement occurred between 1950 and 1954.

A last stand

The indigenous population's hopes that colonial land division and allotment would be revised after the defeat of the Germans were, therefore, soundly dashed. Nonetheless, various groups were determined to fight for their land. Chief Mandume, for example, took a

stand against British-South African territorial demands in Ovamboland.

The frustrated hopes concerning the transfer of power in Windhoek, combined with South Africa's interference in the line of succession of chiefs among one of the most powerful Nama groupings, the Bondelswarts, gave rise to a major Nama uprising against the South African administration in 1922.

Unfortunately, whether resistance came from Chief Jacobus Christiaan, who lost 64 warriors, or the Rehoboth Basters, who had hoped for more autonomy after the South African takeover, the Nama had no chance against an enemy that was militarily far superior. Even the battle-hardened Bondels, for example, who had long held their own in guerrilla fighting against the German colonial forces prior to World War I, now found themselves fighting an adversary which, having been through similar experiences in the Boer War, was well-versed in those very same tactics.

The South African government responded by sending in wave upon wave of fresh troops. Retribution for the unrest was heavy; the Basters lost even the right to appoint their own "kaptein", or leader. Instead, they now had to submit to the authority of a white magistrate, a situation which continued until 1976.

beyond the so-called Red Line – an area which the Germans had tended to avoid. The extreme northern and Kalahari border regions to the east were, however, largely unaffected.

Yet despite their efforts to grab control of as much land in the territory as possible, the South Africans invested very little in Namibia's infrastructure. An exception was the construction of several railway lines – from Swakopmund to Walvis Bay, from Otjiwango to Outjo and from Karasburg to Upington in South Africa, as well as from Windhoek to Gobabis. The continent's very first automatic telephone exchange was installed in Windhoek in 1929.

Divide and Rule

Continuing the policies of the German administration that preceded it, the South African mandatory government consistently interfered in the succession and appointment of local chiefs – with varying degrees of success. Its main tactic was to bring the black population under control by installing lackey chiefs, ready to do its bidding. In this way South Africa's area of influence was gradually extended into Ovamboland and the northern territories lying

LEFT: mine workers and supervisor in cheerful mood.
ABOVE: passing on medical advice (with the aid of a translator) to workers in the Caprivi area.

The isolated, time-warped flavour of Namibia at this time is well expressed by the missionary Dr Heinrich Vedder in the foreword to his book *Old South West Africa* (1934): "This book should only be read by people who love South West Africa; for it contains many things which are of lesser importance in comparison to the major world events of this period, things which could only be of value to someone who has already become attuned to our sunny country."

But in the end, it was these "major world events" that were to determine Namibia's fate – affecting as they did the political consciousness of the white settlers. Essentially, the settlers were divided into two camps, differentiated by language: Afrikaans-speakers loyal to the South African Union advocated a complete union with South Africa; the majority of German-speakers were, by contrast, largely faithful to the Geneva Mandate. It was their hope that, once Germany had recovered its former strength, it would bring a swift end to South Africa's administration of Namibia and usher in a new age of independence for the territory.

The war years

In the 1930s, National Socialist propaganda and agitation served to exacerbate these divisions. The South African government empowered the

territorial administration to forbid foreigners (such as German immigrants) the right to join political organisations – but there was a large loophole: many German-speakers had become naturalised citizens, or carried two passports. The *Deutscher Bund* (German Union) and *Die Verenigde Nasional Suidwes Party* (United National South West Party, VNSWP) were the major political forces of the time, one in favour of the mandate, the other for annexation to South Africa.

The outbreak of World War II put an end to these disputes. In most cases, speaking fluent German was sufficient grounds for the South African officials to detain men of army age in internment camps, regardless of whether they were naturalised British-South African subjects, had dual German-South African citizenship, or were recent immigrants.

During the war years, the women tended the farms. As had been the case in World War I, German property and possessions were placed under the jurisdiction of a "Custodian for Enemy Property". The fate of Germans and their families interned in the South African prison camps of Andalusia and Baviaanspoort remained uncertain until long after the outbreak of peace.

Dr Malan and his National Party's (NP) narrow victory in South Africa in May 1948 put a final stop to all actions directed against South West Germans, even to the threat of deportation, and the last detainees were allowed to go back home to their farms. Until the mid-1970s, South West Germans thanked the NP by adhering to it with unswerving loyalty, although Pretoria's racial policies did not always meet with their approval.

Defying the United Nations

In 1947, South Africa formally announced to the United Nations its intention to incorporate Namibia as a fifth province, arguing that local chiefs had supported the annexation in a communal vote. However, they played down the dissenting voices of many Herero and Nama chiefs, as well as those of the African National Congress (ANC) and South Africa's Communist Party, both of which had always demanded that the UN provide for an honest administration for South West Africa, as specified by the UN General Assembly.

The UN rejected the plan, however, and from that moment on, South Africa's guardianship of the territory was increasingly called into question. Over the next 21 years, the General Assembly and Security Council convened the International Court of Justice in The Hague at least six times in reference to South West Africa. However, a binding, clear statement of the territory's international status, as well as a definition of the limits of South Africa's responsibility, remained lacking.

South Africa chose to ignore the UN's legal pressure; from 1948, for example, the country simply ceased to file the annual reports it was supposed to present on its "trust territory".

The great wave of African independence at

the end of the 1950s and beginning of the 1960s swept over the continent without touching Namibia, although it left clear traces behind in the minds of the country's black population. Yet where black Namibians managed to organise themselves to protest against their lack of political and civil rights, they were met with heavy-handed repression, as in the events of December 1959 when 13 black demonstrators in Windhoek were felled by club-wielding police. The victims had been protesting against their forced resettlement to the new blacks-only township of Katutura.

According to South Africa's policy of

the South African Senate. During all this time, only a few black Namibian nationalists – such as Mburumba Kerina and Fanuel Kozonguizi – managed to get their voices heard by the United Nations Committee on South West Africa.

However, this era did see the founding of the Ovamboland People's Organisation (OPO), which led to the founding of the South West Africa People's Organisation (SWAPO) in 1960. Although SWAPO initially concerned itself only with labour-related issues, it was increasingly identified as an independence and liberation movement – all the more so after 1966, when

apartheid, the black population within the territory of the mandate was nominally permitted to regulate its own affairs. However, all the crucial issues – such as international relations – were left up to the government in Pretoria and the Cape Town Parliament.

An uphill struggle

Between 1949 and 1977, the white population of the mandated area was represented by six delegates in Parliament and four members in

LEFT: South African transport workers.
ABOVE: SWAPO leader Sam Nujoma in combat gear. The organisation was first founded in 1960.

A SAD RECORD

There can be no other country in the world – especially one with such a small population – that matches Namibia's sad record as far as clarifying its international status is concerned. In its decades of transformation from colonial protectorate to mandate to bone of international contention to – finally – universally acknowledged independent state, Namibia has amassed a collection of verdicts, papers, requests and related literature that is unequalled. Despite this, it was not until 1968 that the South Africans' presence was ruled illegal and The Hague demanded that South Africa terminate its South West African administration.

the organisation took a decision to fight for freedom with arms.

Bolstered by their administration's complete disregard for the UN's resolutions, whites, on the other hand, must have felt sure that nothing was likely to change.

Political developments were one thing, the establishment of an infrastructure in Namibia entirely another. In the 1960s, for the first time since German rule, the country underwent a period of rapid development: roads, water and energy resources, telecommunications, agriculture, tourism and other areas reached a level which placed Namibia a cut above the average

Faced with increasing international pressure, South Africa did make a few fainthearted gestures towards granting civil rights to the black population. In 1973, Prime Minister Vorster created a "native council" for South West Africa – just as SWAPO attained observer status at the UN. In September 1975, a constitutional conference was summoned; since it met in the old German *Turnhalle* (gymnasium) in Windhoek, this assembly was to go into the annals as the Turnhalle Conference. Its task was to create a constitution for an independent Namibia, and delegates were strictly divided into 11 groups; political parties were still excluded.

African state in terms of living conditions. In the heavily-populated rural north, however, this process only affected marginal areas and was by and large limited to police zones.

The fifth province

Pretoria's determination to annex Namibia came to a head when, in 1968 and 1969, two constitutional ordinances formally declared the territory to be the fifth province of South Africa. Over the next few years, thousands of young Namibians left the country, either to struggle for independence from abroad or to attend an educational facility not under South African control.

Resolution for change

Some 18 months later, in March 1977, a first draft of the constitution was presented; much influenced by South Africa, it presented a model for an ethnically segregated country. Meanwhile, the five Western members of the Security Council – the United States, West Germany, Great Britain, France, and Canada – closed ranks. This group urged South Africa to guarantee that the Turnhalle Conference would be nullified, and that general and free elections would be held in order to exercise every Namibian's right to self-government – something which had already been demanded by the United Nations in countless resolutions.

Though the Turnhalle Conference did not produce any tangible results, it did succeed in loosening the knots of apartheid. For the first time, black, white and coloured people sat round the table, striving to reach a consensus in lengthy negotiations.

South Africa only partially yielded to the suggestions of the five Western powers. In 1977, General Administrator Marthinus Steyn was appointed to govern the territory until its independence, serving as a counterpart to the UN Special Commissioner

AN INVALID ELECTION

In the general election of 1978, the Democratic Turnhalle Alliance took 41 seats and the Nationalist Party six. Three smaller parties received one seat each.

supervision of the UN. For the first time in the country's history, elections were held on a one-person, one-vote basis. Despite SWAPO's call to boycott elections, 81 percent of the 421,600 registered voters took part. The five Western powers declared the election to be invalid.

On the advice of South Africa, the representatives formed a national congress. However, this legislative body was limited in its powers and constantly subject to South African intervention – as happened when it attempted to implement

for Namibia, Martti Ahtisaari. In keeping with the spirit of the Western demands, which were officially formulated in the international arena as UN Resolution 435 a year later, Steyn removed several mainstays of the hated apartheid laws before the year was out. Segregation also began to be lifted in urban residential areas, a process that lasted until 1980.

Defying the dictates of Resolution 435, South Africa initiated general elections in Namibia in 1978 under its own auspices, without the

a law against racial discrimination, and when it wanted to drop South African holidays.

In January, 1983, the DTA, unable to govern under these conditions, stepped down. In the years that followed, Pretoria laboriously attempted to re-establish some measure of Namibian self-government – for example, the general administrator, a South African official, was effectively left to stand alone as the territory's sole administrator.

In 1985, what was to become the very last "temporary government of national unity" was formed. It, too, lacked credibility, however, for in constitutional questions South Africa again demanded the consensus of all parties.

LEFT: San (Bushmen) trackers were recruited by the South African army during the mandate years.
ABOVE: UN troops assisted during the 1989 elections.

Armed conflict

At the beginning of the 1960s, SWAPO took a joint decision with the Organisation for African Unity: they would resort to arms in the struggle for independence if diplomacy should prove fruitless. The historic first skirmish with the South African police took place not far from Ongulumbashe, in northwest Ovamboland, in August 1966 (today, 26 August is Namibia's Remembrance Day holiday). This marked the start of years of guerrilla and border warfare which were to end only in April 1989.

After Angola's independence in 1975, the armed conflict in Namibia became more and

remained in place right up until shortly before the 1989 elections.

After 1975, Namibia's volatile northern regions became a deployment area for South African military intervention and action in Angola. SWAPO's Angolan headquarters also came under repeated fire, most infamously on 4 May 1978, when an air attack destroyed their camp at Cassinga. Several hundred uniformed men, as well as women and children, were killed.

Superpower involvement

Despite the propitiatory announcement of a plan for the solution of the Namibia question, it

more bound up with the geopolitical interests of the superpowers and their representatives in southern Africa. The Soviet Union and Cuba supported Angola's Marxist MPLA government in Luanda; on the other side, the United States contributed aid to the pro-Western resistance movement UNITA. As long as Namibia's political parties adhered to one or the other of these alliances, all attempts at Namibian unity were doomed to failure.

After a general strike in 1971 involving Ovambo workers in particular, followed by uprisings in Ovamboland in 1972, martial law was imposed in the north for the first time, and controlled by the South African army. This

would be another eleven years before Security Council Resolution 435, which had met with a broad consensus in 1978, was realised. Time and again, the parties accused one another of setting unrealistic conditions which interfered with the plan's execution. Positions became completely entrenched when the US and South Africa made the enactment of Resolution 435 contingent on Cuba's withdrawal from Angola (the so-called Cuban linkage).

In light of the threat from UNITA, the withdrawal of its defending power's troops was totally unacceptable to the MPLA government in Angola. Nor could the United Nations make progress on the Cuba demand, as Resolution 435 was aimed specifically at a solution in Namibia, rather than addressing the security and balance of powers in neighbouring countries.

Finally, in 1988, under the direct supervision of the USSR and the US, the three countries of South Africa, Angola and Cuba met a number of times in Cairo, Brazzaville and New York, until Resolution 435 was inextricably linked with the total withdrawal of Cuban troops from Angola.

LENDING A HAND

The independence process was aided by the United Nations Transition Assistance Group (UNTAG), consisting of some 7,000 people from 110 countries.

Agreement at last

Once agreement between the three countries was reached on 22 December, things moved fast. Administrators and observers from more than 100 countries started to pour into Windhoek.

Yet the Namibia question was threatened anew when, on 1 April 1989 – the very day set aside for the resolution's implementation – heavily-armed SWAPO units moved in along a broad front from Namibia's northern border with Angola. Although Martti Ahtisaari, the authorised UN representative, was prompted to mobilise army units under South African command, conflict was luckily averted. After a quick conference between South Africa, Angola and Cuba, the independence process finally got underway in early May.

Not only did South Africa now lift all its remaining discriminatory laws, but SWAPO fighters were given the option of returning to Namibia as civilians. The withdrawal of all Namibian and South African soldiers still under South African command and their subsequent demobilisation went without a hitch. In June, those SWAPO leaders who had been living in exile abroad were at last able to come home – in triumph.

The repatriation of some 40,000 Namibian exiles and refugees from Angola and Zambia was carried out between May and August, aided by the UN. The next step was to register the Namibians, so that they could take advantage of their unconditional voting rights. More than 700,000 voters were registered, often under exceptionally difficult conditions.

LEFT: delegates at the historic Turnhalle Conference.
RIGHT: San (Bushman) woman voter from the Tsumkwe area at the 1989 elections.

Free elections

In November 1989, Namibia went to the polls to elect a constituent assembly, whose brief it was to create a new constitution for the country. Three parties – the National Patriotic Front of Namibia (NPF), the Federal Convention of Namibia (FCN), and the Namibia National Front (NNF) – each returned a single delegate to the Assembly. Aksie Christelik Nasionaal (ACN) had three delegates; the United Democratic Front (UDF) four. The absolute majority, however, was held by

SWAPO, which, with votes from 57 percent of the electorate, was represented by 41 seats in the Assembly; the strongest opposition was the Democratic Turnhalle Alliance, with 28 percent of the electorate and 21 seats.

In 22 of the 23 total electoral districts, the two major parties were locked in a head-to-head race. Only in Ovamboland, the most heavily-populated region and SWAPO's home base, was the party able to use its home advantage and win the day. None of the other nine parties won a single seat here.

The UN confirmed that the election had been free and fair – the proud culmination of 70 years of bitter struggle in Namibia. ❏

THE MODERN REPUBLIC

While independent Namibia has remained relatively stable and prosperous, regional security issues look set to prove the country's biggest headache

Namibia's new constitution was unanimously adopted on 9 February 1990 and the country became independent just after midnight on 21 March 1990. Few people present on that historic night will ever forget the feeling of elation that swept through the country when the South African flag was lowered and the red, blue, green and yellow Namibian flag took its place – a moment witnessed by a jubilant crowd gathered at Windhoek's Independence Stadium.

For decades, Namibia – one of the last colonies left in Africa – had been at the centre of innumerable debates in the United Nations and round upon round of international negotiations. Ever since the late 1960s, a low-level civil war instigated by the guerilla movement SWAPO had also been simmering, resulting in increased political pressure on the South African administration. Yet only in 1988 did South Africa finally bow to international pressure and agree to terminate its colonial administration. At last, Namibians had the right to elect their own independent government.

The independence celebrations attracted dignitaries from all over the world, including the then secretary-general of the United Nations, Javier Perez de Cuellar, who presided over the ceremony. The outgoing colonial administration was represented by F.W. de Klerk, the then State President of South Africa.

As Dr Sam Nujoma, SWAPO leader and first President of the Republic of Namibia, pointed out in his inaugural address, the struggle for independence had been shaped by the nature of Namibia's colonial experience. As he put it in his speech, "it pleases me to state that we are gathered here today not to pass yet another resolution, but to celebrate the dawn of a new era in this land and to proclaim to the world that a new star has risen on the African continent.

LEFT: old and new architectural styles side by side in the republic's capital, Windhoek.

RIGHT: SWAPO fans at an election rally. There remains a strong popular desire for political continuity.

Africa's last colony is, from this hour, liberated... we have been sustained in our difficult struggle by the powerful force of conviction in the righteousness and justness of our cause. Today history has absolved us; our vision of a democratic state of Namibia has been translated into a reality... we express our most sincere

gratitude to the international community for its steadfast support."

The building begins

The 1989 elections finally saw a victory for SWAPO, which was granted a mandate to form a government.

Prior to independence, a Constituent Assembly representing each of the country's political parties had been given the task of drafting a constitution enshrining the principles of multiparty democracy. And so it does; it's an impressive document, paving the way for a new system of Namibian government consisting of three branches: an executive branch, a parliamentary branch and the judiciary. It also incorporates specific checks designed to guard against the possible abuse of power, allows for substantive judicial review by the courts and assigns broad investigative powers to an independent ombudsman.

Members of the legislature are elected through a system of proportional representation, thus giving minority parties a chance to have their voices heard. There is a strong system of regional and local government, while a Council of Traditional Leaders advises the president on issues pertaining to traditional laws.

A series of national symbols were also

Namibia's early years as an independent state were marked by a mood of unbounded optimism. Brian Atwood, president of the Washington-based National Democratic Institute, compared the state of the nation before and after independence in a paper delivered to the institute. The old Namibia, he said, had been "a static society, full of fear for the future". In November 1989, however, he had returned to monitor the elections and found "a highly ... emotional campaign" where "attitudes ... had changed tremendously". People were now "working together" to build a multiparty system and make it work".

designed to promote the concepts of nation-building and unity. The flag, for example, consists of three coloured bands, arranged diagonally across. The top left hand corner is blue – symbolising the sky and the country's water resources – and contains a golden sun with 12 triangular rays. The bottom right-hand corner is green, representing Namibia's agricultural potential, while the broad red band in the middle depicts the heroism of the people.

The flag also forms the centrepiece of the coat of arms, supported on either side by one of Namibias best-known antelopes, the oryx. Along the base runs the motto, "Unity, Liberty, Justice", the key principles of the Constitution.

Namibia since independence

Initially, all went smoothly for the new state. South Africa handed back the disputed territory of Walvis Bay in February 1994, and relations between the two countries remain amicable.

December 1994 saw SWAPO returned to power in the general elections, winning 53 out of 72 seats. Nujoma was re-elected president for a further five years.

The general elections of December 1999, meanwhile, saw a landslide victory for the president, who captured a convincing 77 percent of the vote. His party, SWAPO, also won 55 parliamentary seats, which gave it the two-thirds majority necessary to amend the constitution.

Although the election was deemed free and fair, these were some controversial results, because the previous SWAPO parliament had used its predominance to alter the constitution anyway, to allow a third term for Nujoma (previously, the constitution had stated that no president should be allowed to serve more than two terms in office).

Still tainted by its links with the former South African administration, the Democratic Turnhalle Alliance (the traditional opposition) won just seven seats, as did a new party – the Congress of Democrats, led by a disaffected SWAPO activist called Ben Ulenga.

SWAPO's opponents continue to attack the government over the country's unemployment rate of 35 percent and over allegations of official corruption. Articles are constantly appearing in the newspapers denouncing another outrageous fiddle or incidence of everyday racketeering that has become taken for granted. For example, it is alleged that the government car pool – mainly consisting of people carriers – has higher fuel consumption per vehicle than a fleet of HGVs. The implication is that members of the administration are taking fuel from government cars for their own private usage.

Regional tensions

Nujoma made the economy the focus of his electoral campaign, going so far as to promise his fellow Namibians that they would have living standards on a par with the developed world in just 30 years. It is true that since 1990, most Namibians have better living conditions and access to basic social services, but the average per capita income remains low. What's more, productivity is still narrow, with little industrialisation outside the mining sector.

Dr Sam Nujoma decided not to stand for the presidential elections of November 2004, but he remained the leader of SWAPO and his chosen successor, Hifikepunye Pohamba, won a landslide victory as the representative of the same party. Although this result was fiercely disputed by the opposition parties, the majority of impartial observers noted there was minimal evidence of voting irregularities. A former exile and founder member of SWAPO, the 70-year-old Pohamba was inaugurated as President in March 2005, and has since pursued his predecessor's policies, including following up on proposed land reforms and starting to tackle corruption. ❏

LEFT: Namibia becomes independent under its first president, Dr Sam Nujoma.
ABOVE: the parliament building, Windhoek.

THE ECONOMIC BALANCING ACT

*Most Namibians enjoy a better standard of living since independence,
although the productive structure remains narrow, with little industrialisation*

For almost a quarter of a century – from the first resolution of the General Assembly ending South Africa's League of Nations mandate in 1966 to Independence Day on 21 March 1990 – Namibia's political future made international headline news. A succession of General Assembly and Security Council resolutions, plus decisions of the International Court of Justice, charted the country's passage through the political reefs.

By the end of this period, Namibia's (mostly white and conservative) business community had come round to the idea of independence for three reasons: nothing else seemed to have worked; the white regime in South Africa, afflicted by even worse troubles, was in no position to help; and the few members of the newly-elected government they had met seemed to be reasonable men prepared to abandon the rhetoric of the past and deal pragmatically with the economy.

Once the country had actually won its independence, however, a rather different picture emerged. Wealthy members of the international community who had previously seemed enthused by the Namibian cause (and who, indeed, had jointly spent US$800 million on the year-long transition supervised by the United Nations) now lost interest. Faced with more interesting prospects in Eastern Europe, they were not disposed to be particularly generous to the newest – but by no means the poorest – member of the community of nations.

In short, the new Namibian government had to work very hard to attract grants and investment. Proximity to South Africa proved (and continues to prove) a double-edged sword: it is an advantage for export trade, but then South Africa tends to attract much of the aid and inward investment to the region. Aid donors meeting in New York in 1990 pledged funds totalling US$696 million to Namibia. Between

two-thirds and three-quarters of this was promised in the form of grants, the balance in concessionary loans. Namibia's proposal to the World Bank that it be regarded as one of the "Least Developed Countries" was, however, turned down, as its per-capita Gross Domestic Product (GDP) exceeded US$1,000, the maxi-

mum for this category. Acceptance as an LDC would have given Namibia access to a wider range of concessionary bank funding.

Communications

Namibia has received US$600 million worth of aid as part of its 1996–2000 development plan from 30 donors under the United Nations Development Plan (UNDP). The UNDP describes the country as having "a stable political and economic climate and low tax rates. Namibia is well placed to serve as gateway to South Africa, boasting good communication networks and port facilities able to handle up to 800 vessels per day." The EU is the largest con-

---

PRECEDING PAGES: tired of tyres.
LEFT: skyline of modern Windhoek.
RIGHT: the fishing industry is crucial to the economy.

tributor of aid to the region, while the biggest bilateral donors are Sweden and Germany.

Measured by per capita gross domestic product, Namibia is the third wealthiest country in southern Africa, after the Republic of South Africa and Botswana. It is well served with infrastructure: major towns and cities are linked by some 5,450 km (3,400 miles) of asphalt roads, while another 37,000 km (23,000 miles) of gravel and unsurfaced roads traverse the rural areas. Some 2,400 km (1,500 miles) of railway

ROOM TO BREATHE

Although it is a very large country – more than a third larger than the UK and Germany combined – Namibia is sparsely populated, supporting fewer than 2 million people in 2006.

to over 150 countries and has some 80,000 subscribers. About 90 percent of the country is served by FM radio stations, with the Namibia Broadcasting Corporation offering programmes in nine languages, including English and German. Much of the country is now able to receive a variety of TV programmes through the publicly owned Namibian Broadcasting Corporation as well as satellite stations from South Africa and Europe, although the small advertising market imposes a limit on further expansion.

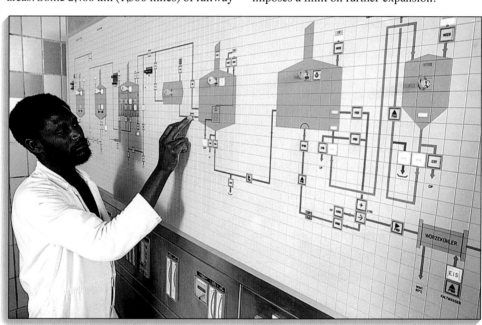

lines, carrying both freight and passengers, are integrated with the South African rail network and thence with the rest of the subcontinent. More than 350 airstrips and airports, including an international terminal outside Windhoek, serve the national carrier, Air Namibia, smaller charter operations and private pilots.

Two harbours – Lüderitz, a fishing port to the south, and Walvis Bay, a deep water harbour in the centre of the coast – provide access from the sea. Constitutional title to the Walvis Bay enclave was the subject of a long dispute with South Africa, which was settled amicably by negotiation in 1994.

The telephone service permits direct dialling

Mining, ranching and fishing

In African terms, Namibia is potentially rich – given its small population – with valuable mineral resources, exceptionally rich fishing waters and a strong livestock farming industry. Diamond, uranium and base metal mining, and beef cattle and Karakul sheep ranching have accounted for some 90 percent of Namibia's exports in the past, as well as about 40 percent of its GDP.

Namibia's fishing grounds, in the nutrient-rich waters of the southeast Atlantic ocean, abound in several pelagic (pilchards, anchovies) and demersal (hake, white fish) species and support a small, but thriving, rock lobster (crayfish) industry at Lüderitz. As Namibia's 200-mile (320-km) exclusive economic zone was not recognised before its independence and there was much pirate fishing, these waters have not yet provided the economic returns of which they are capable – with prudent management. The government believes that a combination of royalty payments by foreign fleets and the value of local catches processed in Namibia could greatly increase the revenue from this sector.

Livestock ranching on the southern and central plateau constitutes almost 90 percent of the value of Namibia's agricultural output for commercial purposes. The agricultural sector itself

the number had risen again to 2 million. Most cattle sold commercially are transported by rail or truck to South Africa for slaughter there, but the government maintains an annual export quota from the European Union.

Changing trends

The pelts of Karakul lambs – once known as Namibia's "black diamonds" – were traditionally auctioned in London, but since 1995 the twice-yearly sales have been held in Copenhagen, where the pelts are sold under the Swakara brand. Karakul farmers have been vulnerable to shifting fashions in the fur industry. At the

contributes only about 10 percent of GDP, but almost 70 percent of the population is dependent on ranching and farming for their survival.

Poor rainfall in most of the country and cyclical droughts make crop cultivation impossible in the absence of irrigation. Even cattle ranching (which in Namibia means hardy beef species like the Brahman and the Afrikaner) can be precarious. The number of cattle declined from 2.5 million in 1979 to 1.3 million in 1984. By 1990, the drought having broken,

LEFT: beer is still brewed German-style in Windhoek's major breweries.
ABOVE: the industrial sector is comparatively small.

peak of demand, there were 4 million Karakul sheep in the country and no fewer than 3 million Namibian pelts were sold in London alone, in a single year. Prices recovered only slightly after the collapse of the market in the early 1980s, only to crash again in 2001. Today, annual output is only about 120,000 pelts, and many farmers have shifted to joint wool/mutton production to protect themselves against the vagaries of the market.

As for minerals, the value of Namibia's mining output ranks fourth in Africa, behind South Africa, Zaire and Botswana, and comprises on average over 75 percent of the country's export earnings. The mining industry pays the bulk of corporate taxes and is the largest private sector employer. Little processing or beneficiation is undertaken in Namibia, however, and most of the products are exported; the industry is thus at the mercy of shifting market prices, reflected in volatile value added output. Employment levels in the industry have fallen in recent years and Tsumeb mine closed in 1998.

> ### A GLITTERING RECORD
>
> Namibia produces 1.3 million carats per year – over 8 percent of world diamond production – which earn more than US$450 million of foreign exchange.

Diamonds are mined from coastal deposits 30 km (19 miles) off the coast of Lüderitz and on the Orange River – Namibia's southern

Rössing Uranium, 68.6 percent owned by the British company Rio Tinto, together with a number of South African mining interests and Minatome of France, operate the world's largest open-cast uranium mine 65km (40 miles) from Swakopmund (www.rossing.com). Careful financial structuring – including a lengthy tax holiday – and long-term supply contracts at high prices, concluded in the nuclear-friendly 1970s, enabled the mine to post excellent profits throughout the early 1980s despite the low-grade ore.

boundary – by NAMDEB. The corporation is owned in equal shares by the government of Namibia and De Beers, although the latter retains all exploitation rights. Production fell throughout the 1980s from a high of 1.56 million carats in 1980 to just over 900,000 carats by 1990, but higher prices have enhanced profitability and encouraged new exploration.

The production includes a high percentage of larger gems, although the average size is falling, and mining conditions are increasingly difficult. The lifetime of deposits depends on the results of new prospecting and the assumptions made about the depths at which it is possible and profitable to mine.

A change of fortune

A combination of circumstances has, however, since made the mine vulnerable. Uranium spot prices fell sharply as plans for nuclear reactors were shelved in the aftermath of the Three Mile Island (1979) and Chernobyl (1986) accidents and new, higher grade, deposits were developed in Australia and Canada. Political and legal pressures were also brought to bear on purchasers by the UN Council for Namibia.

As its long-term contracts drew to a close, Rössing had difficulties signing new agreements after independence in 1990. Uranium sales in the United States were also seriously inhibited in the few years before independence by the passage, at the end of 1986, of the Anti-Apartheid Act, which treated Namibia as part of South Africa. Although one new long-term contract was signed with the French EDF in 1990, a 25 percent production cut-back was announced by the Rössing board in 1991, and the decline continues, with no end in sight.

The Namibian government controls 50 percent of the voting rights and 3.5 percent of the equity in Rössing Uranium. At least three other uranium deposits near the Rössing mine were discovered in the 1970s.

Most base (copper, lead, zinc, cadmium, pyrite, arsenic trioxide and sodium antimonate)

primary gold mine at Navachab near Karibib. Navachab began production in 1989 and is intended to produce 1,900kg (2 tons) of gold each year, over a projected 20-year lifespan.

Zinc has been discovered in the south near Rosh Pinah and is bringing an influx of investment to the area around Lüderitz.

Local manufacturing

Because South Africa administered Namibia pretty much as a fifth province until the end of the 1970s, there was little scope or incentive for the development of local manufacturing industry. Manufacturing contributes only about 5 percent

and precious (gold and silver) mineral production used to be derived from four mines operated by the Tsumeb Corporation (TCL), which closed in May 1998. A lead refinery and copper smelter are owned by Gold Fields (Namibia), a public company whose shares are, however, largely held by Gold Fields of South Africa (GFSA), with Rio Tinto (through BP Minerals) and Seltrust Investments owning smaller blocks. Anglo American Corporation and De Beers have a joint 70 percent stake in Namibia's first

LEFT: almost 70 percent of Namibians depend on farming and ranching for their survival.
ABOVE: Himba women from rural Kaokoland.

to GDP and the sector employs under 10,000 people – about the same percentage of the workforce in formal employment. About half of these work in the food and beverage processing area.

The small size of the manufacturing sector is further illustrated by the fact that the incorporation in 1994 of the fish processing and marine engineering activities in Walvis Bay, after the territory was handed back by South Africa, doubled the value of Namibia's manufacturing output. The government actively encourages domestic and foreign investment in this sector as a means to add value and create jobs. Unilever, Guinness and Lonrho are among the companies which have entered the market.

Water and power

Although the return of some 40,000 SWAPO cadres from exile in 1989 greatly increased the population of Windhoek, most Namibians still lead a rural existence. Development of the physical and social infrastructure in the rural areas, particularly the more populated north, is thus an obvious priority. The improvement of schooling and preventative health care facilities and the provision of jobs, either on the land, or in small-scale, labour-intensive, informal manufacturing enterprises, requires electrification of the rural areas. Improved crop production and better use of grazing lands by livestock

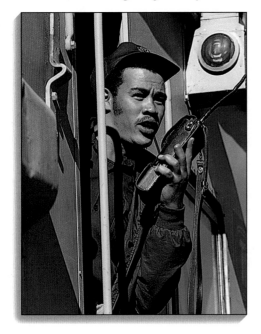

are dependent on the availability of water at points far removed from its sources.

Although most of Namibia is arid, the country has enormous water resources within its borders, particularly in the north, where the Okavango system alone has more water than all the rivers of South Africa together. However, plans for the final phase of the Eastern Water Carrier, which would have brought water from the Okavango River to the central part of the country, were shelved in the 1980s because of a lack of funds for capital works. Likewise, Namibia has the capacity to become the largest net gas exporter in the region through its gas deposits in the Kudu field in the Orange Basin.

Tourism is a promising growth area, which now contributes more to the economy than the manufacturing sector. Direct flights to Europe, improved tourist facilities and increased travel to South Africa are all encouraging this trend.

South Africa remains the country's biggest trading partner, accounting for 80–90 percent of Namibia's foreign trade, and holding as much as 80 percent of the investment in the key sectors of banking, mining and insurance.

Challenge for the future

The country's greatest strengths are the tolerance bred into the political culture since the mid-1970s and reinforced by its exemplary constitution; the free and active press; the basic health of the economy, despite its deficiencies; and the pragmatic approach of the government. Its weaknesses are high levels of unemployment; inequalities of income and opportunity between rural and urban areas and between black and white; over-dependence on the mining sector; insufficient industrial capacity due to an underdeveloped manufacturing sector; and a shortage of critical skills in key sectors of the economy and administration.

Deprived of the ideological shibboleths and divisive loyalties of the past, Namibians since independence have had the chance to unite in support of new social and economic programmes and give substance to the idea of nationhood. The challenges are enormous: combatting unemployment, promoting rapid skills development and effecting economic restructuring in order to maintain growth, holding down inflation and reducing present inequalities of opportunity.

The end of the civil war in Angola has gently boosted development in Namibia, the two countries co-operating productively to their mutual benefit. Angola is rich in minerals and energy sources and shares close cultural and ethnic ties with Namibia. Moreover, fruitful avenues are opening up toward regional co-operation – with South Africa as the economic motor of the whole region. In this way, the necessary progress can take place to enable Namibia to face the economic demands of the 21st century. ❑

LEFT: keeping pace with developments.
RIGHT: rig drilling holes for planting explosives, Rössing Uranium mine.

THE PEOPLES

*Namibia is a rich tapestry of cultures, with at least 11 major
ethnic groups speaking dozens of different languages*

Namibia's population is as varied as its landscape: colourful and rich in different languages and lifestyles. The peoples of this thinly populated expanse of land – which ranges from the river landscapes of the Caprivi Strip, through dry forests and savannahs, to the deserts along the Atlantic – have been compared to a colourful carpet, with fringes that reach deep into the countries around it. This young country combines a palette of peoples and tribes in a geographical area whose borders were drawn through tribal lands between 1884 and 1890 to suit the interests of colonial powers. As a result, many peoples were thrown together in what was to develop into the modern state of Namibia.

The people's socio-political orientation is as many-sided as their culture. At one point, they'll seem conservative; at another, enlightened and progressive. Social isolationism is not uncommon, but neither is upward mobility. Thus, segregation – often the legacy of the apartheid laws abolished in the late 1970s – - alternates with giant steps forward in national reconciliation, after decades of open and dormant conflicts.

The mobile Namibians

Long ago, the nomadic herdsmen of the Herero and Nama moved with the seasons to find good pasture; today, the inhabitants of Kaokoveld still follow this practice. In adjoining territories, competing cowherders quarrelled over pastures, water rights, and ownership of the cows themselves.

Meanwhile, the oldest inhabitants of southern Africa, hunter-gatherers known to outsiders as the San (Bushmen), wandered through huge desert territories which had seemed inhospitable both to the roving herdsmen and to the settled agricultural, herding and fishing clans in

PRECEDING PAGES: going to church; two's company for these Herero women.
LEFT: staying in tune.
RIGHT: farmer's daughter and friend.

Ovamboland, Okavango and the Caprivi Strip.

The first mixed-race and white settlers moved onto the land with wagons and herds of cattle. Settlement and territorial conflicts at the beginning of the century forced native peoples, the Hereros and Namas in particular, from their homelands into outlying areas of the country.

But despite colonial dominion by German and South African settlers, the native population was able to maintain its cultural identity.

The occupation and development of the central and southern region, and the expansion of the mining industry, brought about a great demand for labour. Workers were drawn from the more thickly populated north, in Ovamboland, where "migrant workers" were common. Migrant work, which was strictly regulated according to a contract system until the 1970s, brought together people from every region of the country. The mandate government, however, attempted to prevent migrant workers from settling permanently in the south by means of pass laws. For this reason, the central and southern regions of Namibia were virtually a foreign country for northern natives. In order to obtain a temporary residence permit, they had to have a steady job, and these were hard to come by.

In 1977, the pass laws were repealed. The contract-labour system was no longer practical. Since then, migrant labour has followed its own course: thousands seek employment in industry, trade or administration in order to escape, if only temporarily, the country's "vicious circle of sub-

CITY-SEEKERS

The pattern of urban migration is most obvious in Windhoek, where the population has grown from around 100,000 at independence to around 250,000.

Deportation and emigration

After World War I, in the period between the Armistice (11 November 1918) and the signing of the Treaty of Versailles (28 June 1919), the South African military government deported 4,900 Germans from occupied South West Africa, most of them soldiers, officials and "undesirables". This was a considerable number in a population of only about 15,000, of whom 12,300 were native German speakers. It hit the country's economy as well, since the skilled labourers

sistence economy". Many return periodically to visit their families and villages; others are sucked more quickly into the maelstrom of big-city life.

This syndrome of urban migration has affected every part of the population, whether in the overpopulated areas of the north or the thinly populated deserts to the south and west. Independence has accelerated the process to a remarkable degree. The country's few cities and population centres – Ondangwa and Oshakati, Windhoek and Swakopmund – are faced with the tremendous task of quickly creating reasonable housing for all of these people, to prevent the development of urban slums.

that were needed could not simply be brought in from South Africa. After the deportation ordinance was lifted, some 1,000 of those who had been turned out returned to Namibia.

During the period in which apartheid laws were in effect – over 25 years – many thousands of black Namibians left the country illegally, emigrating to Botswana, Zambia, and later Angola. They were following the patriotic call to take part in the fight for Namibian independence, or hoping to receive higher education in foreign schools and universities. Before the great repatriation in 1989, many Namibians had spent up to 30 years in exile.

With the country's first attempt at independence in 1978, political uncertainty and economic recession induced the white population to emigrate in droves. This group shrank in number from its record height of 110,000 to about 74,000. Emigration occurred primarily among that class which had either been transferred or came looking for work from South Africa only a few years before. But the final, successful, independence process in 1989–90 did not lead to any significant emigration of white Namibians – although the withdrawal of the South African military presence which accompanied independence in 1989 meant that several thousand white family members, who had for years

the ownership of land and inevitably on its use. However, the influx of immigrants to South West Africa never reached anything like the scale of the prodigious migration of people from Europe to the Americas and Australia. Immigrants to Namibia never numbered more than a few thousand.

The most recent large-scale influx was the repatriation of exiles in 1989, the year when the international community realised plans to solve the Namibian question. The Refugee Commissioner of the United Nations set up an "air bridge" to Windhoek and Grootfontein for all Namibians living in exile in Angola, Zambia

lived in various military facilities within Namibia, now left the country.

The newcomers

Originally, South West Africa was regarded as a "settlement area" among the former German colonies, rather than merely as a source of raw materials, such as Togo or Cameroon. European settlers – mainly Germans before 1914, after the two world wars primarily homeless South African Boers – had a major effect on

LEFT: Himba city dwellers on a home visit.
ABOVE: many farms are still owned by descendants of the German pioneers.

RETURN OF THE TREKKERS

One distinct group of 20th-century immigrants were Boers from Angola, who were resettled in the regions of Outjo and Gobabis in 1928, on the initiative of the South African government. The newcomers were mainly survivors and descendants of the legendary "Dorsland trekkers", who had left Transvaal in 1878 in search of land free from British colonial rule. Doggedly refusing to yield to thirst or tropical diseases, these indefatigable trekkers had driven their cattle and ox-drawn wagons through the Kalahari and South West Africa, finally settling in South Angola, where they had remained for about half a century.

and elsewhere. Every repatriate of voting age could take part in the preparations and then in the historic vote for independence in November 1989. In this way, 42,000 refugees returned to their homeland. Many of them were children and adolescents who had never seen the country of their fathers.

Official language, many tongues

The authors of Namibia's constitution selected one of the two languages which had historically been official in Namibia: English. Thus the common vernacular language of Afrikaans, after serving as an official language for some family in the country, with some 680,000 native speakers. Thus, limiting the official language to English is equally unfair to members of every other linguistic family – that is, virtually the entire population. It accommodates neither the majority nor any dominant minority. Linguistic experts calculate that it will take some two generations for the change fully to be implemented; in urban surroundings, the process will be somewhat easier.

However, the mastery of English carries with it hopes of greater social and economic mobility. By means of this international language, the country has been able to hook up with inter-

60 years, was retired to a secondary position as first among 20 or so other tongues recognised in the country. The authors of the constitution deliberately chose not to use the language of the country's erstwhile colonial rulers, German (a customary practice among newly-independent African states).

At least 97 percent of Namibia's population does not speak English at home. Although it is the country's official language, fewer than 2 percent of Namibians are raised as English speakers – a number approximately equal to that of those raised speaking German.

The Ovambo dialect, including both written versions of it, represents the largest linguistic

SPRECHEN SIE DEUTSCH?

German, historically Namibia's first "official" language, has been able to retain its force as a means of communication and vehicle of culture. This is perhaps because of the multilingual abilities of those who speak it, rather than their numbers, which are still relatively small. Mainstays of the German language in Namibia are several schools and churches, a whole range of athletic and cultural organisations, two German newspapers, a radio station and a part of the business world, as well as the tourist and service trades – although, in the latter, people are happy to switch back and forth to English and Afrikaans.

national information exchanges. English has helped to forge links with neighbouring countries, and will also serve, perhaps, as the vehicle for the creation of a new national unity.

Afrikaans, by contrast, is stigmatised as a "language of oppression" because of its connection with apartheid. On the other hand, it is the native language of various extremely vital cultural groups, so there appears to be little danger of its dying out in the future.

The survival of Namibia's other languages will depend on the vigour of the cultures of the individual groups that speak them. The Ovambo dialects, which are rooted in solid, living cultures, are less endangered than the countless smaller border languages, such as those of the Bushmen (San) or some of the Namas.

In sport, languages vary from one discipline to another. English is generally spoken on the football field and the bowling green. Afrikaans dominates at rugby matches; riding, nine-pins and hang-gliding tend to be carried out in German; and at the spectacular athletic jumping game of *omupembe*, Oshivambo is the language you'll hear.

From the very beginning, residents of Namibia have had to be multilingual. As a rule, those who live here can make themselves understood in two or three local languages without any trouble; mastery of four or five is not unusual. Anyone who remained monolingual in a country with as many different languages as Namibia would risk social isolation. And, if anyone complains that this is an unreasonable situation, somebody is sure to point to the matter-of-fact multilingualism of the Swiss.

The quest for culture

Apart from the flag, the national anthem and the civil rights' ordinances that apply to all citizens and every part of the country, there's not much, culturally speaking, that all Namibians can immediately identify with to the same degree. However, the forms of cultural expression of certain sectors of the population are distinctive and characteristic. The traditional Victorian folk costumes of the Herero women, for example, are unique to Namibia. Such a

LEADING LANGUAGE

Over 100,000 Namibians – coloureds, blacks and most whites – speak Afrikaans as their first language, far more than the total of English and German speakers.

synthesis of European and African folk cultures is typical of this country.

Each sector of the population is a tile in the mosaic of Namibia's culture. The ceramics, basket-weaving and decorative woodcarvings of the peoples in the rainy north are as much a part of Namibian culture as the prize songs of the Nama or the Bushmen's dancing rituals. Choral singing is popular and common. Songs accompanied by the rhythm of drums, or classical instruments, on the Okavango river or the Caprivi Strip, or

the church choir, or the 1902 Men's Singing Association in Swakopmund – each has its own sound, its own appeal.

Is this Namibian culture? No, but this country's culture has many different faces. And Namibia is in a position to attract creative individuals from other places – those who wish to explore the cultural legacies of small, fast-vanishing minorities. In the annual music contest, or the visual arts competition, Namibian artists seek out new forms, tones and colours. Faces, environment, social problems: all provide ample subject-matter for their work.

After a hard day's work, the whole population are masters in the art of unwinding – and

LEFT: uptown girls. **RIGHT:** herdsman with his flock.

doing it, when possible, in company. Inviting barbecue fires, by day or under the night sky, blaze throughout the country for festivals and holidays. At sundown, they signal the locations of safari camps, or indicate a lively celebration going on in somebody's back garden.

Meat dishes, of every variety and quantity, are a part of the Namibian diet. Grilling over the glowing coals is a special part of the hospitality one extends to friends and guests. In this country with so many remote

farms and rural communities, such hospitality plays an important role.

The last of the hunter-gatherers

The San people – also known as "Bushmen" – live mainly in the easternmost reaches of northern Namibia along the border with Botswana, a region which the South Africans called Bushmanland. These slight, lean, apricot-skinned people still live in traditional villages, although most of them now wear western clothing and trade painstakingly-made jewellery for money to buy basic foodstuffs. Some still retain their remarkable tracking skills (they can recognise an individual by their footprints), and obtain

> **PEOPLE WITH NO NAME**
>
> Although the "Bushmen" are a distinct ethnic group, they have no collective name for themselves. Instead, they identify themselves as members of the !Kung clan, or the Ju/'hoan, or any one of a dozen other clans.

most of their food from hunting and gathering.

Spending time with these humble, self-deprecating people is a moving experience, for they have a strong sense of fun, a profound understanding of the natural environment and a certain unrushed quality about their lives that has long since disappeared in the west. It is possible for small parties to visit some of the San people in Bushmanland, to see their dances and possibly go out with them on hunting and gathering expeditions.

To do so you should contact the Nyae Nyae Development Foundation, PO Box 9026, Windhoek; tel: 061 236327; fax: 061 255957; www.nacobta.com.na. You can stay at Tsumkwe Lodge from where visits to the Ju/'hoan people are organised by Arno Oosthuysen, PO Box 1899, Tsumeb; radio telephone: 09 264 64 203581 and ask for 531, or fax: 09 264 67 220060.

Togetherness

Namibia's new constitution calls upon the government to distribute goods and social services in equal measure throughout the country. Discrepancies between the central regions and the under-developed border territories, in terms of modern comfort, formal education and structural economic development, are also to be resolved. This development will accelerate the process of adaptation and acculturation, particularly for smaller ethnic groups.

While the existing cultural diversity and regional customs will protect the country from becoming uniform and flat, they will not prevent Namibians from coming together as a people, and growing into a new, identifiable nation. The manifold, colourful peoples of Namibia have already demonstrated this multiplicity in many different situations. A chorus in five different languages sums it up thus:

Namibia, Namibia, ti oms, ti saub,
 geskenk van God;
Namibia, oshilongo shetu, country –
 Heimat Namibia. ❑

LEFT: Himba youth in traditional regalia.
RIGHT: you'll see Herero women in these eye-catching costumes in central and northern Namibia.

RELIGIOUS BELIEFS

Officially, Namibia is a Christian country. In practice, many traditional African beliefs maintain a powerful place in religious life

Africa, the melting pot of many different cultures and languages, is also the meeting-point of a wealth of religions. Namibia is no exception and, when considering local traditions, there is no question of speaking about a single, unified religion. The country's indigenous peoples have their own individual beliefs: for example, many vastly different taboos are observed by different Herero clans, while the Damara used to have many different names for their god.

Despite this wide diversity of religious forms, one can perceive common threads among the colourful fabrics of the various indigenous beliefs. Virtually every one of them espouses the view that God created the world and has guarded it ever since. Certainly, various clans have given quite different names to the supreme being, and developed wildly differing conceptions of this god. But ultimately, all Africans are referring to the same God when they speak of the Creator and Guardian of the Earth.

In their countless myths, Namibia's indigenous peoples also tell of the original link and covenant between God and Man, which was broken through some mistake committed by a man or a beast. But God did not cease to exist; his importance for the collective African peoples remained intact.

Missionary misapprehension

Time and again, Christian missionaries were astonished to find there were no formal religious services of worship among the indigenous population; they took this as an indication of the lamentable degree to which heathen practices had spread.

But it was a mistake to make such judgements solely on the basis of European tradition. For in Africa, God is a being so holy and so thoroughly above Man that one hardly dares to speak his name aloud. If his name is uttered, it must be very guardedly – just as one is reluctant to dis-

turb one's king or chief with trivia or unimportant daily concerns. Men on earth contact the deity through the agency of beings nearer to him: the ancestors, more pithily termed "the living dead".

In traditional religion, the belief is that those who have died are not truly dead; they have

taken on a new form of existence, but remain in contact with the living. They continue to belong to the family, even after their names have been forgotten.

European missionaries were quick to conclude that "true worship" was displaced, in indigenous cultures, by this human "ancestor cult". Again, this is to assess the situation in narrow European terms, leading to the wrong conclusions. For African traditions recognise no difference between the sacred and the profane; religion and daily life form a single unified whole. Each can be observed and discussed in terms of its details, but the two are never actually separated.

LEFT: young Ovambo nun.
RIGHT: a Herero woman worships at a chief's grave.

Traditional religion today

"Official" statistics declare that around 91 percent of Namibia's population is Christian. Only a small fraction of the population, it would seem, continues to observe traditional religious practices. Such traditionalists tend to be found more in the northern regions, among peoples such as the Himba in Kaokoland or the San people, or Bushmen. This fact demonstrates the zeal with which the missionaries pursued their goal: to introduce Christianity into every corner of the land.

Yet to conclude that the entire Namibian population follows Christianity as it is practised in the major churches of Europe would be fundamentally false, for many old African traditions have permeated the Christian denominations – not a homogeneous mixture, as such, but not a separation, either.

Ancestors' Memorial Day

This celebration of the Hereros is a fine example of this religious "co-existence". Most indigenous traditions have, as a rule, remained closed to outsiders; but, in Namibia, the various Herero clans celebrate their national holiday with much fanfare and public display in Gobabis, Okahandja and Omaruru. While these

DUALITY OF DEITIES

At least two groups of San (Bushmen), the !Kung and the G/wi, traditionally believe in two "great chiefs" or gods. Yasema is the powerful god of good who lives in the east. He makes the sun rise, created all things and is the stronger god, on whom one calls for healing. Chevangani is the lesser god, who lives in the west, makes the sun set, and causes evil, sickness and death. When the Dutch Reform Church (NGK) began to work among the Bushmen in the 1980s, missionaries reported that, while the San had no problem in identifying Yasema with God and Chevangani with Satan, converts to Christianity were few.

festivities may not adhere strictly to the letter of religious law, both traditional and Christian elements are clearly evident.

In the case of Gobabis, events focus on a farm cemetery just outside town, where important chiefs and leaders of the East Hereros (Mbanderu) are buried. For Nikodemus' Day (named after one of the chiefs), Hereros journey here from every corner of the land. If they arrive before sunset of the previous day, they must first visit the graves. Before doing this, their presence is made known to the ancestors, and they must undergo a test around the Ancestral Fire to determine whether or not their presence is also welcome to the ancestors. The cult priest pulls the visitor's fingers; if a joint cracks, the candidate has passed muster. If not, he had better keep his distance.

For those admitted, there follows a ritual purification: a master of ceremonies sprays a mouthful of water over the guests. Now they may have access to the graves. At the entrance to the cemetery, the master of ceremonies kneels to the ground and introduces every visitor; through his voice, the ancestors command the petitioner to draw nearer. Each person kneels by the

ancestors cannot have access to them. While Christianity concentrates on sins committed against God, the indigenous tradition addresses itself to the sins which men have committed against other men. It is for this reason that cooperation between the two traditions is seen as important.

The first missionaries

In 1805 the London Mission sent two German brothers, Abraham and Christian Albrecht, to Namibia to begin missionary work among the Khoi-Khoi (Nama). Only

grave of the oldest chief, lays his hand on a stone and gives his name and his place of origin. The other "living-dead" are greeted by touching their gravestone, or by laying small stones on the grave. Visitors can then move freely among the graves. On Sunday, this ceremony is repeated; then, gathered around the graves, worshippers hold a service as if in church.

The thinking is that people's sins determine the course of events. Anyone who has disregarded the commands and wisdom of the

someone who has crossed the dry, infertile regions in the south of the country will fully appreciate the difficulties they faced; indeed, in order to do their job and survive, they had no choice but to move with the nomadic Nama. Abraham died in 1810, but Christian continued their work, eventually establishing the first Christian community in Warmbad.

In 1814 another London Mission-backed German missionary arrived in Windhoek. Heinrich Schmelen's achievements were many: not only did he found a station at Bethanie (his one-room house can still be seen there today), but he discovered a new route west to the coast in the course of his missionary work.

LEFT: Holy Communion in Ovamboland.
ABOVE: traditionally, cattle skulls replace the Christian cross on Herero graves.

Variety of churches

It may sometimes seem to visitors that Namibia has churches at every turn. In fact, they fall quite neatly into three groups, one of which dates back to the missionary era. Originally nurtured by the Rhine Mission and the Finnish Mission, the Evangelical Lutheran Church has the largest following in this category today.

Then there are all those churches that developed when the white settlers came, such as the Roman Catholic Church, which also practises mission work – as does the Anglican Church – and the German Evangelical Lutheran Church.

The influence of the third group, the truly

African, independent churches, cannot be judged by its church buildings alone: its congregations are based, for the most part, in black sections of the cities or on former reservations, where they remain unobtrusive and hidden. But if you pass through one of these neighbourhoods on a Sunday, you will run across people singing, clapping their hands, or dancing around a candle in front of a house, under a tree, or in a simple room. It is not only priests and bishops who work here: prophets and charismatics do as well, while prayer healing and talking in tongues are seen as signs of the efficacy of the Holy Ghost.

Song plays an important role even in the large communities of the former mission churches. No organ is needed; the congregation always sings in four-part harmony. There are also many smaller choirs. Today, they prefer to sing songs written and composed by black Namibians, rather than ones which have been translated from some European hymnal. Services tend to last for a long time, too – often up to two hours.

Striving for unity

There is no question that the South African policy of apartheid also influenced church life in Namibia for years. The Catholic Church and the Anglican Church, at least, ignored the question of race and refused to segregate communities – unlike the South African Dutch Reform Church (NGK) – but on the whole their white adherents preferred not to align themselves directly with anti-apartheid action.

It was the black Lutheran churches (ELCRN and ELCIN) in Namibia that took the first steps towards unity, with each other and with the German Lutheran church. While the German-speaking community would have been content with a federation of churches, the black churches favoured complete and total unity. Yet even the two black Lutheran churches have not been able to achieve this, so wide is the gap between different languages and traditions. Thus, the present objective is simply closer cooperation on a community level between the black and white congregations.

The reforms in South Africa have undoubtedly had profound impact on the Namibian Reform churches as well; they now have to work to reunify churches which have hitherto been divided by race into white, coloured and black. In the light of all the years of theological justification of apartheid, this will be a Sisyphean task.

However, the Council of Churches in Namibia has been able to hold its own; it also played an important role in the transition phase following the country's independence. Its goal is not to establish a "super-church", but rather to achieve cooperation in questions concerning the people of Namibia – which is, after all, just another way of practising Christian unity. ❏

LEFT: traditional healer at work.
RIGHT: Windhoek's graceful Christuskirche (Christ Church) is an Evangelical Lutheran church.

EATING AND ENTERTAINMENT

With no shortage of restaurants in Windhoek and on the coast, the cuisine has a richness and diversity that reflects Namibia's cosmopolitan culture

There's one word almost every Namibian understands: *brötchen*, the German word for "bread roll", which has penetrated every linguistic group in the country. Indeed, European visitors will find all sorts of familiar breads and pastries in the bakeries here, from dark, thinly-sliced pumpernickel loaves to *apfelstrudel*, feather-light *Sachertorte*, sumptuous *Schwarzwaldkirschtorte* (Black Forest Cherry Cake) and many others.

You'll find plenty of other German staples on Namibian menus, too, from frankfurters to *sauerkraut*. Not to mention the beer, of course, which is brewed strictly in accordance with German purity laws.

When it comes to local produce, carnivores have a field day. There are all sorts of exotic cuts such as oryx (gemsbok), kudu, ostrich, springbok and crocodile to choose from in the form of main-course steaks, roasts or stews. Smoked venison and pâtés, meanwhile, often head the choice of *hors d'oeuvres*. You may even spot warthog, zebra, hartebeest and eland on the menu, although these are less frequently encountered

On a more conventional note, the locals will tell you Namibian beef is the tastiest and healthiest in the world, because the cattle are free-ranging.

Superb seafood

Fish fans can look forward to fresh *kabeljou* (cob), kingklip and sole, all caught off the Atlantic coast. The oysters farmed at Swakopmund are a much-prized local delicacy, as are the crayfish (rock lobster) fished in the Lüderitz area.

Other specialities to look out for include the Kalahari truffle *(nabas)*, an indigenous tuber with a slightly nutty flavour. Sliced thinly, it adds a delicious depth to salads, sauces and

casseroles. Also much in demand are the tasty *omajavo* mushrooms which sprout on termite hills after the summer rains. They're either sautéd in garlic butter and enjoyed with steaks, schnitzels and in salads, or served in soups.

Most of Namibia's fresh produce is imported from South Africa, so if you're shopping for

fruit and vegetables in the smaller towns, you're unlikely to find a wide variety; what's more, it may be expensive and of poor quality to boot.

South African influences

The South Africans have also exported their national pastime, the *braai* (barbecue), to Namibia, which means that every weekend in summer, gardens turn blue with smoke as hunks of meat are grilled. Visitors should be sure to sample the *boerewors*, or "farmer's sausage", made from beef or game and flavoured with spices and herbs – as well as the *potjiekos,* a meat stew simmered for hours on the coals in a little three-legged cast-iron pot.

LEFT: cooking up a storm at the Country Club in Windhoek – a good option for Sunday lunch.
RIGHT: scrambled egg, San style: this ostrich egg is equivalent to two dozen hen's eggs.

The pleasures of the palate are usually rounded off with Cape wine. Reds include Pinotage, Shiraz, Cabernet Sauvignon and Merlot, while amongst the white varieties are Chenin Blanc, Chardonnay, Cape Riesling, Blanc Fumé and Sauvignon Blanc.

Eating out in Windhoek

Namibia's cosmopolitan capital is well-supplied with good cafés and restaurants, catering for most tastes and pockets. The ever-popular Gathemann Restaurant in Independence Avenue (on the first floor of the Gathemann Building) has prime seating on a balcony over-looking Zoo Park and is an excellent place for Namibian specialties such as game, Lüderitz crayfish and fresh asparagus from Swakopmund. Vegetarians are well catered for, and there's an extensive wine list.

Practically opposite Joe's Beerhous, on Nelson Mandela Avenue, O Portuga, is a good place to sample the distinctively spicy cuisine associate with the former Portuguese colony of Angola, as well as a wide selection of top-notch seafood dishes. Also renowned for its seafood, Luigi & the Fish is a popular place for a lingering dinner, situated along Sam Nujoma Drive close to the intersection with Nelson Mandela Avenue.

DESERT DELICACIES

Here in this hot and largely arid land, the indigenous peoples have had to adapt their diet to the resources available – which they have done both imaginatively and inventively.

Take the ostrich egg, for example, which is equivalent to some two dozen hen's eggs. The San (Bushmen) know many ways of preparing it; cooks will make a hole in the upper half of the shell and use a twig as a spoon to mix the yolk and the white. A hollow in the earth is filled with hot coals, the egg is poured in and an omelette produced.

But what would the life of the desert nomad be without the !nara? This nutritious fruit grows on river-banks, its deep roots drawing up water; for the Nama it has become a multi-purpose staple. Pressed, the fruit yields up a sweet, thirst-quenching liquid, while the pulp can be made into cake. Baked into a dry breadstuff, it can keep for up to two years, while its roots are used to make medicine.

Meat is a special treat for desert-dwellers, whose poisoned arrows kill game on contact – even giraffe. Hunters expertly dismember the carcass on the spot; specially marked arrows leave no doubt as to whose property the game is. Some claim the head as their special portion. This is buried in a pit filled with glowing coals and left to cure for a day, after which it is removed and the skull broken open – thus exposed, the brain is the greatest delicacy one can hope for.

For lunchtime fare, the Mugg & Bean, with its first-floor balcony overlooking Post Street Mall, serves aromatic coffee as well as a wide selection of sandwiches and light meals. Other good options in the café style include the Café Zoo in the central but surprisingly tranquil Zoo Park, the Craft Café in the Namcrafts Centre on Tal Street, and the more out-of-town Jenny's Place on Sam Nujoma Drive

After dark

For a capital city, Windhoek offers surprisingly little in the way of nightlife and entertainment. Visitors seeking pubs and bars will have to be

Industrial Area) and Club Thriller in Katatura. Live music venues are similarly thin on the ground but include the popular Pentagon Entertainment Centre southwest of the city centre, which doubles as a nightclub after 10pm weekends, and the Tower of Music (open from 6pm Wed, Fri and Sat) in the Namcrafts Centre on Tal Street.

You'll find Windhoek's only cinema, the five-screen Ster-Kinekor, in the Maerua Park Centre in Centaurus Road. Both international and South African releases are shown here, and prices are extremely reasonable in comparison with Europe and the US.

content with the facilities offered by the big hotels, most of which are open to non-residents. Good options include the beer garden at the Thuringer Hof, along with O'Hagan's Irish Pub near the corner of Jan Jonker Road and Robert Mugabe Avenue, Bulldogs in the Hidas Centre, Sam Nujoma Drive, and (most popular of all) the aforementioned Joe's Beerhouse.

As for nightclubs, these tend to come and go, but the more long-serving options include La Dee Das (off Lazarett Street in the Southern

Visitors who want to try their luck at gambling can visit the Windhoek Country Club Resort on the Western Bypass road, as well as the casino at the Kalahari Sands Hotel, in the Gustav Voigts Centre on Independence Avenue.

A varied menu in Swakopmund

Aside from the usual Namibian fare, Swakopmund is renowned for its fresh fish and seafood cuisine. The best place to try it? Look no further than the Hansa Hotel in Roon Street, which has an award-winning restaurant serving good-quality "international" cuisine, from seafood to meat and vegetarian dishes. They also have an impressive selection of South African wines.

LEFT: merriment in a Swakopmund drinking-hole.
ABOVE: a diverse range of live African music is on offer in the capital.

Another fine place for seafood is The Tug, with a great setting down on the beachfront, next to an iron jetty (watching the sun dip down into the sea is an added bonus). It's very popular, though, so make sure you book in advance.

Then there's Kücki's Pub, one of the liveliest and most popular restaurants-cum-bars in Swakopmund. You can sit inside or in a spacious courtyard, but either way, the food (which is traditional German) is very good, Seafood's a speciality here too and, again, it's wise to book in advance.

Swakopmund is also renowned for its traditional German cafés. The Hotel Schweizer-

haus's Café Anton on Bismarck Street is one of the best places to indulge in calorific cakes and pastries, and there are nice sea views, too.

Out on the town

In direct contrast to Windhoek, Swakopmund has a pretty lively nightlife for such a small place, especially during the summer season. Some of the best bars for hanging out include the Rafters Action Pub in Moltke Street (known for its draught beers and choice of imported beers), Fagan's Bar in Roon Street (a lively Irish style pub which sometimes has live bands), and O'Kelly's Pub right next door, which stays open until the wee hours and is a favourite with any-

one who likes to kick up their heels and dance.

If you're feeling lucky, the Swakopmund Entertainment Centre next to the Swakopmund Hotel has a casino, and a cinema too.

Superb seafood in Lüderitz

There's not much nightlife to be found in Lüderitz, and most people retire after enjoying a few drinks at their hotel bar. Foodwise, however, visitors are in for a treat: the speciality here is crayfish, although all the usual meat dishes are also available, too.

Bush cuisine

Out of town on safari, the restaurant choices are few but fortunately most lodges offer ample amounts of food, even if the quality is variable. In many places you'll find your evening meal served in a traditional *boma*, an open-air enclosure lit by a roaring fire, where meals are prepared and served.

Usually, you'll be offered buffet lunches and dinners comprising a wide range of meats, salads, vegetables and desserts. If you want to try something authentically Namibian at breakfast time, look out for (or request) *mahangu* (millet) porridge, a staple food of many black Namibians; it's surprisingly tasty.

Guest farms and smaller establishments – particularly those in the remoter areas – serve a rather more limited selection of meals. Here, it's a question of whether or not the chef's on form the day you arrive in camp, but in the main, the food is fresh and well-prepared. Indeed, the standard of the cooking at some of the more far-flung places like Kulala Lodge in the Namib is remarkably good, considering the difficulties of supply and preparation.

On a camping safari guests will usually be offered a traditional *braai* (barbecue) in the evenings, complete with lots of different kinds of salads and *potjiekos* (stew).

If your itinerary includes the northern regions, you'll be able to supplement your diet with all sorts of indigenous fruit and nuts from roadside stalls – depending on the season, of course. Look out for marula fruits, the *embe* or *omuve* (bird plum), and succulent monkey oranges – great for quenching thirst on a boiling hot day. ❏

LEFT: a scene from Windhoek's biggest knees-up, the Karneval, which usually takes place in early May.
RIGHT: wedding celebration, northern Namibia.

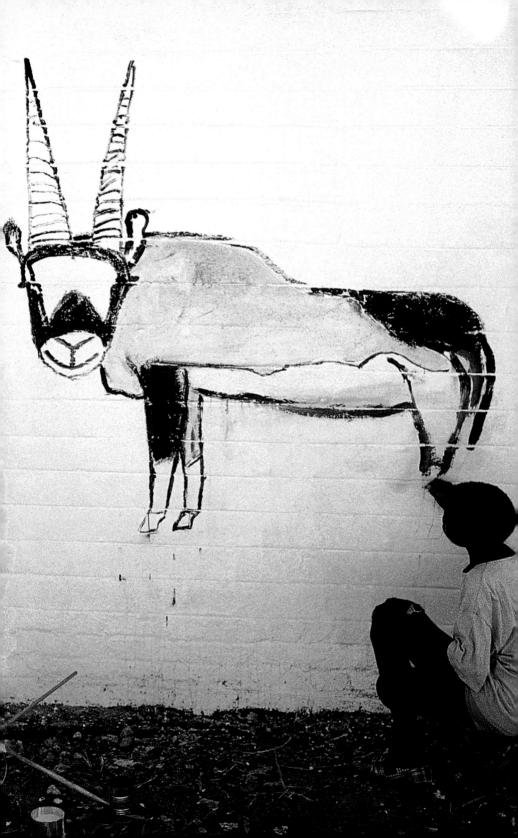

THE ARTS

Contrary to most visitors' expectations, Namibia's cultural scene is a flourishing blend of myth, township art and modernity

Most people think of Namibia as a country of wild landscapes and stunning scenery. Less well-known, however, is the country's urban environment, which has given rise to a rich cultural scene. For decades, white immigrants – particularly in Windhoek and Swakopmund – have worked to preserve their European culture and build up an art scene within the country itself. Since independence in 1991, black artists, too, have made their presence known.

Soon after World War II, artists and artistically-minded citizens and patrons of Windhoek and Swakopmund started to found cultural associations with their own exhibition spaces which presented a wide range of local and foreign works. Their aim was to promote local talent, as well as introducing it to the international art scene.

Neighbouring South Africa was a major force behind Namibia's artistic development – yet even in the days when apartheid was the status quo, local art societies were open to members of all races. Today, galleries and exhibitions display the works of black artists, as well as works about Africa, while the National Art Gallery in Windhoek contains an extensive collection of Namibian art works old and new.

African crafts

Since independence in 1991, the country has been in a pioneering phase, artistically speaking. In Okavango, Ovamboland, Caprivi and in the south of the country, there has been a revival of traditional craft production, with locals being encouraged to create anew – without falling into the rut of mass-production.

Pottery and basketry – the latter traditionally woven with Makalani palm leaves – are practised by women in northern Namibia, from the Caprivians to the Ovambo and the Kavango.

Woodcarving, too, is part of the northern tradition, although it's usually practised by men.

As for beadwork, the San (Bushmen) and the Himba are traditionally the most skilled practitioners. Authentic San crafts (bags and clothing decorated with beads made from ostrich egg shells, seeds and porcupine quills) are eas-

iest to find in the Tsumeb area; for Himba crafts you have to go to Kaokoland – or check out Windhoek's private galleries.

Tapestries woven from karakul wool also occupy a special place in the local crafts scene. Wall-hangings and floor coverings from the large weaving establishments such as Ibenstein and Dorka near Dordabis *(see page 176)* can reach a very high standard.

Oil and watercolour landscapes

Namibia's extraordinary scenery has fascinated European artists ever since colonial times. After all, even the most barren stretches of the Namib Desert can be bewitching, whether because of

LEFT: black artists are now making their presence felt – sometimes in the most unlikely places.
RIGHT: Ovamboland in northern Namibia is a good place to find authentic local crafts.

the bizarre light effects in the early morning or the unusual play of intense colours as evening approaches. From this land of stones and vast distances, artists have often created landscape images depicting unspoiled Edens and romantic panoramas.

Even the renowned colonial painter Ernst Vollbehr, in general a rather distanced observer, bathed his work *Lüderitz Harbour* in a gentle pink afternoon light. The oil landscapes of Carl Ossmann, exhibited in Berlin, started a tradition in Namibia before World War I of naturalistic depictions of nature; this school remained the major artistic force in the country

Animal subjects

Axel Eriksson, Zackie Eloff, Hans-Anton Aschenborn and other artists often include peacefully-grazing antelopes in their depictions of nature: for them, wild animals – so remote from the rest of the world – are an important part of this tranquillity.

Fritz Krampe, however, who had sketched elephants and gorillas in the Berlin Zoo as a child, chose African wildlife as a central theme of his work, filling entire canvases with it. Krampe spent much of his time exploring the Etosha region and other areas of Africa rich in wildlife. He was less interested in gentle

until new stylistic conceptions and subjects came onto the scene in the 1970s, forcing it into a secondary position.

The calligraphic brushstrokes in the works of Adolph Jentsch, a landscape painter recognised and acknowledged far beyond the borders of his own country, are meant to establish a mystical connection between one's own heartbeat and the rhythm of surrounding nature. Jentsch, strongly influenced by Far Eastern philosophies, often meditated for hours in the wilderness before starting on a watercolour. Other significant names to look out for in local galleries are Otto Schröder, Johannes Blatt and Jochen Voigts.

gazelles or picturesque ostriches than in the large, threatening animals: lions, elephants, buffalo, hyenas and vultures.

His trademark became the representation of action: his brushstrokes were quick, strong, often sketchy. The viewer almost recoils from these oil paintings, drawings and lithographs of fighting, hunting or fleeing animals – as if he or she could feel the hot winds of the steppe and smell the danger.

Focus on man

All of the above artists occasionally produced portraits or figurative works. But it wasn't until the 1980s, probably as a result of socio-political developments associated with the country's move towards independence, that man, his environment and his perceptions, were seen as challenging subjects for the visual artist. In retrospect, the discovery of the human figure can already be seen in the landscape paintings of Anita Stayn and François de Necker.

Photography, as well – an art which has reached a high level of technical development in Namibia – now tends to concern itself more with *Homo sapiens* than with the microcosmos of nature which it used to depict: the devastation of border wars in Kaokoveld, or the jubilation of independence ceremonies.

Sculptors are a rare breed in Namibia; Dörte Berner from Dordabis is the only one who has successfully exhibited abroad so far. Sculpted from local steatite (soapstone), her massive, monumental works depict persecuted, lonely, scorned men, or mothers and groups of children seeking protection.

Black art

A new, vital artistic category is currently making headlines in Namibia, township art. This term, coined in the black slums of South Africa, describes the work of a new generation of artists in Namibia, who have been able to receive an artistic education at the Windhoek Academy, today the University of Namibia, or private art schools in Lüderitz Bay, with the help of grants and scholarships. Joseph Madisia, Andrew von Wyk and Tembo Masala have already attained renown.

In black parlance, "sharp" is the superlative form of "good"; and the drawings and paintings of these young artists, depicting existence in the crowded township huts, telling of suffering, poverty and protest, are sharp – as well as aggressive, funny, cynical and penetratingly realistic. Colours tend to be loud and jarring; simple actions are magnified into lofty expressiveness. These are pieces which captivate the viewer by means of their unmitigated realism. At the same time, they present a balance between daily city life and African myth.

LEFT: not only are carpets woven from the wool of the karakul sheep, a Namibian speciality...

RIGHT: ...almost any design can be commissioned.

> **PICTURE THIS**
>
> John Muafangejo – who confined himself exclusively to the restricting black and white of linoleum prints – was the first black man to have his art exhibited in Namibian galleries.

One of the best-known names on the modern Namibian art scene belongs to the Ovambo John Muafangejo. This artist, who died tragically young, remained impressively uninfluenced by European stylistic elements even after he had visited South Africa and travelled in Europe. His lino-cuts of traditional life among the Ovambos, and his visions of Biblical history are absolutely original and unique, and so unparalleled that they fetch high prices on the South African art market.

The Performing Arts

Song and dance were among the first artistic expressions of the Namibian indigenous peoples. As early as the late Middle Ages, Portuguese sailors to Africa witnessed local musicians playing reed flutes in settlements along the coast. Other travellers documented performances of vocal music in black *kraals* as early as 1668.

The Namas in the centre and south of Namibia possessed a whole range of handcrafted and technically advanced musical instruments which were taken over, in part, by the San and the Khoi-San: bowls covered with stretched hides to serve as drums; a stringed instrument called the "gora"; and the "ramki", a kind of guitar with three or more strings made from cattle tail-hair or plant fibres.

Reed flutes were used to stimulate and arouse during traditional religious rituals – when worshippers imitated the movements of animals in order to summon spirits – bone rattles provided a rhythmic accompaniment. Indigenous clans also used hand-rattles made from gourds, as well as signal trumpets made of antelope horns. In the north of Namibia, the Ovambos and Kavangos used tall wooden drums. In Caprivi, xylophones were added to complete the rich sound texture.

In Okavango, traditional drums and other instruments are still used today in ritual dances, and even in Christian services.

European influences

For decades, the official music and theatre scene of Namibia was dominated by European tastes and styles as an élite group of "culturally aware" Windhoek and Swakopmund residents attempted to transplant the cultural heritage of Germany, Britain and South Africa into the "wilderness". After World War II, the founding of artistic organisations meant that exhibitions, ballet and theatre performances could be arranged, and foreign artists brought in.

In 1902, the Swakopmund Men's Choral Association was established, followed by the Men's Choral Association of Windhoek and numerous other choirs (mixed as well as men's) throughout the country. Thanks to a lack of trained choir directors, music teachers from the schools were conscripted after 1963. In 1971 the State Music Conservatory was founded in Windhoek; since then, an able staff has provided voice lessons.

Since the abolition of South Africa's apartheid system, black and white Namibians alike have begun to explore their joint cultural traditions. Deluged with critical acclaim on European and American tours, the mixed-race Cantare Audire Choir performs religious and classical European music, as well as spirituals, African and Namibian compositions.

Theatre and dance

Namibia's formal theatrical tradition stretches back to its earliest days as a colony. Long before SWARUK, the Southwest African Council on the Performing Arts, was founded in 1966, talented laymen were staging such difficult works as Goethe's *Die Mitschuldigen* or Tennessee Williams's *The Glass Menagerie*.

These days, in addition to the work of the National Theatre in the capital, sundry community theatres have formed in the townships. In its School of Arts, the University of Namibia has its own theatre department. The Space Theatre and the Warehouse Theatre, two experimental stages, let young Namibian actors and playwrights display and fine-tune their skills while finding new points of departure.

As for the indigenous dramatic tradition, song and dance have always played an integral role. Since independence, various cultural organisations have established programmes where actors are sent to outlying areas – not just to entertain, but also to involve members of the community, young and old, in creating and acting out a story.

Even in traditional ceremonies, dramatic elements have always been powerfully deployed. Sensations and experiences are elevated into a magical sphere through the use of dance, rhythm and music. ❏

LEFT: although choral music stems from Namibia's élitist colonial heritage, choirs have now become part of local culture.

The First Artists

The wealth of paintings and engravings found in rock shelters and on rocky outcrops in Namibia are the only remaining archaeological traces of the hunter-gatherers who, until about 2,000 years ago, were southern Africa's only inhabitants.

This art is closely associated with shamanic trance experiences, a key religious activity for these societies. Even to this day, the trance dance remains a central ritual amongst the last few remaining San clans living in the Kalahari desert. During such dances, the women will clap and sing special "calling" songs named after things which they believe to be particularly powerful – the eland or the giraffe, for instance – while the men dance slowly and rhythmically around them.

The San believe that this singing and dancing activates a supernatural potency, and that it is the task of the shamans in the group – usually about half of the men and about a third of the women – to harness this energy in order to enter a trance state – or, as they term it, the spirit world. Once in this world, the shamans are said to be able to cure the sick, resolve social conflict and control the movements of game, as well as the all-important rain-animal that is believed to bring rain. Such "work" guarantees the existence of San society.

Shamans entering a trance usually experience a variety of physical and visual hallucinations, and often use "death" and "underwater" as metaphors for their trance experience. In traditional rock art, this state of mind would often be depicted by a dying eland. Think of the similarities: both can bleed at the nose, froth at the mouth, stumble about and eventually collapse unconscious.

When you are trying to decipher rock art, therefore, bear in mind that the commonest themes are trance dancing (women clapping and men dancing), those animals which symbolise supernatural potency (usually an eland), and the visual and physical hallucinations which shamans ritually undergo.

A recent interview with one of the last surviving descendants of a San artist – a woman now in her eighties and living in South Africa's Eastern Cape – has shed new light on the probable ritual use of the paintings. She told how eland were driven up the valley where her (habitually nomadic) clan had temporarily settled, and killed at a spot near the cave where the family slept. Blood from the animals was mixed with paint in an effort to transfer the eland's power to the paintings which decorated the walls of the clan's cave.

In addition, if the clan shamans wanted to increase their level of potency while dancing, they would turn to face the freshly-executed paintings, believing that the potency in the paintings would then flow into them. In other words, the paintings and engravings were not just depictions of things that happened in the spirit world or symbols of powerful creatures, they were also powerful things in themselves – storehouses of the potency that made contact with the spirit world possible.

The San's way of life initially survived the arrival of the Khoi herders, who migrated down from the north of Africa some 2,000 years ago; indeed, they developed good relations with them and lived together in relative harmony. But their society came increasingly under pressure following the arrival of the Boers and the British at the Cape in the 17th century. These white colonists not only took over the San's land and hunting areas, they looked down on them as little more than vermin – and hunted them down accordingly.

Today, a few San groups struggle to survive in Botswana, Namibia and South Africa, but their numbers are so few, they cannot really be said to represent a distinct social grouping any more. ❑

RIGHT: you'll find this engraved elephant at Phillips Cave on Ameib Ranch, a farm in central Namibia.

THE ARCHITECTURAL HERITAGE

The combination of German colonial rule and Namibia's extreme climate spawned a curious but effective style of building

An appropriate architecture for Namibia has to cope with a wide daily temperature range and intense solar radiation. Any functional building has to moderate the effects of daytime heating on the structure and the interior. For many centuries, the indigenous peoples responded appropriately by building a framework of poles sheathed with thick layers of mud and small openings.

The official architecture of the German colonial era found a different solution, adapting the building traditions of Germany to the altered demands of climate and building materials. The result was a verandah architecture – essentially a thick-walled core covered with a saddle roof and surrounded by a perimeter of lean-to roofs. The latter would shield the walls from the sun's rays, thereby retarding the passage of heat to the interior of the core.

The verandah genre was promoted by missionaries who had encountered it all over South Africa and applied it to their buildings in Namibia since the early 19th century. The Imperial Directorate of Building Services – primarily under the directorship of Gottlieb Redecker, the first architect born in Namibia – developed verandah architecture based on contemporary classical interpretations. A good example is the modifications made to the Ludwig von Estorff House in Windhoek in 1902.

In colonial Namibia, the verandah came to serve additionally as the equivalent of an entrance hall, and as a congenial, cool, covered outdoor living space, especially if located on the south of the house. The verandah genre was applied to a wide range and scale of building types, achieving its logical conclusion and monumentality in the Parliament Building in Windhoek, the *Tintenpalast* ("Ink Palace") of

1913, essentially a double-storeyed verandah building with classical elements.

The visitor to Namibia will not fail to see the Wilhelmenian influence in many of the colonial buildings. Obvious examples are the Railway Station, Prison and Hohenzollernhaus in Swakopmund. The moderate climate here per-

haps allows the architecture to blend in with the landscape rather more successfully than elsewhere in the country.

The most prolific private architect was Wilhelm Sander, whose legacies are firmly imprinted on contemporary Windhoek; the Gathemann and Genossenschaftshaus in Independence Avenue are perhaps the first you will encounter. It was Sander who, inspired by a disused military post, recycled and remodelled it as a medieval castle, Schwerinburg, thereby setting the course for the "manor house" of Duwisib in the south of the country and two more castles in the capital by and for himself. Woermann House in Swakopmund, by the

---

PRECEDING PAGES: colourful homes in Windhoek's Katatura district.
LEFT: Swakopmund's Hohenzollernhaus (1906) is a good example of the local *Jugendstil* style.
RIGHT: the early 19th-century Ritterburg building in Swakopmund now houses government offices.

house architect of the shipping line, Friedrich Höft, is based on the design principles of the Arts and Crafts movement while making sparing use of Art Nouveau motifs.

Also Art Nouveau-inspired is the Windhoek landmark, the Church of Christ, completed in 1910. But the centre for Art Nouveau architecture is without doubt Lüderitz, the southern harbour town which developed after 1908 when diamonds were found at Kolmanskop. The town, in a majestic setting focused on the harbour and

> **SHINING EXAMPLE**
>
> Namibia's most important office building is the glass-clad CDM Building in the capital, whose distinctive faceted south façade provides the glare-free conditions required for diamond sorting.

Shark Island, has the homes of the magnates located on the Diamantberg, the paradigm of which is the Goerke House of 1909.

South Africa and apartheid

After the German era, development was hesitant, hampered by political indecision, prolonged droughts and the depression in the 1930s. Things changed in the 1950s when the priority became the incorporation of Namibia into South Africa, which made available massive development aid. The infrastructure was developed and Windhoek matured into today's modern city.

But the ideology of apartheid was packaged along with economic assistance. To architects,

that meant that they had to design into public buildings separate facilities for each of the two races. Examples are the Main Post Office and the terminal buildings of Windhoek's two airports.

A major development was the Windhoek Library, Museum and Archives Building, the result of an architectural competition won by Hellmut Stauch, son of the discoverer of the Namibian diamond fields. A proponent of modern architecture as developed in Brazil, Stauch reaffirmed in his buildings the need to adapt design to the Namibian climate. With rising urban land values came the demand for taller buildings. Stauch's penchant was the external filigree of louvres to shade the core of the building without impeding daylight – in principle a continuation of the verandah traditions of colonial Namibia. The Carl List Haus of 1964 was the prototype.

Architecture since Independence

German colonial buildings are being preserved and renovated on a large scale; for example, the Alte Feste, Kaiserkrone, and Orban Schule (Conservatoire). This style of architecture, termed historicist because it drew upon historical prototypes, initiated the idea of conserving old buildings. The architecture being realised at the dawn of independence in 1990 again drew upon historical sources relating the two periods of the country's past. The hipped gable roof composition of the Wernhil Park Shopping Centre and the mansard roof and clock tower of Mutual Platz echo the roofscapes of the Wilhelmenian past. In Lüderitz, similar historical motifs have been revived.

Bold architectural responses are being made to the country's problems. In a landscape as harsh as that of Namibia, the setting defies the normal set of value judgements. The new buildings complete the urban landscape, perhaps more by similarity than by contrast; nevertheless they add to the totality, its richness and diversity, while the old structures remain relevant to contemporary life in Namibia. ❏

LEFT: indigenous architecture is designed to provide shelter from the intense summer sun.
RIGHT: Windhoek combines many architectural styles.

ACTIVE PURSUITS

For lovers of the Great Outdoors, there are few places on earth
more "outdoors" than Namibia's sparsely populated wilderness

Namibia's desert climate, with clear skies and sunshine throughout the year, together with its wealth of unspoilt wilderness areas and few crowds, makes it an expansive playground for outdoor enthusiasts who can enjoy a diverse range of activities.

Hiking and climbing

During Namibia's winter months, between April and October, hiking and climbing give an opportunity to experience the Namibian landscape – its scale, colours and mountains contrasting with endless plains – together with spectacular views, where you can really feel the freedom of space and appreciate the natural environment. Walking is mainly done in the early morning and evening, with a rest during the heat of the day. One of the main pleasures is that, even on the most popular trails, it never gets crowded.

Hiking trails extend from the Brandberg, Spitzkoppe, Pondok and Naukluft mountains to the Waterberg Plateau and Fish River Canyon. They vary considerably in length, from short walks to serious eight-day hikes across rugged terrain, where you need to carry your own equipment.

It's important to be suitably fit, prepared for hot temperatures, to carry enough water and to wear proper walking boots. Trails need to be booked in advance with the Ministry of Environment and Tourism (MET) in Windhoek *(see Travel Tips, page 286).*

The Brandberg granite massif rises to Konigstein, at 2,575 metres (8,450 ft) the highest mountain in Namibia. It's a strenuous three-hour return hike to see the "White Lady of the Brandberg", but there's a network of other trails, and guides can be hired from the local community. The mountain presents a number of technical climbs for serious mountaineers.

Similarly, the mountains of Spitzkoppe and Pondok give testing rock climbs – the highest peak, Grott Spitzkoppe (1,728 metres/5,670 ft), is "the Matterhorn of Namibia".

Among Namibia's many walking trails, the Naukluft mountains are the setting for one of Africa's toughest hikes – the 120-km (75-mile),

eight-day, Naukluft Trail. It follows the Naukluft river before ascending the escarpment, from which there are expansive views across the plains. Two circular trails – the Waterkloof (17 km/10 miles) and Olive (10 km/6 miles) – provide challenging day hikes.

The steep ascents encountered on each day's hike and the rocky terrain underfoot are physically demanding and the trails are not recommended for beginners or the unfit.

Considered one of the top five hiking trails in Southern Africa is the Fish River Canyon. Following an 80-km (50-mile) stretch of the river, from Hiker's Point to Ai-Ais, it involves rough walking – scrambling over rocks, ploughing

PRECEDING PAGES: camping in the Namib.
LEFT: hikers ascending one of the dunes at Sossusvlei.
RIGHT: canoeing down the Orange River is a must for adrenaline junkies.

through loose sand and sustaining soaring temperatures – but solitude, spectacular scenery and the magnificent colours of the canyon make up for any discomfort. There are no facilities whatever, though, so backpackers must aim to be totally self-sufficient.

The Waterberg Plateau Park has nine short wilderness trails, open throughout the year. Of the longer trails, which require advance booking, there is an unguided, 42-km (26-mile), four-day hike around sandstone kopjes at the southern end of the plateau.

But the park's main appeal is the guided Okarakuvisa Trail, a three- or four-day trek.

Here walkers track animals (white and black rhino and sable and roan antelope, amongst others) through the bush in a pristine wilderness area away from roads and other people, to become absorbed in learning about wildlife issues and the natural environment while staying in camps surrounded by sandstone cliffs.

Take to the water

Canoeing the Orange river along the South African border is very different from canoeing on the Zambezi. Five-day trips in Mohawk two-man canoes traverse a 75-km (47-mile) stretch of the river. There are no hippos or crocodiles,

so swimming in the scorching midday temperatures while gently drifting downstream, is particularly relaxing. The river meanders through stark, arid scenery, interspersed with several rapids, where people are noticeable by their absence. At night, with no unnatural light in the sky, the stars are particularly awesome, and you can experience the eerie silence of the desert.

In contrast, there are game-viewing trips by *mokoro* (dugout canoe) on the northern rivers. At the coast there's sea-kayaking among seals and dolphins around Walvis Bay, and boat excursions to see dolphins, seals and pelagic birds. For an adrenalin rush try white-water rafting which is organised on the Kunene river,

SANDBOARDING

Swakopmund has developed as a centre for desert adventure enthusiasts. The sand dunes of the Namib provide an exciting variation on snowboarding called sandboarding, although techniques are much the same. Most sandboarding is carried out in the dune area between Swakopmund and Walvis Bay, where dunes rise to 120 metres (400 ft) high.

Quad-biking is also extremely popular, on motorised four-wheelers that make it possible to take picnics and sundowner trips in the desert. If you're quad-biking, it's important to go on organised trails, as there are nesting birds in certain areas.

bordering Angola, along a 120-km (75-mile) stretch between Ruacana and Epupa Falls.

Riding

Namibia has a strong horse-riding tradition, based on the farming community, and riding is widely available to visitors at lodges and on private farms, where it's often possible to see game such as oryx and kudu from horseback.

One of the most exciting and challenging rides, giving a flavour of the scale and variety of the Namibian countryside, is the Namib Desert Ride, organised by Reit Safaris. It's a nine-day, 400-km (250-mile) ride which begins

consequently hunting now attracts a high proportion of international visitors, too – particularly Germans and Americans *(see page 127)*. Encouragingly, Namibia's Professional Hunters' Association follows a strict ethical code, with all trophy hunters being accompanied by an experienced professional hunter or registered guide.

Angling

Fishing is an extremely popular Namibian pastime, with a choice of deep-sea fishing and surf angling off the Atlantic coast, and freshwater fly-fishing in the northern rivers of Zambezi,

in the comparatively green highlands of the Khomas Hochland, then descends into the arid lands of the Namib Desert, with its gravel plains and dunes, before arriving at the coast.

Hunting

Hunting is part of an everyday way of life for many Namibian farmers who regularly shoot game for the pot. In the 1980s, as cattle and karakul prices fell, many farmers diversified into offering trophy hunting on their farms, and

LEFT: hiking in the Fish River Canyon offers marvellous views of mountains, sea and sky.
ABOVE: waiting for the wind.

UNDERWATER ATTRACTIONS

The shipwrecks that litter the Skeleton Coast are the prime attraction for divers, the best dive sites being between Lüderitz and north to Spencer Bay, where visibility is good – between 3 and 10 metres (10–33 ft). December to May are considered the best months for diving. Arrangements can be made through the Namibian Underwater Federation (NUF, *see Travel Tips page 280*).

Inland, for experienced cave-divers, there's the opportunity to swim subterranean lakes – including Dragon's Breath Cave, only discovered in 1986, which contains the largest underground lake in the world.

Chobe, Kunene and Kwando, or on the dams.

Prime surf angling spots are found along the blustery Atlantic coastline north of Swakopmund to the mouth of the Ugab river, while deep-sea fishing trips can be arranged from Swakopmund. Shark fishing here compares with the best in the world, with some copper sharks weighing in at around 180 kg (400 lb). Other species like west-coast steenbras, cob, blacktail and white stumpnose are a regular catch, although what you end up with on your hook will largely depend on what bait you use. Red bait is considered a good, all-purpose choice, as are fresh pilchards (unless you're

after galjoen which favours white mussels and red bait). Steenbras are partial to shrimps, while cob (also known as kabeljou) will readily take white mussels. The season here runs from November to March.

Many fly-fishermen gravitate to the Chobe and Zambezi rivers in eastern Caprivi, lured by the ultimate freshwater challenge, the Tiger Fish. Here a serious quest for large specimens – over 9 kg (20 lb) – involves fishing the rapids from a dugout canoe *(mokoro)*. Fishing lodges like Impalila can also provide boat excursions, complete with guides and fishing tackle. Tiger-fishing's usually most rewarding between August and December.

Bream, barbel and African pike are among the 81 fish species found in these waters, along with greenhead, squaker and nembwe. Undoubtedly, part of the attraction of fishing in this region is experiencing the wonderful riverine birdlife and game coming to water.

Sky adventures

Thanks to the near-perfect atmospheric conditions prevailing in Namibia, it's a popular destination for airsports enthusiasts.

Ballooning across the Namib desert at dawn, followed by a traditional champagne breakfast, is a wonderful way to experience the size and emptiness of the desert. Recreational flights over Sossusvlei from Swakopmund give expansive views of the Kuiseb river canyon, star and crescent dunes stretching to the horizon, the pan at Sossusvlei and wreck of the *Eduard Bohlen* which ran aground in 1910.

Bitterwasser, southeast of Windhoek near Uhlenhorst is renowned for its world record-breaking gliding conditions, with some of the best thermals in the world. Microlighting takes place around Windhoek, the Brandberg and the coast and the season usually stretches from October to January, when thermal activity is the most favourable.

Four-wheel drive trails

Namibia's rugged terrain has always attracted 4x4 enthusiasts who relish the wilderness experience, testing their wits and their vehicle's performance against the elements. Unfortunately, with the increase in 4x4 clubs, more people are venturing into remote areas, where their enthusiasm has not been matched with care for the environment. Gravel plains are particularly susceptible, as vehicle tracks can last for centuries.

There are a number of recognised 4x4 trails. Among these are the Windhoek to Okahandja Trail travelling through several farms in the Khomas Hochland; the Dorsland Trail, which marks the Namibian section of the 1878 Dorsland Trek, from South Africa through Namibia to Angola; and the Kalahari-Namib Trail which opened in 1999. They present a driving challenge, but the routes are not advisable to those who have no experience of African 4x4 driving conditions. ❑

LEFT: many remote areas can only be reached by a four-wheel-drive vehicle.

The Sky at Night

The starry heavens as seen from Africa are the most beautiful in the world; high above Namibia, as elsewhere in Africa, it looks as if Atlas himself were bearing them on his shoulders. Seeing them for the first time is an intoxicating experience.

Namibia's position on the Tropic of Capricorn means there is only a short twilight between day and night, so you can see the stars from almost immediately after sunset until sunrise. Still mercifully free of air pollution, the beautiful Namibian night skies allow stars down to the sixth order of magnitude to be discerned with the naked eye. On a clear night, about 2,500 individual stars and up to five planets are visible.

The galaxy that includes our sun, which we know as the Milky Way, contains around 100,000 million stars, which appear in their greatest concentration as a hazy luminous band across the sky. The Namibian Bushmen call it the "backbone of the night".

Many constellations are easily identifiable. Orion is one of the most distinctive, with the three stars in his belt. Orion's "shoulder" is the star Betelgeux, a red super-giant star 300–400 times the diameter of the sun, 10 times the diameter of earth and one of the largest known stars.

The constellation Taurus is clearly visible from November to May. Virgo can be seen from March to August, Aquarius from August to January, and Leo from February to July. The brightest star in Leo is Regulus, a star of the first magnitude. You can spot Scorpio, the brightest of the zodiac constellations, from May to November.

Sirius, the Dog Star, is the brightest star in the sky and forms part of the dog's head of the constellation Canis Major. Since time immemorial the "Southern Cross", named after the shape made by its four brightest stars, has been the compass of camel caravans as they trailed through the desert. The two bright "pointers" that seem to point towards the Southern Cross are Alpha and Beta Centauri – of which Alpha is the nearest star to Earth.

Some stars from the northern hemisphere can also be seen in Namibia: Capella, from December to March; Arcturus, from June to August; and Altair, from July to October. The planets Saturn, Jupiter,

RIGHT: the southern skies.

Mars, Mercury and Venus (the brightest of all, also known as the Morning or Evening Star) can also be seen on occasion, although their visibility varies as they move through space at different speeds in different orbits. You may also see magnificent shooting stars and satellites on a clear night.

The naked eye can also detect "Messier objects", named after the French astronomer Charles Messier (1730–1817) in the southern sky: star clusters, nebulas and galaxies such as Hercules and Omega. Two other galaxies, known as the Magellanic Clouds after the seafarer Ferdinand Magellan, are sometimes visible. The Greater Magellanic Cloud is a star cluster containing some five

million stars and is 160,000 light years from earth, while the Lesser is even farther away and contains around two billion stars.

In February 1986, it was possible to spot Halley's Comet with the naked eye in Namibia. And for many months in 1997–98, the comet Hale-Bopp was clearly visible in the southern African sky.

The largest meteorite that has ever been found struck the earth in Namibia: "Hoba", with a mass of around 55 tonnes, was named after the farm on whose land it fell.

The overwhelming dimensions of the heavens over Namibia seem to be reflected in the land itself: they stretch away unfathomably, much like the desert. ❑

ON SAFARI

Namibia's extraordinary landscape and extensive conservation areas

make a wildlife safari a unique and memorable experience

Shimmering expanses of white at Etosha Pan, apricot and coral dunes in the Namib desert, verdant waterways of the Caprivi, empty, bleached beaches along the Skeleton Coast, barren terracotta mountains in Damaraland, ochre rockfaces of the Fish River Canyon and cloudless azure skies all paint vivid, lasting impressions of the Namibian landscape.

The country is big, raw, wild and often bleak. There's an overwhelming feeling of space, timelessness and distant horizons. It's a desert land of extremes, where even during the winter months, between April and October, temperatures are known to regularly soar to 30°C (86°F) during the middle of the day, dropping to near freezing at night.

Wildlife viewing against this backdrop is a very different experience from other safari destinations in Africa. What makes Namibia particularly special is the number of large mammals found in a desert environment, and the fact that the animals are not restricted to designated parks.

In hostile terrain, sightings of species such as desert elephants, Hartmann's mountain zebra or the elusive black rhino are particularly gratifying, while the renowned Etosha National Park compares with the best game parks in Africa and has sizeable herds of the endemic black-faced impala. The clown-faced oryx (gemsbok), with its distinctive black and white mask and rapier horns, is a desert specialist, and is often seen in the sand dunes.

Birdlife is surprisingly diverse, thanks to the variety of habitats, with 620 recorded species. Raptors are numerous, and it's common to see pale chanting goshawk perched on telephone posts at the roadside, or eagles soaring on the afternoon thermals. In the arid regions of Damaraland, the guttural croak of Ruppell's korhaan can be heard echoing along the valleys in the early morning, mingling with the mewing of longbilled larks.

Plant life is equally intriguing and often bizarre, such as the quaint *Welwichsia mirabilis* (an underground tree with "pine" cones), elephant's foot or the aptly-named bottle tree.

Namibia is geologically rich, and much of its

ancient history is well preserved. There are dinosaurs' footprints, fossilised trees, and magnificent sites of stone age rock art, the most famous being at Twyfelfontein. Remarkably, the descendents of these early artists, the San (also called the Bushmen), still live in the Kalahari today. Other indigenous peoples, like the Himba pasturalists of the Kaokoveld, also still pursue a traditional lifestyle.

Choosing a safari

Namibia does not have a safari heritage like its counterparts elsewhere in Africa. But there is a distinctive Namibian safari style, characterised by well-organised efficiency and a comprehen-

LEFT: camel-trekkers heading through the dunes near Swakopmund.

RIGHT: expedition to the "White Castles" at Hoarusib Canyon, Skeleton Coast National Park.

sive variety of options, ranging from budget tours on scheduled coaches and minibuses, to more expensive special interest tours and mobile 4x4 camping safaris with knowledgeable guides, fly-in safaris with a pilot-guide, self-drive or train travel.

Combined with some of the active pursuits described in the preceding chapter, a uniquely Namibian safari can be designed to suit most tastes and budgets. Travelling is more comfortable in October and November when it's cooler, but if you want to see baby animals or migrating birds, the summer months are best.

The scheduled tours generally cover the most popular and accessible highlights of the country, a typical 10-day itinerary travelling from Windhoek to Sossusvlei, Swakopmund, Damaraland, Etosha and returning to Windhoek. Special interest safaris and mobile camps give the flexibility of travelling on different routes and at a more relaxing pace, with time to appreciate the scenery and to learn about the environment.

If you plan to travel in remote areas, bear in mind that even the more upmarket tours do not offer the camping luxury found in countries such as Tanzania or Kenya; logistically, it's impractical to travel with so much equipment – so the camping is comfortable rather than lux-

NAMIBIA'S NATIONAL PARKS

The country has a broad spectrum of 20 national parks, game reserves, parks and resorts, ranging from the 50,000 sq. km (20,000 sq. miles) of Namib-Naukluft Park to the Popa Falls Game Reserve of 25 hectares (60 acres).

The best known and most visited is Etosha National Park, established in 1907 and now occupying 22,270 sq. km (8,6000 sq. miles). It is home to 114 mammal species and 340 birds. The best time for game watching is May–September, when you can expect to see many antelope species, elephant, rhino, giraffe and lions.

The vast Namib-Naukluft Park is the largest wildlife reserve in Africa and the fourth largest in the world. It embraces flat gravel plains, rugged mountain ranges (the Naukluft), steep river gorges, the sand dunes of the Namib Desert and the lagoons of Sandwich and Walvis.

The Skeleton Coast Park is a true wilderness area, a narrow strip stretching 16,390 sq. km (6,330 sq. miles) along the Atlantic Ocean from the Ugab River all the way north to Angola. Namibia's smaller parks are no less remarkable. They include Fish River Canyon – a spectacle second only to America's Grand Canyon – and the Waterburg Plateau Park, established specifically for the protection of endangered species, where you can see white and black rhino, and roan and sable antelope.

urious. And don't confuse mobile camps (where your tents travel around with you) with permanent tented camps, which are among the best in Africa. In areas like Damaraland and the Kaoko-veld, the road scarcely exists in places, so these safaris will only appeal to those with an adventurer's spirit.

Fly-in safaris are ideal for those on a tight time schedule. They provide a wonderful way to experience the diversity of Namibia, and with such clear flying conditions, they are the best way to

SAFETY FIRST

If you are driving yourself on safari, do stick to the designated speed limits, even if there is no traffic – many accidents result from speeding on gravel roads.

insurance cover details, especially the Collision Damage Waiver (CDW).

Namibia offers a wide range of accommodation, from international standard hotels to lodges, tented camps, guest farms, guest houses, rest camps and campsites. When selecting accommodation from one of the tourism publications, bear in mind that standards are based on the physical infrastructure – number of rooms and facilities offered – rather than on the ambience or quality of service.

Namibian cuisine generally gives excellent

appreciate the scale and geological complexity of the country.

Going on a self-drive safari holiday is easy to arrange, as the country has an excellent road network with well-maintained tarmac and gravel roads. There's a good choice of accommodation, from camping to guest farms, lodges and hotels. Tourism literature on the main attractions in each region is readily available. When selecting a car-hire company for a safari, it pays to scrutinise

LEFT: the waterhole at Okaukuejo rest camp in Etosha National Park.
ABOVE: bushcraft demonstration, Etosha National Park.

value for money, except perhaps at some of the rest camps. The main centres have superb restaurants, serving Namibian beef, mutton, oryx, kudu, ostrich and succulent seafood from the coast, a speciality being Walvis Bay Oysters. South African wines and Namibian-brewed beer are readily available.

Train travel for tourists has recently come of age, with the introduction of the Desert Express in 1998. A luxury service, it travels between Windhoek and Swakopmund, with several stops on the way, including a sunrise excursion to the Moon Valley in the Namib desert. Other trains are the Shongololo Express and Rovos Rail *(see Travel Tips, page 260).* ❏

THE PREDATORS

There are cats, there are dogs, there are relatives of the weasel – and plenty of other creatures besides – all aiming to stay alive by hunting and killing

Namibia's wildlife survives despite the harsh regimes nature dictates in this largely arid country. Fourteen major vegetation zones support at least 134 species of wild mammals in niches where they feed, establish territories and reproduce. Some are "Namibian specials", endemic animals which live nowhere else. Most have developed unique and interesting adaptations which help them survive in their dry and hot environment.

All of Africa's "Big Five" (elephant, rhinoceros, buffalo, lion and leopard), plus the well-known prey animals, are present in Namibia. Some are specifically adapted to the desert; others display unique survival mechanisms.

The **lion** *(Panthera leo)* is by far the largest African predator: an adult male may weigh anything up to 240 kg (530 lb). Lions are unique among the cats in that they live in social groups or prides which hunt co-operatively and there is much greater sexual dimorphism (differences between the sexes) than in the other species.

A pride consists of a coalition of males, generally two or possibly three brothers who defend and hold a territory, up to 15 females who are themselves probably related, and usually some youngsters. It is the females who do the hunting, bringing down prey as large as buffalo and as difficult as young elephants.

Like the other big cats, lions hunt by ambushing prey and then sprinting after it for a short distance. They have little stamina and unless their quarry is only a short distance away when they break cover, they have little chance of success. Although it is the lionesses that do the work, once they have killed it is the males and the cubs that feed first.

Occasionally, lions make their way down the river valleys into the Skeleton Coast National Park, where they struggle to make a living,

scavenging the tide line and occasionally hunting Cape fur seals. They are likely to be shot as soon as they leave the park.

Resting lions will barely flick a tail or twitch a foot for hours at a time. Only if you come across playful young cubs or a mating pair are you likely to witness any activity. Lions are

more active after dark and you may see them on a spotlit night drive from a private lodge or at a floodlit water hole.

The next largest African cat is the **leopard** *(Panthera pardus)*, about 2 metres (6 ft) from nose to tail, with a male weighing 60 kg (130 lb) or more. This muscular and solitary nocturnal hunter is one of the most secretive of cats.

Leopards creep up on their quarry in the darkness, only making a dash at the very last moment. In order to prevent lions or hyenas from stealing their prey, these powerful beasts will haul their food up into a tree and cache it there, sprawling over a nearby branch in the shade of the dense foliage during the day.

PRECEDING PAGES: Burchell's zebra at a waterhole; ostriches at the edge of the desert.
LEFT: a lion stands guard over a killed giraffe.
RIGHT: a brown hyena scavenges a shark carcass on a Skeleton Coast beach.

Alternatively, they will crawl into impenetrable thickets or deep grass.

Only the very fortunate will spot a leopard in daylight in Etosha – although waterhole watchers may be rewarded by one coming to drink at night. Nevertheless, it is always worth checking any likely looking trees, where a luxuriant bell-rope of a tail is frequently a giveaway.

The leopard, and the third of the big cats, the **cheetah** *(Acinonyx jubatus)*, are both persecuted by Namibian farmers for stealing stock. They are snared, trapped and shot – and for cheetahs this is a significant problem. Namibia has around 2,500, the largest population in the world, but they live mainly on farmland where they constantly come into conflict with man.

The cheetah is the fastest land mammal and, once it breaks cover from its ambush, this lithe cat, weighing around 50 kg (115 lb), can achieve speeds of 100 kph (60 mph) over short distances.

As with lions, coalitions of brothers hold territories but they do not consort with the females except to mate with them, and take no part in rearing the young. The female does this alone, defending and feeding her litter until the cubs are almost full-grown and have learned to hunt for themselves.

NAMIBIA'S SMALLER CATS

The lynx-like **caracal** *(Felis caracal)* is found throughout the country except for the Namib coastal strip. It is a robustly built cat, over a metre (3 ft) in length and weighing around 16 kg (35 lb). It varies in colour from sandy brown to silvery grey, with very distinctive ear tufts and a fairly short tail. The caracal is nocturnal, solitary and a very swift and adept hunter, even catching birds in the air as they take off. As well as mainly ground-living birds, it also eats mammalian prey up to the size of impala.

The **serval** *(Felis serval)* is much the same size as the caracal but slighter, weighing only around 11 kg (25 lb). It has long legs, a small head, upstanding ears and a fine black-spotted coat on a gold background. Mostly found in the north of Namibia, it hunts at night, either by itself or in pairs, and feeds mainly on small mammals although it will also take birds and reptiles.

The **African wild cat** *(Felis lybica)* looks very much like a pale domestic tabby, but with distinctive reddish-brown ears. It lives throughout the country, except for the Namib coastal strip, and feeds on mammals up to the size of a spring hare, as well as on birds, reptiles and invertebrates. Although it is largely nocturnal, you may see a wild cat during the day time at quieter watering holes in Etosha, when it might try hunting doves coming down to drink.

Cheetahs cover long distances and have extremely large territories, generally centred around a number of play trees which they scent-mark with both faeces and urine.

Next on our list is the **spotted hyena** *(Crocuta crocuta)*, the second largest carnivore in Africa. Standing 90 cm (3 ft) tall and weighing around 65 kg (140 lb), it is a formidable animal with powerful forequarters and a massive and heavily muscled head. It has a spotted coat and a comparatively short tail. Although often seen

> ### MIGHTY BITE
>
> The spotted hyena, with the strongest jaws of any mammal, can eat large bones – a source of nutritious marrow. Its droppings are usually white because of all the calcium they contain.

The **brown hyena** *(Hyaena brunnea)* is a much smaller animal, weighing only about 40 kg (90 lb). It tends to be a specialist of arid areas and survives throughout the Namib Desert in western Namibia. It is much the same shape as the spotted hyena, but its body is covered with long, coarse, light or dark brown hair. It spends its nights foraging individually, feeding mainly on small mammals, birds, insects, reptiles and wild fruits such as melons.

It is often possible to find the tracks of the

individually, in pairs and in threes, hyenas live in clans which defend a territory.

Though they have a reputation for scavenging, hyenas are extremely competent cursorial hunters, employing their considerable reserves of stamina and often co-operating to run down prey, such as wildebeest, over long distances.

They will steal prey from other predators, including lone lions, and will eat all manner of carrion, making more efficient use of prey than any other carnivore. They are found mainly in Etosha and in the Caprivi Strip area.

brown hyena, showing where it has wandered hither and thither during the night in search of food. In spite of its solitary nature, the brown hyena also holds territories with others in its group of males and females.

The dog family

The **wild dog** or Cape hunting dog *(Lycaon pictus)* is found in the northeast of Namibia. It is a rangy animal, similar in size to a domestic Alsatian, with a short coat randomly patched with black, white and gold. The wild dog lives in a close-knit pack of 10 to 15, which roams a very large territory up to 2,000 sq km (770 sq miles) in size, living a nomadic lifestyle unless

LEFT: Grant's golden mole attacks a locust.
ABOVE: a lioness eyes up zebra in the Etosha Park.

rearing puppies. The pack is a highly specialised and efficient hunting team, pursuing and attacking prey as large as buffalo.

Throughout Africa, the wild dog population is dwindling. It suffers from the same fatal diseases as domestic dogs (notably distemper and rabies), is often a road casualty, and is also heavily persecuted by farmers, being both shot and snared. Attempts to reintroduce the dogs to Etosha have unfortunately failed in the past, and with a global population estimated at fewer

> ### EXCEPTIONAL EARS
>
> The bat-eared fox has very acute directional hearing: it can pinpoint termites moving underground, and digs furiously to unearth them before they can burrow away.

seal colonies at the coast where they are known to suffer from mange from time to time. An omnivore, the jackal eats insects, small mammals, fruits and nuts, and often scavenges around camp sites. Its high-pitched screaming cries are one of the characteristic sounds of the African night.

The little **bat-eared fox** *(Octocyon megalotis)*, is covered with thick buff grey fur, while its legs, muzzle and the tip of its bushy tail are black. Its huge rounded ears are unmistakeable. It is equipped with long claws on its

than 5,000 (excluding animals in captivity), the animal is considered to be endangered.

The black back and black bushy tail of the **black-backed jackal** *(Canis mesomelas)*, make it unmistakable. Its flanks and long legs are chestnut, it has pointy ears, stands about 38 cm (15 ins) at the shoulder and weighs about 8 kg (18 lb). It is capable of living throughout the country and may be seen anywhere from the Namib Desert to the Caprivi Strip.

It is probably the most commonly seen carnivore and may be spotted trotting singly or in pairs through the national parks such as Etosha. It is frequently seen at floodlit waterholes, and large numbers of the animals gather around the

front feet for digging for insects, its primary prey. It will also take other invertebrates, small mammals, birds and reptiles. Although both nocturnal and diurnal, the bat-eared fox is more often seen during the day in the winter when the cold desert nights keep insects inactive.

The silvery buff **Cape fox** *(Vulpes chama)* is a small fox (3 kg/7 lb) with a dark, bushy tail. Generally solitary and nocturnal, it lies up during the day in cool shade or in an underground den. It is an omnivore and takes a range of small prey and fruits.

ABOVE: the endearing bat-eared fox.
RIGHT: a honey badger emerges from its burrow.

Like some other foxes it caches food, and you may spot a hungry Cape fox out in daylight excavating a hidden larder. It lives throughout the drier parts of Namibia. Keep a look out for Cape foxes at dusk, when you may see one or even a pair emerge from a den.

The weasel family

Namibia has two otters but very little permanent water, so both species are confined to the Caprivi Strip. The larger of the two, the **Cape clawless otter** *(Aonyx capensis)*, grows to 160 cm (5 ft) in length and weighs up to 18 kg (40 lb). It is a typical otter with a dense, dark brown coat, flat streamlined head and a broad tapering tail. Its white chin is characteristic. Each foot has five toes and those on the hind feet possess rudimentary claws and are also webbed. It is able to manipulate food with its feet and hold it while the otter feeds. Although most of its diet is aquatic creatures, the Cape clawless otter takes a range of prey including insects, reptiles and even birds.

The **spotted-necked otter** *(Lutra maculicollis)* is much smaller (1 metre/3 ft long and 4.5 kg/10 lb in weight). It too is chocolate-brown but with a mottled creamy white throat and upper chest. Like the Cape clawless, its hind

feet are webbed but in this species they have white claws.

The diet of the spotted-necked otter contains a greater proportion of aquatic prey as this species is more tied to water than the Cape clawless. Look out for a low shape swimming in the water and a tail which often emerges as the otter dives.

The **honey badger** or **ratel** *(Mellivora capensis)* is slightly larger and heavier than the Eurasian badger – 1 metre (3 ft) in length and weighing in at about 12 kg (26 lb). It is black with a broad silvery-grey saddle stretching from the top of its head to the tip of its tail. This gives it a rather ghostly appearance at night

SAND-SWIMMER

Many Namibian mammals have developed unique adaptations for survival in their dry, hot environment. One of the most fascinating is **Grant's golden mole** *(Eremitalpa granti)*, a totally sightless yet ferocious predator only 8 cm (3 inches) long, endemic to the arid Namib Desert. Aided by its streamlined coat of silky pale yellow fur, this nocturnally active mole "swims" beneath the loose sand, covering up to 5 km (3 miles) a night. This adaptation enables the mole to live without burrows in the sliding dune slipfaces, and also to sense through the sand the movements of its favourite prey – web-footed geckos, crickets and beetle larvae.

when the legs are almost invisible and the animal appears to float along.

It is extremely powerfully built with long sharp claws on its front feet. It is a nocturnal animal, usually seen alone or in pairs foraging for small mammals, invertebrates, birds, reptiles, bee larvae and honey. Its tough, thick skin helps considerably in its defence and it is fearless and aggressive in its dealings with other creatures in the bush.

Like the honey badger, the **striped polecat** *(Ictonyx striatus)* is almost entirely nocturnal. It is a black and white striped animal weighing just under a kilogram (2 lb) and is found

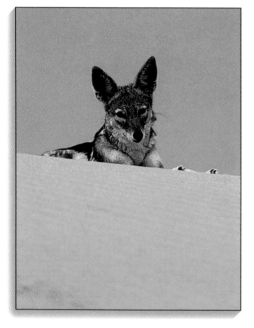

throughout Namibia. It is a solitary insectivore and uses a highly distasteful secretion from its anal glands in self-defence. You may see this animal beside the road at night when it is out foraging.

The **small-spotted genet** *(Genetta genetta)* weighs in at just under 2 kg (4 lb). Its buff-coloured body is covered with small dark spots while its tail is ringed with black and has a white tip. It lives throughout almost all of Namibia, apart from the desert regions, and preys on rodents, small birds, invertebrates and reptiles, hunting and foraging for fruit alone at night. It prefers to live in areas of bush, so that it can climb a tree if disturbed.

Varieties of mongoose

Finally, there are a number of mongooses in Namibia of which the best known is the **suricate** *(Suricata suricatta)* or meerkat. This small mongoose weighs just less than a kilogram (2 lb) and is characterised by a silvery coat with dark bands across the back, a dark burglar's mask, and rounded ears on the sides of its head. It is a diurnal animal, living co-operatively in a family of up to 30 in dens with many entrances.

When they first emerge in the morning, suricates take some time to warm up, standing on their hind legs and facing the sun. The group tends to forage as a pack, feeding on invertebrates and small reptiles. Baby-sitters look after any young in the den and look-outs warn the rest of the group if danger threatens.

Sometimes **yellow mongooses** *(Cynictus penicillata)* live alongside suricates, their slightly larger cousins. This mongoose is yellow with a white-tipped tail in the southern part of the country, which is greyer in the north. It is a diurnal animal and though it lives in warrens with others of its species, it forages individually, hunting for small mammals, invertebrates and sometimes birds. Yellow mongooses are often seen crossing roads, and may also be spotted at some of the waterholes in Etosha, where they sometimes share the holes of ground squirrels.

The **slender mongoose** *(Galerella sanguinea)* often appears black when it is glimpsed running for cover. In fact it is reddish-brown, with short legs, a long sinuous body and a tail with a black tip. Like the yellow mongoose, it is a solitary animal, hunting mainly insects during the day, and is often seen crossing roads.

Both the **banded mongoose** *(Mungos mungo*, weighing 1.4 kg/3 lb) and the **dwarf mongoose** *(Helogale parvula*, just 250 g/8 oz) live in the north of the country and both live in groups. The former is grey with dark bands on its back. It hunts during the day, foraging in open woodland under logs and bark in search of invertebrates and wild fruits.

Dwarf mongooses are black or very dark brown and tend to live in old termite mounds scattered throughout the group range. Like many other mongoose species, it feeds on invertebrates, reptiles and small mammals. ❑

LEFT: a black-backed jackal on a dune.
RIGHT: leopards are rarely seen during the day.

GRAZERS AND BROWSERS

Namibia's vegetarians include the largest land mammal, the world's tallest animal, aquatic antelopes and rodent-like creatures related to the sea-cow

Despite Namibia's aridity, its grasslands and bushlands support a splendid variety of herbivores. The **African elephant** (*Loxodonta africana*) is probably the one animal which gives wildlife watchers in Africa the most pleasure. With its dextrous trunk, high level of intelligence, complex social system and longevity, this is an animal to which many people can relate.

The elephant is also the biggest land mammal. A bull may weigh up to 6 tonnes and stand 4 metres (13 ft) at the shoulder. By standing up on its hind legs – something seen only occasionally – a big bull can reach higher than a giraffe. The large ears, rich in blood vessels, act like car radiators. By waving its ears back and forth an elephant can reduce its body temperature substantially.

The trunk can do most of the same delicate tasks as a human hand, as well as more strenuous work such as lifting logs or ripping bark. It is also used for sucking up water for drinking and bathing. Nearly all African elephants have tusks, incisor teeth composed entirely of dentine, which continue to grow throughout the animal's life.

Elephants live in family units led by an elderly matriarch, with sisters, daughters, granddaughters and their offspring. Male elephants tend to live individually or in loose aggregations and are generally much calmer and easier to approach than breeding herds with their vulnerable calves. Only when a bull elephant is in a mating condition (called musth, a state similar to oestrus in females) does it tend to be unpredictable. Bull elephants in this state are normally found within breeding herds where they seek out receptive females.

Elephants eat almost any vegetable matter and they often spend time by water, grazing the lush water plants growing there. The elephant's digestive system is very inefficient, so they

have to cram in as much food as possible, and sometimes feed for 16 hours out of 24. They also drink a great deal. A bull elephant will consume 230 litres (50 gallons) of water a day, taking on board 100 litres (22 gallons) at a time.

Elephants are generally easy to see in Etosha, especially around many of the waterholes. You

should also look out for them in the Caprivi Strip, where you may come across some of the big herds for which Botswana and Zimbabwe are well known. Namibia is noted, too, for its desert-adapted elephants which live in Damaraland and the Skeleton Coast. These animals are well adjusted to a desert existence, sometimes going without water for up to four days.

Endangered giant

Another large mammal which has adapted to life in the desert is the **black rhinoceros** (*Diceros bicornis*), which stands 1.5 metres (5 ft) at the shoulder and weighs up to a tonne. It is a large grey beast with two horns, each a

---

PRECEDING PAGES: desert elephants in Damaraland.
LEFT: a herd of gemsbok on the run.
RIGHT: elephants live in family units.

dense mass of hair (not attached to the skull), and ears in the shape of funnels. This is a browsing animal, using its prehensile upper lip to grasp food which it cuts from shrubs with its premolars, giving bushes a rounded appearance in areas where it feeds frequently. Black rhino tend to be short-tempered, and often their first instinct is to charge.

Rhinos have been heavily poached in the past, both for traditional Asian medicine and for dagger handles for Yemenis. Fortunately the latter market

> **WATCH MY LIPS**
>
> The black rhinoceros is not black, any more than the white rhino is white. Zoologists today prefer to use the terms "narrow-lipped" or "hook-lipped" for the former, and "wide-lipped" for the latter.

Zebra and giraffe

The **Hartmann's mountain zebra** *(Equus zebra hartmannae)* is a Namibian endemic which thrives in a desert environment. It lives mainly in the mountainous hinterland between the coastal desert and the plateau in the interior. This is a tall, lean zebra, 1.5 metres (5 ft) tall at the shoulder and weighing 300 kg (660 lb). It lacks the distinctive "shadow stripes" of the Burchell's zebra and lives a more nomadic lifestyle, moving on when food is scarce.

is now in decline as other materials have become fashionable but poaching continues, and the black rhino population worldwide has been reduced to only about 2,500.

Anti-poaching schemes in Namibia, pioneered by Save The Rhino Trust Fund, have included intense monitoring, involving local communities in helping to protect the animals and cutting off their horns to remove temptation. After the Ngorongoro Crater in Tanzania, Etosha is probably the easiest place to see black rhino in the wild. They are often spotted at the floodlit waterholes at the rest camps and may be seen at dusk or daybreak moving to and from water in the coolness of the day.

The **Burchell's zebra** *(Equus burchelli)* is slightly smaller, standing 1.3 metres (4 ft 3 ins) at the shoulder and weighing around 315 kg (700 lb). Its stripes are wider than the mountain zebra's and there are grey "shadow stripes" between the black stripes, especially on the sides and the rump.

It lives in the north of Namibia, thriving in areas of open woodland and scrub with grassland. It can be readily seen in significant numbers at the waterholes in Etosha National Park as well as in the Caprivi Strip.

It is impossible to confuse the **giraffe** *(Giraffa camelopardalis)* with any other animal in Namibia. The tallest creature on earth, a male measures 5.5 metres (18 ft) to the top of the horns and weighs up to 1,200 kg (1.2 tons). The giraffe lives in the north of the country where there is sufficient savannah woodland to provide its essential browse, but it is not unusual to see giraffe some distance away from trees of any size.

Giraffe live in loose aggregations and, because of their great height, are able to maintain visual contact over much greater distances than other mammals. They are plentiful in Etosha and can also be seen in the Caprivi Strip.

LINGUAL LENGTH

The giraffe's black tongue is the longest of any mammal's – 45 cm (18 ins) – and mobile enough to curl round the tips of branches.

which form a V-shape on the top of the head.

The gemsbok is at home in the desert and may be seen climbing sand dunes where there is not a speck of green. While they may only be seen in small groups in the desert, in Etosha they form quite large herds at waterholes where fighting between males is a fairly frequent occurrence.

The **springbok** *(Antidorcas marsupialis)* is another desert antelope, standing about 75 cm (30 ins) at the shoulder and weighing 37 kg. It has a chestnut back, a white belly and a darker

Antelopes large and small

The **oryx** *(Oryx gazella)* is frequently known by its Afrikaans name of **gemsbok** (pronounce the "g" like a guttural "h"). It is a heavily-built antelope, weighing up to 240 kg (530 lb). The upper parts of its body are buff, its belly white, and a broad black line divides the two. It also has a black band down the centre of its back and a black tail. Its distinctive face is black with a broad mask of white and a white nose. Both sexes of the creatures have long, straight horns

LEFT: giraffe on the savannah in the rainy season.
ABOVE: the springbok is the most common antelope in Namibia.

DRY RATIONS

Like many of Namibia's desert-dwellers, the gemsbok is well adapted to arid conditions. Although mainly a grazer, it will also dig up succulent roots and eat wild melons for the water they contain. It grazes at night, when the lower temperatures lead to an increase in the vegetation's water content. (Even dead grass that has been baked by the sun all day can absorb 40 percent of its weight in airborne moisture during the night.) As well as using every available source of water, the gemsbok also produces concentrated urine, to preserve fluid, and allows its body temperature to rise without sweating. It can, quite simply, survive without drinking.

brown band dividing the two. Its face is largely white with a black band running through its eyes towards its muzzle. Its ears are long and both sexes carry lyre-shaped horns.

Springbok are both browsers and grazers but they only drink when water is available, surviving on the moisture in their food at other times. In Etosha they may form very large herds and can often be seen during the heat of the day when they are least active, crowded into what little shade the thorn trees offer.

The handsome **kudu** *(Tregalaphus strepsiceros)* is 1.4 metres (4 ft 6 ins) at the shoulder and weighs up to 250 kg (55 lb). It has a buff

grey body with a few vertical off-white stripes, a white V-shaped marking on the face, large, veined ears and, on the male, a wonderful pair of spiral horns.

Kudu live in scrub and savannah woodland and are sometimes known as the grey ghosts of the bush because of their ability to hide in the sparsest of cover. They are graceful, handsome animals and are sufficiently athletic to be able to clear a 2-metre (6-ft) fence with ease. They tend to live in small groups of up to a dozen animals and are most active in the cooler times of the day.

The **impala** *(Aepyceros melampus)* is an elegant, lightly-built antelope, found in the Caprivi Strip area. It stands 90 cm (3 ft) at the shoulder and weighs around 50 kg (110 lb), a browny reddish animal with a pale belly and black markings around the tail and on the heels. The male has a pair of gracefully curved lyre-shaped horns.

A distinct subspecies, the **black-faced impala** *(Aepyceros melampus petersi)*, is found exclusively around Etosha. It is heavier and darker than the common impala and, as its name suggests, has a dark blaze on its face.

The **red hartebeest** *(Alcelaphus buselaphus)* is a chestnut-coloured antelope with whitish flanks measuring 125 cm (4 ft) at the shoulder and weighing around 150 kg (330 lb). Both sexes have horns which grow upwards and then backwards from the forehead.

Though they are found in the north and east of Namibia, red hartebeest prefer fairly open country rather than thick bush and turn up fairly regularly at some of the waterholes on the western end of the Etosha Pan.

An inhabitant of rocky areas, the **klipspringer** *(Oreotragus oreotragus)* is a small, stocky antelope that grows to about 60 cm (2 ft) at the shoulder. It walks on the tips of its hooves like a dancer on points. These dainty feet allow it to move through its habitat with grace and ease. Generally living in pairs they are sometimes visible in the river gorges of the Namib-Naukluft National Park.

An even smaller antelope, the **Damara dik-dik** *(Madoqua kirkii)*, is no bigger than a medium-sized dog – only 38 cm (15 ins) at the shoulder, and 5 kg (11 lb) in weight. It is yellowish grey in colour with a tuft of hair on its forehead, a long, shrew-like snout and large glands below the eyes. This species is endemic

WARTS AND ALL

No African scene is complete without at least one **warthog** *(Phacochoerus aethiopicus)*. Often described as grotesque, but not without appeal, this grey, bristling pig weighs around 100 kg (220 lb) and has large wart-like protuberances on the sides of its face. An adult's canine teeth develop into curved tusks.

A group or "sounder" of warthogs usually consists of sows and their young, or unattached bachelors. They are active during the day, feeding on grasses and roots, often kneeling to graze, but will scuttle away when you approach, their thin tails held erect. They spend their nights underground, generally in aardvark holes.

to Namibia and is found in the central and northern areas in thick scrub. It is worth looking out for them in Etosha where they are fairly commonplace, though not easily spotted.

Squirrels and mice

The **ground squirrel** *(Xerus inauris)* is a common resident of Namibia's most arid areas. Its kidneys are among the most efficient in the animal kingdom when it comes to conserving water, and because of this it can survive without drinking throughout the dry

> **NIGHT VISITORS**
>
> If you are at a camp or lodge in woodlands, look out for tree mice at night. They are frequently in attendance at camps but, being nocturnal, are often overlooked.

it will attack fearlessly. Consequently, the ground squirrel provides shelter for the mongoose, and its guest repays the host by repelling dangerous intruders.

The **tree mouse** *(Thallomys paedulcus)* is a small grey-yellow rodent with white underparts and dark rings of fur around the eyes. Its other distinguishing feature is a tail that is longer than the head and body together. As the name suggests, tree mice are totally arboreal, living in holes in trees or abandoned birds' nests. Although they prefer

season, which can last up to a year in the desert.

It is a small grey rodent with a single white stripe along its sides and a bushy tail which it can use as a sunshade when necessary. It lives in colonies of up to 30 other squirrels, and digs burrows which it sometimes shares with members of the mongoose family. This partnership apparently benefits both species – while the vegetarian ground squirrel is the pioneering type, given to digging warrens, the mongoose is an alert predator with a dislike of snakes, which

LEFT: ground squirrels live in burrows.
ABOVE: the timid Damara dik-dik is one of the smallest antelopes in the world.

> **MONKEY BUSINESS**
>
> The **Chacma baboon** *(Papio ursinus)* is an agile primate that is found in most of Namibia except the desert – anywhere with drinking water nearby, and rocky cliffs or tall trees in which to retreat when threatened. An adult male weighs around 32 kg (70 lb), with powerfully built shoulders, but the female is considerably smaller. It is a highly gregarious species that lives in troops of up to 100, led by a dominant male. The baboon feeds mainly on fruit, seeds, leaves and flowers, and digs for roots and bulbs, but is not averse to insects and other invertebrates, and will even take rodents and birds if it can catch them.

acacia trees, they live throughout Namibia's savannah woodlands.

The **rock hyrax** or **dassie** *(Procavia capensis)* is a curious brown animal that resembles a large guinea pig, about 60 cm (2 ft) long and weighing in at 4 kg (9 lb). Scientists, at a loss to classify this unusual creature, have placed it and its close relatives in their own order, the Hyracoidea. Their evolutionary development is quite distinct from the rodents they resemble – in fact, unlikely as it may seem, their closest living

---

MINUSCULE MOUSE

Namibia's smallest rodent is the **desert pygmy mouse** *(Mus indutus)*, which measures 10 cm (4 ins) from nose to tail, and weighs just 6 grams (¼ oz).

---

largest and most obvious of these is the **hippopotamus** *(Hippopotamus amphibius)*, a 1.5-tonne barrel-shaped herbivore. It spends its days semi-submerged in rivers and waterholes and likes these to be deep enough for it to sink out of sight if danger threatens. Hippos emerge in the evening to graze, returning to the safety of water during the day. Dominant bulls mark their territories by scattering dung with a vigorous flicking of the tail. Being large and lying around in "schools" of around 12 or more, hippos are easily seen in the rivers of the Caprivi.

The **Cape buffalo** *(Syncerus caffer)* is a massive, black, ox-like animal that weighs about 750 kg (¾ tonne). It has impressive horns, especially on the male. Buffaloes need abundant grass, shade and water to survive and live in large herds, often several hundred strong. They seek shade during the day, and move to and from water at dawn and dusk. They love to wallow, especially the old males which often live in a solitary state and are notorious for being dangerous if disturbed accidentally, charging blindly at the perceived danger.

The **red lechwe** *(Kobus leche)* is limited to the Okavango and surrounding areas. It is a chestnut-coloured water-loving antelope, about 1 metre (3 ft) to the shoulder and weighing 100 kg (22 lb). The male has elegant lyre-shaped horns, but its special distinction is elongated hooves to assist it when walking in muddy places. Lechwe are generally seen resting on dry ground during the day but feed in shallow water, and will flee into the water if disturbed.

An even more specialist water antelope is the **sitatunga** *(Tragelaphus spekei)*. It is slightly larger than the lechwe, and confined to almost the same geographical region. It has a long, coarse brownish coat with white markings on the face, neck, chest and feet, and the male has spiralling horns.

Sitatungas are the most aquatic of antelopes. They spend most of their time in dense reedbeds, in water up to 1 metre (3 ft) deep. Their hooves are widely splayed to enable them to walk on mats of reeds and other floating vegetation and they lie up in reed beds, trampling down the stems to form platforms. ❏

relatives are probably the elephant and the dugong or sea cow.

Hyraxes live in colonies among rocks and feed on whatever vegetation grows nearby. You have a good chance of seeing them in rocky areas in the south of Namibia, such as around Hardap Dam. White urine stains on the rocks are a sure sign that dassies are around.

Water-loving mammals

A number of mammals are found only in the Caprivi area. These usually demand wetter conditions than are generally available in the rest of Namibia and consequently tend to overlap into neighbouring Botswana's Okavango Delta. The

LEFT: hippos spend all day in the water.

Hints for Hunters

Since the early 1970s, Namibia has been Africa's number-one hunting destination, especially for German-speaking Europeans. The Professional Hunters' Association, which includes virtually every professional hunter or hunting guide in the country, takes pains to ensure that high ethical standards and fair hunting practices are upheld.

In fact, most of the game killed each year – more than 90 percent – is killed by local people for food, either for individual consumption or resale. Trophy hunting by visitors accounts for the other 10 percent. There are about 300 state-licensed hunting farms, which are usually over 5,000 hectares (12,500 acres) in area. The supply of wildlife on these holdings, as well as standards of accommodation and hunting rules, are fixed by law. Outside these areas, visitors may only kill animals on non-registered farmland when accompanied by a professional hunter. For either type of hunting, you need a state-issued licence, which is accompanied by a catalogue of the species you are permitted to shoot. The official documentation also sets out the conditions for the export of trophies.

The backbone of all hunting in Namibia is farm hunting, when the guest lives with the farmer and his family on their land. The hunting party sets off at dawn in open jeeps, looking for game. Once the animal is sighted, the hunt continues on foot – which can take minutes, or hours, or a whole day, depending on the guest's wishes and stamina and the chances of hitting the animal. For lunch, people generally return to the farm, or eat a little something in the bush. After a siesta during the hottest hours – when the game also retreats into the shade – the hunt may continue until sunset.

In contrast to farm hunting, a safari hunt is led by a professional hunter, accompanied by local helpers. The advantage is that the hunter is allowed to lead his guest onto land that is not a part of a registered farm. A stationary base camp is generally the point of departure for the day's activities. If you prefer to rough it, some organisations offer "adventure trips", on which you sleep in the middle of hunting territory, in tents or around the campfire under the starry sky.

The hunting season for foreign trophy hunters lasts from February to the end of November. In the rainy season (February to April) and for a while after, the land is still green and lovely, but it's harder to make out the animals in the bush. By August the plant life begins to thin out and dry up.

The unpredictable rain, and regional variations, mean that the wildlife population of hunting areas is extremely variable. If a farm normally rich in wildlife has a dry year, the animals simply leave. So when you are planning a hunting trip you should collect up-to-date information about the situation in the area before you book. On farms that are fenced to keep the game in, or with safari organisations that are licensed to hunt territories throughout Namibia, this is less important.

Importing weapons into the country is not complicated: you declare your gun(s) to Customs officials or police officers on entry to Namibia (no fully automatic weapons) and a permit of limited duration is issued. When you leave the country, present your weapons again at Customs, and the permit will be revoked.

The price of a day's hunting, accommodation, guides and staff, transportation and trophy fees is fixed every year by the Professional Hunters' Association. Though there has been a steady increase in recent years, the cost of hunting in Namibia is still among the lowest in Africa.

See Travel Tips for more details of organisations who arrange hunting trips. ❑

RIGHT: a gemsbok makes an impressive trophy.

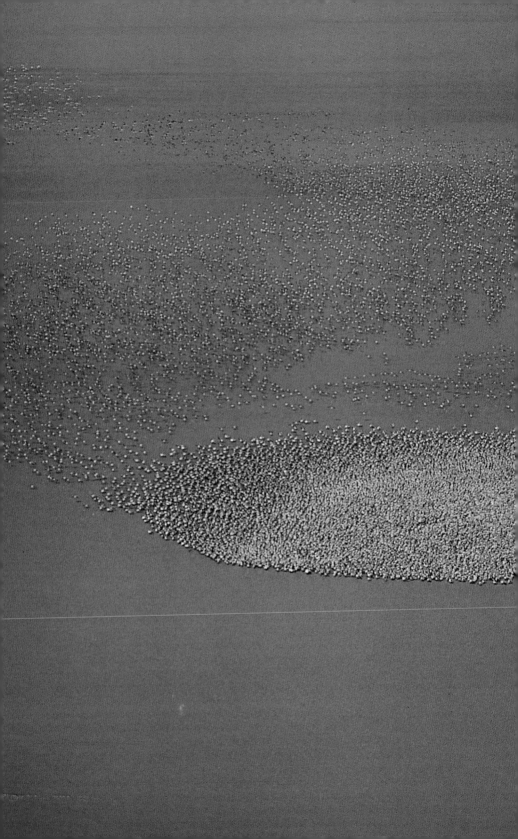

NAMIBIA'S BIRDS

From seashore to arid desert, from savannah to riverine forest,
the varied landscape is home to a wide diversity of birds

The diversity of habitats in Namibia is reflected in the number of birds to be found there. To date, 620 of the 887 bird species listed for southern Africa have been recorded. Of these, about 500 species breed locally while the remainder are migrants.

Coastal habitats include rocky and sandy shores, lagoons and saltworks (the latter are found in all of Namibia's major coastal towns, and have a pronounced effect on the local bird populations). These give rise to some remarkable birds, from the **white pelican** *(Pelecanus onocrotalus)*, so characteristic of the coastline round here, to the **greater** and **lesser flamingos** *(Phoenicopterus ruber and Phoeniconaias minor)* which occur in very great numbers along these shores, and whose sonorous honking can be heard all night when the tides are right for night-time foraging.

Birdwatchers in these coastal regions can also expect to see large skeins of **cormorants** (four species), accompanied by **Cape gannets** *(Morus capensis)* flying offshore. Closer inshore, enthusiasts are quite likely to encounter several species of terns and gulls, the most common of which are the **kelp gull** *(Larus dominicanus)* and **Hartlaub's gull** *(Larus hartlaubii)*.

One of the most interesting birds of the Namib coast is the tiny **Damara tern** *(Sterna balaenarum)*, whose world population numbers only about 7,000 individuals. They breed along the Namib coast in summer and migrate northwards to Nigeria in autumn. Their nest consists of a shallow scraper on the gravel plains of the desert, usually couple of kilometres (1 mile) inland. Only one egg is laid; shortly after hatching, the chick leaves the nest and wanders about, probably to avoid predators such as black-backed jackals which are

common in the region. Parents and offspring keep in touch by means of contact calls. The main threat to the survival of the Damara tern is the large number of thoughtless off-road drivers who crush the eggs.

Jackass penguins *(Spheniscus demersus)* are occasionally seen near the shore, but these

delightful birds prefer to forage out to sea, breeding on islands off the coast. Their call is a loud, donkey-like bray.

Desert habitats

The gravel plains north of the Kuiseb River and the sand dune complex to the south support a small but distinctive bird population. The most obvious of these is the **ostrich** *(Struthio camelus)*, the world's largest bird, which occurs in large numbers in even the most barren habitats, and may often be spotted in the distance, running elegantly through the desert mirage. They are usually seen in pairs or groups, sometimes with large crêches of young birds.

PRECEDING PAGES: a vast flock of lesser flamingos feeding at Etosha Pan.
LEFT: the distinctive bateleur eagle.
RIGHT: the dramatic plumage of the crimson-breasted shrike.

Equally memorable, though very much smaller, is the **Namaqua sandgrouse** *(Pterocles namaqua)*, huge flocks of which can be seen making spectacular daily visits to desert waterholes. This little bird is related to the pigeon, but it has a longer tail and lovely sand-speckled markings.

Other birds found in these areas include the stately bustards and korhaans. Frequently seen in Etosha is the **kori bustard** *(Ardeotis kori)*, reputedly the largest flying bird in the world – although it is reluctant to take to the air unless threatened. The male has a dramatic display in the breeding season. It inflates its throat to fan out the white neck feathers, arches its tail up along its back and emits a deep, resonant "oom-oom-oom" call.

Ruppell's korhaan *(Eupodotis rueppellii)*, found almost exclusively in the Namib desert, is nicknamed the desert frog because of its strange croaking call.

A number of raptors including the lovely little **red-necked falcon** *(Falco chicquera)* turn up in this area. So too do several species of larks, buntings and chats which are of particular interest to keen birdwatchers since many of the creatures are extremely specialised and limited in their distribution.

DRINKS CARRIER

The Namaqua sandgrouse is well adapted to its arid environment, having evolved a method of collecting water for its young and transporting it over long distances. (There is precious little liquid to be obtained from the bird's usual diet of dry seeds.)

The adult sandgrouse's breast feathers are specially modified to absorb and hold moisture. The bird visits a waterhole in the early morning and completely immerses its breast in water, then flies back to the nest site – up to 50 km (30 miles) away – laden with precious liquid, which the chicks then release by nibbling at the parent's breast feathers.

The semi-desert escarpment

There are 15 species of birds that are endemic or near-endemic to Namibia. ("Endemic species" occur nowhere else in the world, while 80 percent of the known range of "near-endemics" falls in one country.) An important area for endemics in Namibia is the transition zone between the desert and the arid savannahs.

The birds found here include a small green and pink-marked member of the parrot family much loved by caged bird enthusiasts, the **rosy-cheeked** or **rosy-faced lovebird** *(Agapornis roseicollis)*, which is generally found in small and quite noisy groups and, because it needs to drink regularly, is never too far from water.

Also look out for that striking, self-assured little harlequin, the **white-tailed shrike** *(Lanioturdus torquatus)*, and the **rockrunner** *(Achaetops pycnopygius)*, a small brown bird with an enchanting liquid call, which scuttles around rocky outcrops like a little mouse, darting for cover into long grass. Other species you may see here include **Hartlaub's francolin** *(Francolinus hartlaubi)*, often seen in small groups scurrying over rocks, **Bradfield's swift** *(Apus bradfieldi)*,

> ### BALANCING ACT
>
> A distinctive bird of prey found in the semi-desert is the *bateleur (Terathopius ecaudatus)*. It has the shortest tail of any eagle, so rocks from side to side as it flies. This gives it its unusual name: *bateleur* is French for "tightrope-walker".

in places in these regions is the **sociable weaver** *(Philetairus socius)*. This species is noticeable mainly for its communal nests, which are enormous structures woven from twigs into the shape of a dome. Straw is then used to fill in the gaps, giving the nest a thatched appearance, and to make separate chambers inside the communal nest. You'll often come across them weighing down substantial branches of sturdy trees, or even wrecking telephone poles; some nests have

the cackling **violet woodhoopoe** *(Phoeniculus damarensis)*, and the tiny **Herero chat** *(Namibornis herero)*.

The arid savannah

The southern Kalahari, the central highlands and the north-central regions reaching as far north as the Etosha National Park all comprise a number of acacia-dominated vegetation types. One of the most striking species of birds found

---

LEFT: white pelicans are numerous on the coast.
ABOVE: the martial eagle *(Polemaetus bellicosus)*, one of the largest birds of prey.
RIGHT: common waxbills *(Estrilda astrild)*.

been in continuous use for up to 100 years.

These nests can attract squatters, too. Other bird species who use them include rosy-faced lovebirds and tiny grey **pygmy falcons** *(Polihierax semitorquatus)*, whose entrance holes can by distinguished from those of the weavers by their coating of white droppings.

Telephone poles are also good places to spot a **pale chanting goshawk** *(Melierax canorus)*, a light grey bird with long orange legs and orange base to the bill, which uses these poles as hunting perches.

Keep an eye out for dramatically marked **crimson-breasted shrikes** *(Laniarius atrococcineus)*, black and white above, with an improbably scarlet breast (or, very rarely, a buttercup yellow one), and dainty **violet-eared waxbills** *(Uraeginthus granatinus)*, with their distinctive violet cheeks.

Other residents of these parts include **helmeted guineafowl** *(Numida meleagris)*, noisy grey birds with blue faces and red caps which live in flocks and look especially comical as they bustle along in single file, and the enchanting **lilac-breasted roller** *(Coracias cordata)* and **purple roller** *(Coracias naevia)*. The former is more conspicuous than its quieter cousin, but both perform spectacular and noisy display flights of rolling aerobatics – hence the name.

some interesting raptors, from the **little banded goshawk** *(Accipiter badius)* to its cousins the **gabar** *(Micronisus gabar)* and the **dark chanting goshawk** *(Melierax metabates)*.

Then there are the **kingfishers**, including the **woodland** *(Halcyon senegalensis)* and the **grey-hooded** *(Halcyon leucocephala)* varieties; the latter's wings in flight are as brilliant in colour as the European kingfisher's, and take you by surprise in this waterless environment.

In forested areas, birds often rely heavily on vocalisation to locate other members of their species. Some of the birds in these dry woodlands have particularly beautiful calls, for

These areas are also very much characterised by **hornbills** including the **grey** *(Tockus nasutus)*, **red-billed** *(Tockus erythrorhynchus)*, **yellow-billed** *(Tockus leucomelas)* and **Monteiro's** *(Tockus monteiri)*, all characterised by long, heavy, downward-curving bills, some (such as the grey hornbill) with a casque on the upper mandible.

The dry woodlands

The northeastern parts of Namibia comprise one of the country's smallest habitats, but they do contain many large and spectacular species of deciduous trees, growing from a substrate of deep sand. In these areas you can expect to see

HORNBILL HIDEAWAY

The hornbills have unusual nesting habits. The female lays her eggs in holes in trees, then seals herself completely into the nest with a mixture of mud and sticks, cemented together with saliva – presumably to ensure maximum safety while the eggs are incubated. She must then rely totally on the male to feed her through a small slit, and while incubating the eggs she moults all her wing and tail feathers.

Later, when the eggs have hatched, the female breaks out of the nest, and helps the male to feed the young. The young repair her escape-hole and remain incarcerated until they are ready to fly.

example, the liquid whistles of the **African golden oriole** (*Oriolus auratus*) and the **black-headed oriole** (*Oriolus larvatus*), and the musical twitter of the **orange-breasted bush shrike** (*Telophorus sulfureopectus*).

The riverine forests

Namibia's inland wetlands consist of a varied collection of systems, ranging from perennial to episodic rivers, and from large man-made dams to ephemeral pans and small springs. The riverine forests here form a

> **ARTFUL ANGLER**
>
> The skimmer gets its name from its fishing technique – flying low with its bottom jaw dipped just below the water. If it encounters a fish, the bird snaps its bill closed, neatly trapping its prey.

parrot (*Poicephalus robustus*), and **black-collared barbets** (*Lybius torquatus*), and some attractively marked insectivores such as the **Natal robin** (*Cossypha natalensis*), **tropical boubou** (*Laniarius bicolor*), **grey-headed bush shrike** (*Malaconotus blanchoti*), and the spectacularly beautiful red and green marked **narina trogon** (*Apaloderma narina*), which has a booming hoot of a call.

Other remarkable birds include the handsome **African skimmer** (*Rynchops flavirostris*), a

link with the tropical and eastern regions, where rainfall is higher.

A host of large and obvious birds are found by water: giants like the **goliath heron** (*Ardea goliath*); smaller but wonderfully plumaged egrets such as the **great white egret** (*Egretta alba*); and odd-looking species such as the **hammerkop** (*Scopus umbretta*) which builds a round haystack of a nest 2 metres (6 ft) across.

Typical and characteristic birds of the riverine forests include brightly coloured fruit-eaters like the **Knysna lourie** (*Tauraco corythaix*), **Cape**

large tern-like bird with dark brown upper parts, white underparts and a large orange-red bill. It can often be seen flying low over rivers with slow, leisurely wing beats.

Lucky birdwatchers may also be treated to a view of the magnificent **Pels fishing owl** (*Scotopelia peli*), a gentle-looking giant of a creature which feeds on a diet of fish and crabs, along with the occasional small mammal. Look out for it on tree branches near rivers.

Finally, no list would be complete without the **African fish eagle** (*Heliaeetus vocifer*), which is common near water all over southern Africa, and whose haunting cry is powerfully evocative of the whole region. ❑

LEFT: a rosy-faced lovebird peeps out of a nest hole.
ABOVE: a Cape parrot feeds on a clementine.

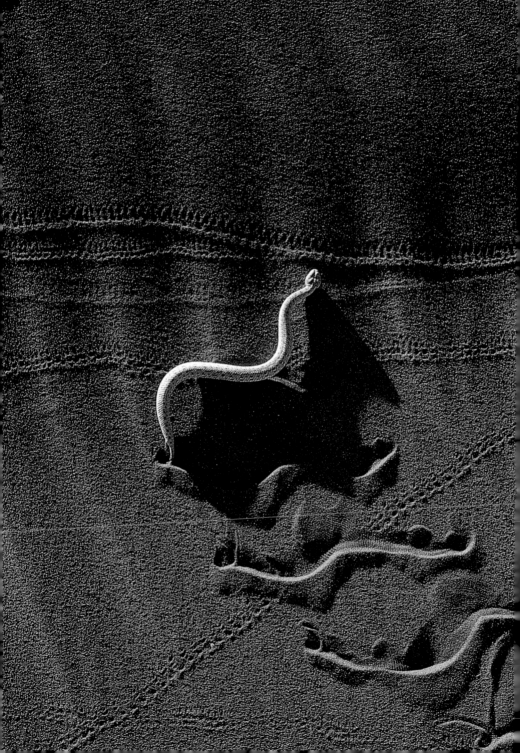

AMPHIBIANS AND REPTILES

From mighty crocodiles to tiny sand frogs – not to mention garish tortoises

and lethal snakes – Namibia has no shortage of cold-blooded inhabitants

The great variation in Namibia's altitude, and geomorphology, the extreme differences in the levels of rainfall, and the varied vegetation which results are reflected in the diversity of the country's reptiles and amphibians. Species normally associated with the tropics are found in the northern border rivers of the Kunene and the Okavango. These include the impressive **Nile crocodile** *(Crocodylus niloticus)*, which feeds mainly on fish when young but then begins to take larger mammals as it attains adulthood. A big Nile crocodile can reach 6.5 metres (20 ft) in length and weigh 1 tonne (2,200 lbs).

The **Nile monitor** *(Varanus niloticus)*, the largest of Africa's lizards at 2 metres (6 ft) long, tends to share the same habitat and is known to dig up crocodiles' nests and feed on the eggs. The **African soft-shelled turtle** *(Trionyx triunguis)* is also found in the Kunene River, and **green turtles** *(Chelonia mydas)* collect in the warm water of the river mouth to find respite from the cold Benguela current.

The casual visitor will encounter most reptiles and amphibians by accident, often when travelling by car. It is not unusual, especially after rainfall, to come across a large **leopard tortoise** *(Geochelone pardalis)* on the road. It is a good idea to stop and move it off the carriageway. Put into the roadside grass where it cannot be seen, for these are considered to be a delicacy by many Namibians. While the leopard tortoise is found over most of southern Africa, the **Nama "padloper"** *(homopus sp. nov.)* is the only one of Namibia's six tortoise species that is endemic to the country.

If you are very lucky, you may spot a running chameleon. The **Namaqua chameleon** *(Chamaeleo namaquensis)* is one of 55 endemic reptile species and has adapted to life in the Namib Desert and the adjacent arid areas. Entirely ground-living, it feeds on beetles and

other insects and even lizards. The fact that it can actually run for a short distance is just one of its peculiarities.

The arid parts are particularly rich in specially adapted species. There are a great number of geckos, many of which have a very restricted range. The most unusual is probably the **web-**

footed gecko *(Palmatogecko rangei)*, which inhabits the wind-blown sands of the Namib. The toes of this delicately-marked nocturnal animal are webbed, similar to a duck's, enabling it to walk nimbly up the slip-face of shifting dunes and, in particular, to dig burrows in the fine sand to escape the deadly heat of the day. Six species of diurnal geckos are found in the Namib. Their perfect camouflage enables them to remain unnoticed most of the time but, if they are spotted, they will quickly dive under a rock for shelter.

Sharing this environment are other Namib endemics such as the **side-winding Namib adder** *(Bitis peringueyi)* which has evolved a

LEFT: the side-winding adder lives up to its name, leaving very distinctive tracks.
RIGHT: a blue-headed agama basks on a rock.

number of characteristics to enable it to thrive in a desert environment. Its eyes are on the top of its head so that, when it sinks into the sand to escape detection or to get away from the heat of the sun, it still has a view of the world. It has also developed a lateral "side-winding" motion which enables it to move up sand dunes as steep as 45°. Other species of dwarf adders also occur, some, such as the **horned adder** (*Bitis caudalis*), with horn-like scales above their eyes. None are seriously poisonous, but they

are in great demand from snake-lovers, who like to keep them in their terrariums.

The snakes that are more dangerous or even fatal to humans, such as the **puff adder** (*Bitis arietans arietans*), **Egyptian cobra** (*Naja naja annulifera*), **western barred spitting cobra** (*Naja naja nigricincta*) and **black mamba** (*Dendroaspis polylepis*) do occur, but are seldom encountered. The last three will generally make themselves scarce if you approach them, but puff adders often lie on or beside paths, relying on their camouflage to escape detection, and it is then that the unwary may be bitten.

Like the leopard tortoise, snakes are most often seen on roads, either crossing as swiftly as the flitting shadow of a passing bird, or coiled up in the evening on the tarmac when they relish the warmth stored in the blacktop during the day. Many are killed at this time and their crushed bodies at the roadside offer the opportunity to inspect these often beautifully marked reptiles in safety – but do make sure they are dead before going too near!

One infrequently seen snake is the rare **Angola dwarf python** (*Python anchetae*) which lives in the mountainous areas from the northwest of Windhoek into Angola. In the same habitat lives a very active endemic, the diurnal **Damara** or **Namibian rock agama** (*Agama anchietae*). The male, with its orange head and tail and black or blue body, tends to sit in a dominant position on a rock, from where, with bobbing head, it scans its territory for a yellow-headed female or other males which might want to challenge him.

Quick-change artists

The desert climate rarely gives amphibians much time to lay eggs in what are often ephemeral pools, or for the tadpoles to metamorphose into the adult form. Consequently this happens very rapidly, a process enhanced by the high temperature of the sun-warmed shallow water, and very soon young froglets and toadlets, such as baby **bullfrogs** (*Pyxicephalus adspersus*) are leaving the water and disappearing into the surrounding grass. When they emerge the young often spread out over tracks near their birth pool and, if travellers are passing in a vehicle, it becomes impossible to avoid them all.

The melodious and continuous trilling call of **Lelande's sand frog** (*Tomoptema delelanii*), combined with the regular, snoring croak of the **guttural toad** (*Bufo gutturalis*), provide an interesting backdrop to summer nights around a Namibian campfire. Come sunset, the clicking chorus of the **barking geckos** (*Genus ptenopus*), calling from their burrows, will make those nights under the Southern Cross something to remember. ❑

LEFT: a Damara rock agama soaks up the sun.
RIGHT: most chameleons are arboreal and catch their prey with their long tongues.

PLANT LIFE

A wide range of curious plants thrive in Namibia's diverse habitats, including species that manage to live where there is minimal rainfall

In the dry season, a visitor to Namibia might have the impression that the country is almost barren and the vegetation monochromatic and colourless. Broad expanses of golden-brown grass, rugged mountainsides and plains dotted sparsely with scrub are characteristic of many regions of this desert land. But as spring begins, in August and September, the acacias, such as the **camel-thorn acacia** *(Acacia erioloba)*, start to deck themselves out with mimosa-like bunches of flowers. After months without rain, this reawakening always seems like a miracle.

When the first rainfall comes, generally in October, broad, dusty plains are transformed overnight by a covering of green fuzz. In a few days, this has developed into a thick yellow carpet of **morning stars** or **devil's thorn** *(Tribulus zeyheri)* mainly on disturbed ground, especially roadsides and around waterholes, while countless bulbs and buds quickly unfold colourful flowers. Annual plants suddenly appear, ornamented with magnificent flowers of every colour and transform the veld. Some 2,400 flowering plants, along with 345 different grass species, have been recorded in Namibia.

The cold Benguela current which runs along the entire coast prevents rainfall from the west. The result is a strip of desert running northwards from the Orange River on the southern boundary to the Kunene River on the border with Angola – the Southern, Central and Northern Namib. This can be further differentiated as the outer Namib, a 56-km (35-mile) wide strip along the coast, which receives almost no rainfall and obtains most of its moisture from coastal fogs, and the semi-desert of Namib to the east, which gets a meagre 50–100 mm (2–4 ins) each year.

In the transition area between the two, the famous **welwitschia** plants *(Welwitschia mirabilis)* sprawl across the sand, their twin leaves shredded by the wind. Some of these living fossils are over 1,000 years old. Other desert dwellers include several species of **stone plants** *(Lithops spp.)*, also known as Bushmen's buttocks, which look for all the world like stones until their beautiful flowers emerge.

More humble but tremendously important for the desert ecosystem is the **ganna** or **brackbush**. There are two species, *Salsola aphylla,* which grows mainly in the beds of the seasonal rivers, and *Salsola nollothensis* or coastal ganna, which is found in the dunes. Although apparently growing on top of a dune, in fact the brack-bush grows first and the dune forms around it helping to retain moisture and protect it from the wind.

In dune areas, especially around Sossusvlei, you should come across that staple of the Namib desert, the **!nara melon** *(Acanthosicyos horrida)*, a Namibian endemic. It has protective stems with long, bare, evil-looking thorns

---

LEFT: the fruit of *Welwitschia mirabilis*, a plant that lives for centuries in the desert.

RIGHT: the flower of the curious ice plant, whose stems are covered with water-filled papillae.

but somehow oryx, brown hyena and porcupine penetrate its defences in order to get to the watery melon.

Slightly further inland are two more noteworthy plants. One is the **elephant's foot** (*Adenia pechuelii*) which grows among rocks and has a thick grey-green stem about a metre (3 ft) tall with woody twigs on top. The second is *Euphorbia damarana*, quite a large plant with many individual, grey-white stems whose milky latex is poisonous to man – although both black rhino and gemsbok appear

PALM PRODUCTS

The hard fruit of the makalani palm are known as vegetable ivory. They are frequently carved into ornaments with animal motifs.

herbia albida) which can easily reach heights of 15 metres (50 ft).

Among the dark red rocks and kopjes in this area, **sterculia** trees (*Sterculia quinqueloba*) are common. Their thin, light grey, bark is made even whiter by a white bloom which covers it as an adaptation to the dry climate. They stand out in graphic contrast to the dark, rocky background. In the same general habitat are what appear to be small baobab trees. In fact they are **moringas** (*Moringa ovalifolia*) which have the same

to be able to eat it without apparent ill effects.

In the north of Namibia, the semi-desert gives way to the mopane savannah, which characterises mountainous Kaokoland and the western half of Ovamboland. Here, **mopane** (*Colophospermum mopane*) appears as shrubs or trees. Although apparently providing welcome shade in the middle of the day, the mopane often fools the innocent traveller for its paired leaves fold together to save moisture, thus casting little shade, while small black mopane bees descend on any source of moisture and collect, irritatingly, around the eyes and nose. The dry river beds, or *arroyos*, are lined with white-flowering **ana trees** (*Faid-*

bloated-looking trunks and branches that more closely resemble the general pattern normally made by roots – giving rise to the legend that they have been planted upside-down.

In many areas where there is enough water, especially on the Kunene, tall **makalani palms** (*Hyphaene petersiana*) with their odd but strangely appealing scent grace the landscape. In the rainy season, the area is regularly flooded, and various beautiful water plants spring up, including water-lilies, different types of Aponogeton, and the sensitive mimosa-like *Neptunia oleracia*, which closes its feathery petals at the slightest touch.

The northern Kalahari consists for the most

part of an open dry forest, which reaches all the way to the Caprivi Strip. In the Kavango region the **false mopane** *(Guibourtia coleosperma)* or oshivi tree and others are harvested and used by the Kabangos for their wood carvings.

In the Strip itself you will come across a wide variety of trees. One of the most noticeable is the so-called **sausage tree** *(Kigelia africana)*. It is named after its large sausage-like fruits which hang from the tree on long stalks and occasionally drop to the ground where they are eaten by animals such as rhino and baboon. They have exquisite blowsy, blood-red, velveteen flowers which fall to the ground and lie scattered under the lush green canopy.

Bordering on southern Ovamboland, Etosha National Park covers 22,270 sq. km (8,685 sq. miles). Within it, a basin or pan 4,950 sq. km in area (1,930 sq. miles) is classified as a salt desert and contains virtually no vegetation. Only in the west, after the rainy season, is it lightly bedecked with a species of salt-loving grass. To the north and west, this basin is bordered by grassy plains and to the south, by a savannah of small shrubs, which gives way to the mopane savannah.

Here, at the beginning of the rainy season, **omuparara** trees *(Pettophorum africanum)* explode into yellow blossom; in autumn, the **purple-pod terminalia** *(Terminalia prunioides)* leaves large red blotches of colour on the landscape. **Marula** trees *(Sclerocarya birrea)* produce fruits that are a particular favourite of elephants. It is probably a myth that they become drunk by eating them when they are fermenting, although marula fruit is turned into a creamy liqueur for human consumption.

Further east in Bushmanland you may come across the **poison grub tree** *(Commiphora africana)* under which are found Diamphibia beetles. The Bushmen dip the shafts of their arrows in the deadly juice of these insects but keep the tips clean in case they stab themselves accidentally.

In this area you should find some huge **baobab trees** *(Adansonia digitata)*. These

> ### SWEET-SMELLING SHRUB
>
> Although most acacias are trees, *Acacia nebrownii*, the **gland acacia**, grows in small bushy clumps. In the evenings its yellow balls of blossom waft a sweet fragrance across the savannah.

ancient trees with their enormously thick trunks have an edible pulp often sought by elephants who can literally tear one of these giants to pieces. Even when they are totally hollow these trees somehow survive, supported by their shell of bark.

The central highlands, with altitudes of up to 2,000 metres (6,560 ft), are the highest part of Namibia. Characteristic plants here include the **mountain thorn** *(Acacia hereroensis)* and **wild sage** *(Pechuela loschea-lubnitzia)*. In the spring, the

worm-bark tree *(Albizia antheimintica)* is thickly covered with large yellow blooms which resemble downy chicks.

South of here, once you leave the mountains at Rehoboth, the broad expanses are covered by dwarf shrub savannah. Here, large trees can only be found in dry river beds in small stands. The **quiver-tree** *(Aloe dichotoma)* is an exception. Although an aloe rather than a true tree, it grows to a reasonable size and its branches, hollowed of their cellular interiors, were used as quivers by Bushmen in this area. It is possible to make out its distinctive mushroom shape on plains and stony hillsides, especially in May when it has shining yellow blossoms. ❏

LEFT: the !nara melon is a staple food of the Topnaar.
RIGHT: stone plants look more like pebbles than plants – until they bloom in the rainy season.

PLACES

A detailed guide to the entire country, with principal sites
clearly cross-referenced by number to the maps

Named for the ancient desert that stretches the length of its Atlantic coast and dominated by thousands of square miles of sand and rock, Namibia has a landscape that is always extreme. Yet while it may not seduce with the bountiful charms of neighbours like cosmopolitan South Africa, or Botswana with its profusion of wildlife, it is Namibia's desert with its extraordinary flora and fauna, gutsy people and vast distances that brings visitors back – and back again – for another taste of an untamed wilderness.

There's more to this enormous country (it's nearly as big as France and Italy combined) than just the desert, too. Its northern borders are well-watered by rivers, while other parts of the country offer landscapes of spectacular, rugged mountains, deep canyons and wide-open plains.

The Namibian adventure usually begins in Windhoek, a city still dominated by the graceful buildings erected at the turn of the 19th century when the great scramble for African territory brought a sudden influx of German missionaries and colonists to this wild land. The capital acts as a useful jumping-off point for a range of intriguing journeys into the interior, including the majestic (and surprisingly little-visited) Fish River Canyon in the south and the mysterious Skeleton Coast to the west. Legendary among anglers, this coast's perilous mists and huge swells made it the graveyard of many an unwary mariner in times gone by.

Wildlife fans will probably already have heard of the Etosha National Park, one of the finest game reserves in the world, where the huge diversity of southern Africa's wildlife (including all of the "Big Five") can be viewed at close range.

For intrepid travellers in search of a true wilderness experience, off-the-beaten-track Namibia has much to offer. The Kaokoveld in the northwest is home to some extraordinary desert-adapted flora and fauna as well as the proud Himba people. Then there's remote Damaraland, strewn with archaeological finds dating back to Stone Age times. While it's only accessible to expeditions with 4-wheel-drive vehicles, the lush wilderness of the Caprivi region, on the other hand, is easily explored by car. ❑

PRECEDING PAGES: each coloured pebble a unique creation; surprisingly, the semi-desert of the Kalahari is home to plenty of plant life; the vast, wide-open landscape of barren Damaraland.
LEFT: on safari in the Caprivi.

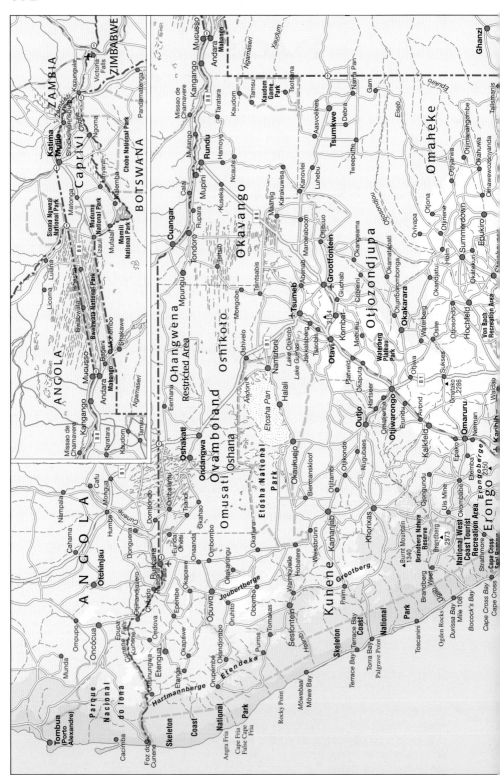

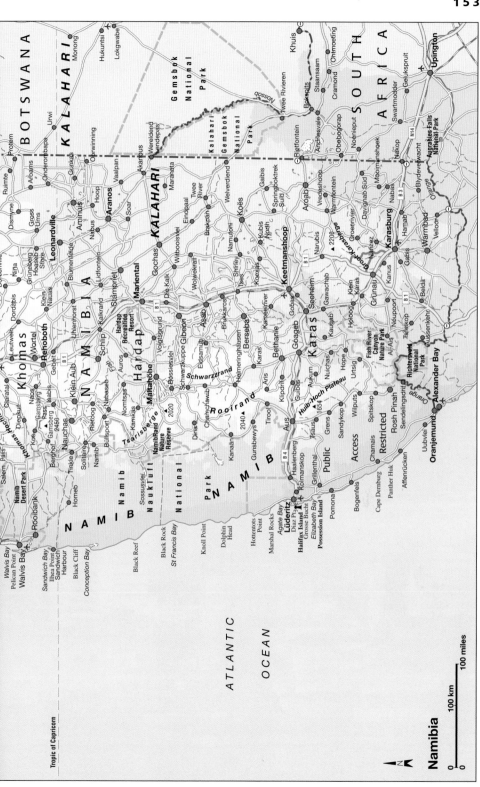

Namibia

ATLANTIC OCEAN

Tropic of Capricorn

100 km
100 miles

WINDHOEK

*Set at the geographical heart of the country in the rolling
Central Highlands, Namibia's cosmopolitan capital is a
sprawling African city with a marked Teutonic flavour*

Map
on page
158

Windhoek

Cupped in a valley bounded by the Auas Mountains to the south, the **Eros Mountains** to the northeast and the hills of the **Khomas Hochland** ("Highland") to the west, **Windhoek** is Namibia's capital and its commercial, financial and administrative hub. Yet it's not just a busy transit point. The town and the surrounding countryside have plenty to offer visitors, too.

At first glance, the place seems unusually small for a capital city, but appearances are deceptive – several outlying suburbs are tucked away in the surrounding valleys. Windhoek's overall population is around 280–300,000, a colourful ethnic mix of Europeans, Ovambos, Hereros and Damaras, with smaller numbers of Nama, San and "Coloured" (mixed-race) people as well.

Despite its name, which translates as 'Windy Corner', the place is not particularly windy – in fact, thanks to its relatively high altitude (about 1,650 metres, or 5,400 ft) it enjoys a dry and pleasant highland climate most of the year round. However, high summer (January–February) can be very hot and humid, with temperatures often hitting the 35°C (94°F) mark. What's more, nearly two-thirds of the city's average annual rainfall (365 mm/14.4 ins) is recorded in the first three months of the year, with occasional showers in November and December. Summer gardens, in other words, can be spectacular.

A town of many names

Although Windhoek itself is little more than a century old, the hot springs in the area have attracted settlers in one form or another for many thousands of years. The original site (in today's Klein Windhoek valley) was called *Aigams* ("fire water") by the Nama and *Otjimuise* ("place of smoke") by the Herero, although since then it has also been known as Elbersfeld, Concordiaville, Esek and even Queen Adelaide's Bath – although it's unlikely that the blue-blooded one ever set foot here.

In around 1840, the Nama chief, Jan Jonker Afrikaner settled at the springs with his followers and renamed the site Wind Hoock – apparently a corruption of the name Winterhoek, after the South African mountain range where he had been born. This name stuck and, by 1850, "Windhoek" was in general use.

In 1890, during the German colonial occupation, a military outpost was established in the town to house the headquarters of the German *Schutztruppe* (Defence Force) under Major Curt von François, whose brief it was to broker a peace between the warring Nama and Herero. That same year, Windhoek was declared the administrative capital of German South West Africa and began to evolve into the busy commercial and financial centre it is today – although the city itself wasn't officially founded until 1956.

PRECEDING PAGES: a Windhoek skyline.
LEFT: Hereros big and small at this city-centre souvenir stall.
BELOW: the graceful Christuskirche, one of Windhoek's best-known landmarks.

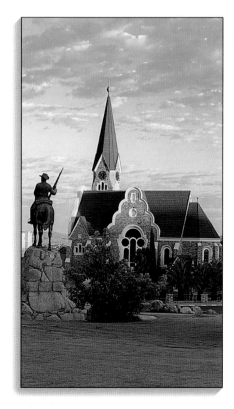

A walking tour

Thanks to the city's compact size, it's easy to take in all the main sights on a self-guided, two-to-three-hour-long walking tour. Set out early in the morning or late in the afternoon to avoid the hottest temperatures, and wear a pair of good walking shoes (and a sun-hat).

Our walk begins at the bus terminal at the corner of **Fidel Castro Street** and busy **Independence Avenue**, slicing through the heart of the city centre (the Kalahari Sands Hotel which dominates the skyline here is a useful orientation point). Close by is Windhoek's newest landmark, a millennium clock; perched on 13 poles to represent Namibia's 13 regions, it's topped by a metal version of the city's emblem, the aloe.

A short walk north takes you to tranquil **Zoo Park Ⓐ**, past a busy pavement market selling Namibian indigenous arts and crafts. Although you won't find animals at the park any more, there was a small zoo here from German colonial times right up until the early 1960s, along with an elegant café where an orchestra played classical music. Look out for the sculpted column commemorating a Stone Age elephant hunt which took place here some 5,000 years ago (an elephant fossil and some quartz tools were unearthed on the spot in 1962). Nearby to the south is the **Kriegerdenkmal**, or War Memorial, dedicated to the memory of German soldiers who fell in the 1893–1898 Nama wars.

The park also offers a good view of three fine old colonial buildings, set just across the street on the west side of Independence Avenue. The Erkrathaus (1910), the Gathemann House (1913) and the Kronprinz, built in 1902 as an hotel, were all designed by renowned local architect Willi Sander and are known collectively as the **Old Business Façades**.

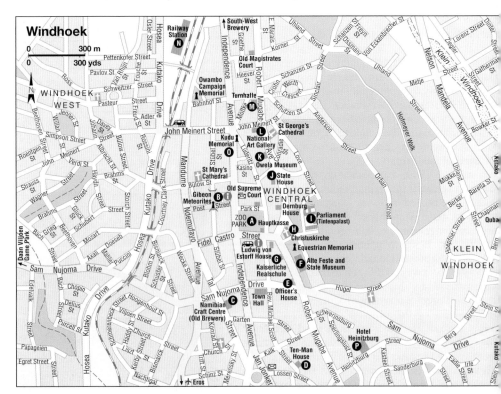

Around Independence Avenue

A short step north up the avenue takes you to Windhoek's main post office, past the **Post Street Mall** on your left (the striking Clock Tower near the top of this street is a replica of a turn-of-the-century structure which once crowned the Deutsche-Afrika Bank). The mall itself is a good place to shop for souvenirs, with its profusion of curio shops, craft stalls, chain stores and street cafés. Its centrepiece is the curious **Gibeon Meteorite National Monument B**, an open-air display housing 33 relics of the largest known meteorite shower ever to have hit the earth – probably about 500 million years ago, when it scattered debris over an area of 360 by 110 km (210 by 65 miles) centred on the small town of Gibeon. The individual stones on display, which weigh up to 555 kg, were collected over the period 1911–13, but the meteorite shower was first documented by the explorer J.E. Alexander in 1838, prior to which the metallic rocks (an iron-nickel alloy) were used by local hunter-gatherers to shape into tools.

The Post Street Mall fountain comprises one of the largest collections of meteorites in the world.

Now retrace your steps down Independence Avenue; walk south as far as Sam Nujoma Drive and turn into it, heading west. A left turn from here into Tal Street takes you to the **Old Brewery C**, where Namibia's favourite tipple, Windhoek Lager, was once produced – it's now home to a thriving arts complex, including the trendy Warehouse Theatre, the Namibian Craft Centre, and Tower of Music.

After a break for refreshments at the centre's small café, turn left into Garten Street to find Independence Avenue once more. Cross it and head east for one block to reach the Rev. Michael Scott Street, leading south to the H-shaped, fortress-like **Ten-Man House D**. Designed by Adolf Matheis in 1906 to provide accommodation for unmarried government officials, it's another fine example of the local colonial style.

BELOW:
street scene,
Katatura suburb.

Historic heart

The next section of the walk takes in some of the most interesting German-era architecture Windhoek has to offer, as well as some great city views. Head north up Rev. Michael Scott Street back to Sam Nujoma Drive and turn right onto Robert Mugabe Avenue, the city's colonial heart. The **Officer's House E** (closed to the public), on the corner, with its decorative Putz-style brickwork, was built in 1906–7 to house senior officials, while just up the road is Windhoek's oldest building, the white-washed **Alte Feste F**. Built in 1890 as the headquarters of Captain von François' *Schutztruppe*, it's now part of the State Museum (Mon–Fri 9am–5pm, Sat and Sun 10am–12.30pm and 3–5pm; closed public holidays, no entrance fee, donation requested). Exhibits include a particularly well-thought-out display on Namibia's struggle for independence.

Just north of the Alte Feste stands an **Equestrian Memorial** (actually, it's pretty hard to miss), erected in 1912 to commemorate the German soldiers who fell in the Herero and Nama Wars of 1904–1909. The turreted structure opposite is the **Kaiserliche**

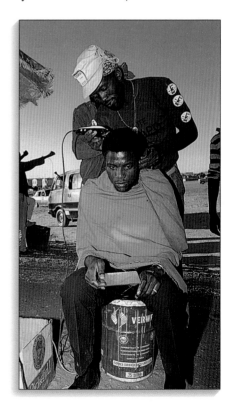

You'll find indigenous crafts such as these drums at the Werhill Mall.

BELOW: Alte Feste, Windhoek's oldest building.

Realschule , built in 1907 as the first German primary school in Windhoek. Later it became the city's first German secondary school, then an English school; it now houses government offices.

Immediately north of the memorial is the graceful German Lutheran **Christuskirche** , or Christ Church. Designed by Gottlieb Redecker in an adventurous blend of neo-Gothic-meets-Art Nouveau *(Jugendstil)*, it was built between 1907 and 1909 from local sandstone and remains one of Windhoek's best-known landmarks (guided tours Wed 4pm, Sat 11am; tel: 061 236002).

Across the street is the **Ludwig von Estorff House**, named for a *Schutztruppe* commander who lived here between 1902 and 1910. Originally built as a canteen for military artisans, it was subsequently used as a residence for senior officers such as von Estorff. One block north lies the equally impressive **Haupt-kasse**, once the colonial government's revenue office – it too, now houses government offices, namely the Ministry of Agriculture.

Another Gottlieb Redecker design crowns the hill behind Christuskirche to the east. The imposing **Parliament** buildings with their splendid gardens once housed the colonial government's administrative headquarters and were nicknamed the **Tintenpalast**, or "Ink Palace" – a sly reference to the vast quantities of ink the toiling bureaucrats seemed to get through (guided tours are available but must be pre-booked, tel: 061 2882605).

Back on Robert Mugabe Avenue, a short stroll north takes you past **Dernburg House**, built especially to accommodate the German Secretary for the Colonies when he paid a visit to Namibia in 1908 (it was subsequently used as government offices). **State House** , the official residence of Namibia's President, is a little further on. The graceful colonial governor's mansion

which once stood here was flattened in 1958 to make way for this modern building; all that remains today is a section of garden wall.

Map on page 158

More city-centre sights

While the walk outlined above offers a basic tour round the core of Old Windhoek, there are plenty of other interesting buildings to explore nearby. A short walk north of State House on Robert Mugabe Avenue is where you'll find the **Owela Museum ⓚ**, containing the State Museum's worthwhile natural history section (Same openings times as affiliated Alte Feste). It offers some information on Namibia's diverse local cultures, but the excellent displays on cheetah conservation are the biggest draw here. Worth a quick look, too, is the church in Love Street, a block away from the museum to the east – known as **St George's**, it's the smallest cathedral in southern Africa.

Back on Robert Mugabe Avenue and heading north, you'll soon reach the **National Art Gallery of Namibia ⓛ**, which is definitely worth a visit. Temporary exhibitions complement the permanent art displays, which cut across a broad range of styles and periods. Look out particularly for the outstanding linocuts by John Muafangejo, and paintings by the colonial artist Adolph Jentsch (Mon–Fri 8am–5pm, Sat 9am–2pm, Sun 11am–4pm; free Mon–Fri, entrance fee Sat and Sun).

On the corner of Robert Mugabe Avenue and Bahnhof Street you'll find the **Turnhalle ⓜ**, built in 1909 as a gymnasium. In the 1970s it was turned into a conference centre, springing to fame in 1975 when the South African government staged the first Constitutional Conference on Independence for South West Africa here. This historic gathering brought a range of white and black Namibian political leaders and groups together for the first time to discuss the country's future; it subsequently became known simply as "the Turnhalle Conference".

Castles and kudus

Walking westwards along Bahnhof ("Station") Street, you'll find Windhoek's gracious old **Railway Station ⓝ**, built by the Germans in 1912 and later expanded in the same architectural style by the South African administration. If you're planning to catch the Desert Express to Swakopmund, this is where it departs from *(see Travel Tips page 259)* but, even if you're staying put, the building's still worth a look. Train buffs should head for the upper level and the little **TransNamib Transport Museum**, which covers the history of train travel in Namibia (Mon–Fri 10am–1pm and 2–5pm; entry fee).

Diagonally across from the station, at the entry to the car park, stands a large stone obelisk. The **Owambo Campaign Memorial** was erected in 1917 to commemorate those South African and British soldiers who fell in the fight to bring down Mandume, king of the Kwanyama, the biggest Owambo tribe; Mandume himself was also killed during the campaign.

Other interesting buildings nearby include the **Kaiserliche Landesvermessung**, the old colonial

BELOW: this gaily painted mural adorns the Namibian Craft Centre.

The Herero

The Herero *(OvaHerero)* were originally a pastoral people who migrated to what is now Namibia some five hundred years ago. According to oral tradition, they came from the Great Lakes of East Africa, travelling through present-day Zambia and southern Angola and arriving at the Kunene River in about 1550.

After a sojourn of some 200 years in Kaokoland, many migrated further south. Towards the middle of the 18th century their vanguard reached the Swakop River Valley; by the 19th century, the Herero were establishing themselves firmly in central Namibia. Today, they number more than 100,000 and are still regarded as expert cattle breeders.

The Herero nation includes a number of subdivisions:
● The Herero proper, including the traditional chiefdoms of Maherero (Okahandja region), Zeraua (Omaruru), Kambazembi (Waterberg) and others. In Kaokoland, the Ndamuranda

and the Tjimba Herero also belong to this subgroup.
● The Mbanderu in the east of Namibia (especially in the district of Gobabis).
● The Himba and other smaller factions living in northern Kaokoland and in southwest Angola.

A particularly striking feature of their social order is the double descent system. Every individual belongs at the same time to a matrilineal *(eandag)* and a patrician *(oruzo)* clan. Traditionally, the matriclans exert control over people's property, especially cattle, and supervise the application of the traditional laws of inheritance. The localised patriclans, on the other hand, take responsibility for sacred objects and the holy cattle *(ozohivirikwa)*, the exercise of authority in the family, succession of chiefs, priesthood, ancestral fires and the ritual food taboos.

As a result of the colonial wars, and particularly the consequences of the Herero Uprising of 1904–05, traditional culture suffered greatly through a decrease in population, the confiscation of tribal land, a prohibition on cattle breeding and restrictive labour regulations. But, even during this bitter period, there were attempts to revive the bonds of family life and tribal solidarity.

In the beginning, the Herero made use of the means of communication offered by Christian congregations to keep in touch with their fellow tribesmen. Later they established their own organisations including burial societies, religious fraternities and paramilitary associations. The transfer and burial of Chief Samuel Maherero, who had died in exile, at Okahandja in 1923 became a demonstration of the Herero's unbroken national consciousness.

Before independence in March 1990, much of Herero political life centred around the so-called Herero reserves where headmen and councillors were elected. Since 1950 "Herero tribal meetings" have been held annually under the chairmanship of a "Chief's Council" led for decades by the revered Chief Hosea Kutako, who directed numerous petitions at the United Nations calling for Namibian independence. ❑

LEFT: Herero women base their striking costume on styles worn by missionaries' wives.

surveyors' offices, on the corner of Independence Avenue and John Meinert Street; these are now occupied by a local tour operator. Diagonally across the street is the bronze **Kudu Memorial ⓞ**, donated by a wealthy Namibian businessman in the wake of the terrible *rinderpest* epidemic of 1896, in which thousands of kudu (and cattle and sheep) perished. The statue, by Professor Behn of Munich, was erected in 1960.

Also within walking distance of the city centre – but only just – are Windhoek's three turreted castles, **Heinitzburg ⓟ, Schwerinsburg** and **Sanderburg**. Designed by the ubiquitous Willi Sander in the early 1900s and set high on a ridge overlooking the city, these quirkily romantic buildings are much-loved landmarks, although only Heinitzburg Castle (now the Hotel Heinitzburg Garni; tel: 061 249597; www.heinitzburg.com) is open to the public – the other two are private homes. A firm favourite with the locals, thanks to its lavish afternoon teas, the Hotel Heinitzburg Garni is worth the effort it takes to walk there. Head south down Robert Mugabe Avenue to the corner of Heinitzburg Street, from where it's a short, steep climb up the hill to the castle at No 22.

Map on page 158

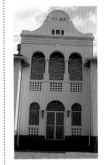

Excursions further afield

There's a distinct lack of inexpensive, reliable public transport in Windhoek, which can be a source of frustration for visitors who want to branch out and explore beyond the city centre. There are, of course, plenty of companies offering city tours *(see Travel Tips page 260)* and taxis abound, too – although they are fairly pricey.

The historic Turnhalle building – now the seat of the National Council.

BELOW: celebrations during the annual WIKA carnival.

Whatever mode of travel you settle for, it's worth considering a trip out to Windhoek's suburbs if you really want to get a feel for the city. **Katutura**, on the city's northwestern outskirts, is a bustling residential district whose name means "the place where we do not wish to go" in Herero. It's a reference to the area's former incarnation as a blacks-only township, established in 1960 by the South African administration, who forcibly evicted Windhoek's black residents from their homes in the Old Location (now known as **Hochland Park**) and moved them here. Since independence, of course, apartheid policies such as these have been swept away and, increasingly, Windhoek's urban areas are becoming differentiated along economic lines, rather than race.

Hochland Park's **Old Location Cemetery** – a national monument – makes a worthwhile, if poignant, excursion. There's a mass grave here where 13 people are buried, shot dead by the South African police on 10 December 1959 during protests against the forced removals to Katutura. The day of the killings, 10 December, is known as Human Rights Day and is a public holiday.

On a lighter note, the **Hofmeyer Walk** is an hour-long hiking trail winding south through unspoilt countryside along the ridge that separates Windhoek from the Klein Windhoek valley. It's particularly rewarding during March and April, when the mountain aloes *(Aloe littoralis)* are in bloom – their bright red flowers attract plenty of birds. At any time of year, the views back over the city are stunning. You

Map on page 158

can pick up the trail in Orban or Anderson streets, just east of the Parliament building, then follow signs to the finishing point in Uhland Street (be aware, though, that recently there have been reports of hikers being mugged along the trail; if you decide to embark on it, don't carry any valuables).

Festivals

A particularly good time to visit Windhoek is during the city's main carnival (also known as **WIKA**), held in the last week in April and the first week in May. The city's best-known knees-up, it's also the one with the strongest Teutonic flavour. Summer's end is celebrated in true German tradition with oompah bands, much good humour and vast quantities of beer.

If, on the other hand, you prefer something rather more African, the **Enjando Street Festival** is a summer programme of art, music, dance and drama which usually takes place in November. A section of Independence Avenue between Fidel Castro Street and the main Post Office is closed off to motorists and becomes an ocean of people instead.

Wildlife

BELOW: this imposing office block dominates the city centre. **RIGHT:** bustling market scene.

Windhoek, like most African cities, is not known for its wildlife viewing possibilities. Nevertheless, there are a couple of worthwhile possibilities within easy day tripping distance of the city centre. Foremost among these is the **Daan Viljoen Game Park** (open sunrise–6pm daily; entrance fee), which lies 20 km (12½ miles) west of Windhoek and is accessible by a good tar road. Of greater interest, perhaps, for its network of day hiking trails rather than its game viewing, this mountainous area is nevertheless a good place to seek out the localised Hartmann's mountain zebra, giraffe and large antelope such as greater kudu, oryx and blue wildebeest. Largely because it is permitted to walk freely, and to get out of your car at whim, Daan Viljoen is an excellent place to tick near-endemics such as Monteiro's hornbill, Damara rockjumper, white-tailed shrike alongside the striking crimson-breasted shrike, shaft-tailed wydah and violet-eared waxbill. A small rest camp offers simple accommodation and camping facilities to those who prefer to sleep outside the bustling capital, and there is a restaurant on site.

For larger wildlife, a somewhat more contrived – but nevertheless worthwhile – experience can be had at **Okapuka Ranch**, a private game lodge situated some 40 km (25 miles) north of Windhoek alongside the surfaced road to Okahandja. Aimed primarily at overnight visitors (it would make a convenient first stop heading northward to Etosha or Caprivi), the lodge also welcomes day visitors for a fee, and facilities include walking trails, game drives and a good restaurant. A pride of captive lions are fed daily at 5pm, while free-ranging wildlife includes giraffe, gemsbok, greater kudu, blue wildebeest and (rare elsewhere in Namibia) the beautiful sable antelope. It's a rewarding spot for birdwatchers too, protecting a similar selection of species to Daan Viljoen. ❑

CENTRAL NAMIBIA

Often overlooked by visitors thanks to its proximity with Etosha, this region is rewarding in its own right, too, from its rolling hills and river valleys to its abundant historical sites

A ll too often, the area north of Windhoek is seen by visitors merely as something to "get through" en route to northern Namibia's big draw, the Etosha National Park. Yet not only does north-central Namibia hold many attractions of its own which repay closer attention, it's also well set up for a self-drive tour. Most roads are tarmac or well-graded gravel, while provisions, banking facilities and fuel are available at all the main towns and most rest camps along the way. Bear in mind, though, that many of the attractions round here are on private land, and require advance booking.

Exploring the highlands

Heading north from **Windhoek ❶** on the B1 highway, you'll pass through the hilly farmland of the **Khomas Hochland**, flanked on the east by the Onyati mountains. **Okahandja ❷** 71 km (44 miles) north of Windhoek was established in 1849 by the German missionary Friedrich Kolbe, only to be abandoned in 1850 after repeated attacks by the Namas under Jonker Afrikaner. It was a timely escape; the following year, little **Blood Hill** (to the east of the B2) was the scene of a massacre where the Namas killed around 700 followers of the Herero leader Tjamuaha. Today, however, Jonker Afrikaner lies side by side with several distinguished Herero chiefs in a graveyard opposite the Rhenish Church in Kerk Street (open by appointment only).

Okahandja is the main Herero administrative centre, and a place of great historical significance for these people as a whole, too. The **Green Flag Herero** or **Mbanderu** assemble here each June to pay homage to their forefather, Kahimemua Nguvauva, executed in Okahandja on 13 June 1896 for his involvement in a revolt against the German administration. Then, at the end of August each year, the streets come alive at the **Red Flag Herero procession**, when men in military-style uniforms and women in billowing red dresses honour the memory of their fallen chiefs.

Lining the southern and northern approaches to the town are curio markets run by the Rundu-based Namibian Carvers Association, which are well worth a visit (open daily). There's also the **Ombo Ostrich Farm**, 3 km (2 miles) northwest of Okahandja on the D2110, offering 45-minute tours packed with facts about these extraordinary birds (tel: 062 501176; small fee), but otherwise there's not much to see here.

Okahandja has a limited selection of hotels, but there is plenty of accommodation just outside town. Although this is some of the best farmland in Namibia – prime cattle-ranching country, in particular – in recent years many farmers have restocked their land with game and opened up as guest farms catering for the tourist trade.

Windhoek

PRECEDING PAGES:
Okahandjo's Red Flag Herero procession.
LEFT: those elaborate Herero outfits dry slowly.
BELOW: German war cemetery, Waterberg Plateau.

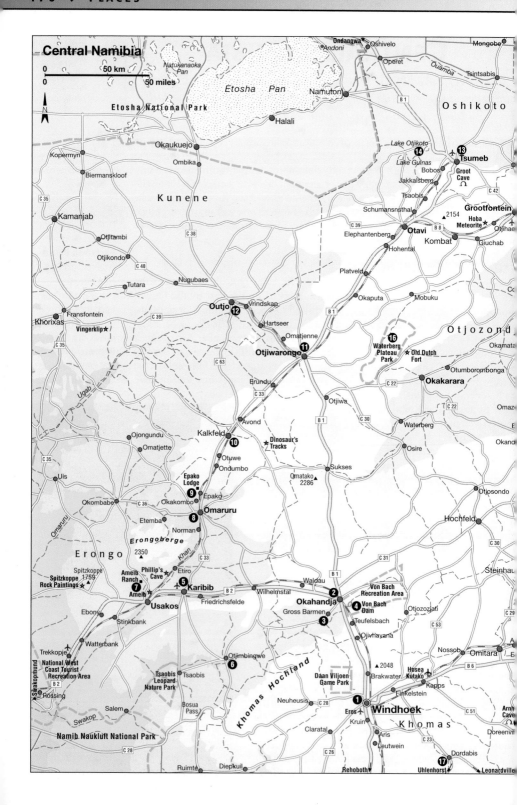

Central Namibia

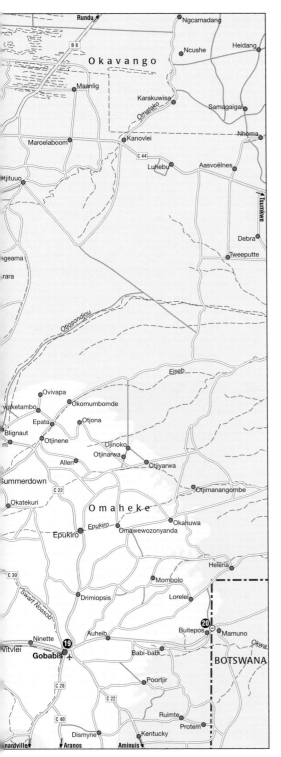

Apart from these, other good stopover places in the vicinity include **Gross Barmen ❸**, another old mission station built round a dam on the Swakop River some 24 km (15 miles) southwest of town on the C87. The main attraction here is a hot mineral spring, feeding a glass-enclosed thermal hall and an outdoor swimming pool. The water has a constant temperature of 65°C (150°F), but is cooled to a more bearable 40°C (104°F) for the thermal pool.

The spa is very popular with weekending locals and visitors passing through en route to Etosha, and there are also some good walks and birdwatching in the surrounding wooded hills.

Stocked with carp, bream, barbel and bass, the **Von Bach Dam ❹**, just off the B1, some 3.5 km (2 miles) south of Okahandja on the D2102, is a big hit with watersports, enthusiasts and fishermen. Game-viewing opportunities are limited, but kudu, Hartmann's mountain zebra, springbok, eland and ostrich are all present in the surrounding park. The accommodation's pretty basic, however.

Outside Okahandja, the B2 turns off in a westerly direction to the coastal resorts of Swakopmund and Walvis Bay. Take this road and at first you'll pass through predominantly featureless bush farmland before the the ochre-pink granite mass of the Erongo mountains come into view in the north, just outside **Karibib ❺**. This little ranching town (112 km/70 miles from Okahandja), is best known for its high-quality marble produced at the Marmorwerke quarry nearby; examples can be seen on floors in the Houses of Parliament in Cape Town and even on wall panels at Frankfurt Airport.

The useful **Henckert Tourist Centre** on the main street should be your first stop here; it began as a gem and curio shop back in 1969 but now houses a Namib-I tourist information facility, a money bureau and a coffee shop too.

From Karibib, you can take a detour south to Otjimbingwe, or continue 30 km (18 miles) along the B2 to Usakos to visit the Ameib Rock Paintings. Sleepy **Otjimbingwe ❻** lies 51 km (32 miles) along the D1953; founded as a Rhenish mission sta-

*Ostrich on a dusty
farm road near
Otjimbingwe.*

BELOW: the
Dordabis region is
home to Namibia's
karakul industry.

tion in 1849, it remained a quiet little place until the early 1880s when – thanks to its strategic position halfway between Windhoek and Walvis Bay – it enjoyed a brief stint as German South West Africa's administrative capital. In 1890, however, the capital was transferred to Windhoek, and Otjimbingwe sank back into small-town torpor once more. It does have some interesting buildings, however, including the Rhenish church (the oldest place of Christian worship for the Herero), and the 1872 powder magazine erected to protect the locals against Nama attacks.

Erongo rock art

The Erongo massif is best known for its rock art sites, of which the vast **Phillip's Cave** – home to a famous engraving of a "white elephant" – is the most rewarding. It's situated on land belonging to an upmarket guest farm, the **Ameib Ranch ⑦** (tel: 064 530803), lying some 27 km (17 miles) from **Usakos**: to get there, take the D1935 for 11 km (7 miles) before turning right on the D1937. The cave is a short drive and then a 40-minute walk from the ranch house. There are also several good walks to the curiously-shaped rock formations scattered around the farm, too – the group of round granite boulders known as the **Bull's Party**, some 5 km (3 miles) from the house, is one of the most picturesque.

Back in Karibib, it's a 65-km (40-mile) drive north through undulating bush farmland to pretty little **Omaruru ⑧** on the C33. Set on the banks of the Omaruru River – dry and sandy for the best part of the year – this former Rhenish mission station came under repeated attack by Herero forces at the turn of the last century and in 1904 was finally besieged. But the day was saved by a German officer, Captain Victor Franke, who petitioned the then Governor for permission to march north with his company from their garrison in southern

PRECIOUS PELTS

Soft, smooth, silky and supple, Karakul pelts are "Namibia's Persians", and the carpets and coats made from them fetch a high price both at home and abroad. Dordabis in the eastern part of Central Namibia is the heart of the Karakul industry; in these dry lands on the fringes of the Kalahari Desert, the hardy Karakul sheep enable many people to make a living where it might otherwise be impossible. The sheep's grazing habits stimulate the growth of many local plants and shrubs, while by treading grass stems into the ground, the herds also prevent erosion; the top level of soil, usually endangered by the wind, is thus saved.

There's only one thing that neither man nor beast can force from nature: rain. When there's a drought in these already arid regions, it has dire consequences on the Karakul industry. Lack of food and water drastically cut down the size of the herds.

The first sheep were imported from Germany in 1907; there are now over 1 million in Namibia, bred in black, grey, brown and white. In 1978, some 2,500 Karakul breeders produced 4.66 million pelts, but since then – thanks to drought and reduced demand – the industry has been in decline, with only 120,000 pelts a year produced recently.

Namibia and lend their efforts to the fight. After a 19-day trek, he galloped into Omaruru and relieved the siege. **Franke Tower** on Omaruru's eastern outskirts was built in his honour; it's usually locked, but ask at the nearby **Hotel Staebe** if you want to get hold of a key.

If you're keen to see more rock art, there's a very well-preserved site with both paintings and engravings outside Omaruru on a farm owned by the Hinterholzer family. Follow the D2315, 3 km (2 miles) south of Omaruru for 24 km (15 miles) and then turn south on the D2316 for 19 km (12 miles). Allow an hour to reach **Erongo Lodge** (not to be confused with the Erongo Wilderness Lodge). It's a short drive to the site from here, along a road that climbs steeply into the thinly-wooded hillsides of the Erongo Mountains, past white-trunked moringa trees striping the ochre rock faces. Visiting arrangements can be made through Erongo Lodge (tel: 064 570852; www.erongolodge.iway.na).

Map on page 170

In Herero, Omaruru means "sour milk", after the milk their cows gave when they'd been grazing on a local shrub, known as the bitterbush.

The road to Etosha

Like Okahandja, Omaruru is well served by guest farms, many of which stock game. Luxurious **Epako Lodge ❾** *(see Travel Tips, page 263)*, 18 km (11 miles) north on the C33, is a particularly good stopover choice if you don't have time to visit Etosha – the wildlife here includes elephant, leopard, white rhino and giraffe, as well as over 180 species of bird. It also has some rock art, although the paintings aren't of the same quality as those found near Erongo Lodge.

Keep going north along the C33 for some 64 km (40 miles) from Omaruru and you'll reach the village of **Kalkfeld ❿**. The only reason for stopping here is to visit the fossilized dinosaur tracks on the extraordinarily-named **Otjihaenamaparero farm** nearby; the most striking are the imprints of a two-legged, three-toed dinosaur, which can be followed for about 25 metres (80 ft). Follow the D2483 for 19 km (12 miles) and turn right onto the D2414; from here it's 10km (6 miles) to the signposted turn off. The tracks are a short walk from the parking area (entry fee).

A 70 km (43 miles) drive northeast from Kalkfeld leads to **Otjiwarongo ⓫**, a rather unremarkable ranching town that has adequate tourist facilities and serves as a popular springboard for eastern Etosha. A more popular stop-off than the town itself, however, is the guest farm called **Okonjima**, which is signposted west of the B1 trunk road about 35 km (22 miles) south of town. Serviced by two small luxury lodges, this vast and in parts mountainous acacia-studded farm is also home to the **AfriCat Foundation** (www.Africat.org), whose pioneering work in the rescue and release of big cats has earned it numerous international ecological and ecotourism awards since 1997, including the Genesis Award (Discovery Channel BBC / Ark Trust Inc), WWF Green Trust Award, and most recently the 2004 World Travel Award for Namibia's leading safari.

A one- or two-night stopover at one of Okonjima's exceptionally comfortable lodges is the ideal way to break up the drive from Windhoek to Etosha, while also offering some superb close-up encounters with habituated leopard, captive lion and rehabilitating cheetah. Ask to be shown around the clinic and information

BELOW: local handicrafts include traditional masks.

Many of Central Namibia's guest farms are well stocked with wildlife.

centre for further insight into this multi-faceted organisation, which rescued more than 850 'problem' cheetah and leopard in its first 13 years of existence, and was able to release a full 86 percent of these handsome creatures back into the wild. AfriCat also plays an important role in educating youngsters about big cats (more than 20,000 children and young adults have passed through its education centre or outreach programme since 1998) whilst also giving refuge to 'welfare' animals which for one or another reason cannot safely be released back into to the wild.

Outjo , a further 68 km (42 miles) northwest of Otjiwarongo along the C38, is an attractive little place set amidst low, grassy hills (the name means "small hills" in Herero) with views of the Paresis mountains. It was first established in 1897 as a *Schutztruppe* control post, although development pretty much ceased during the Herero War (1904–5). There's not really much to see here, although as it is just 96 km (60 miles) from here to Etosha's Andersson Gate, it could serve as a good overnight stop if you're heading on to the park.

To Lake Otjikoto

BELOW:
the hot thermal
pool at Gross
Barmen resort.

If you're heading to Etosha, the other alternative is to stay on the B1 after Otjiwarongo and head northeast through **Otavi** to **Tsumeb** ⑬, a charming, leafy-avenued town in an area of considerable mineral wealth. Vast deposits of copper have been found here, along with over 200 other minerals including silver, lead, zinc and cadmium. The excellent **Tsumeb Museum** (Mon–Fri 9am–noon and 3–6pm; Sat 9am–noon; entry fee), housed in an old German-built schoolhouse in Main Street, has good displays on the area's geology and cultural history, together with an array of German armaments retrieved from nearby **Lake Otjikoto** where they were dumped by retreating forces in 1915.

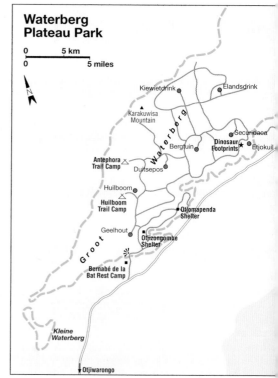

Waterberg Plateau Park

0   5 km
0   5 miles

N

Kiewietdrink

Elandsdrink

Karakuwisa
Mountain

Waterberg

Bergtuin

Securidaca

Dinosaur
Footprints

Etjokuil

Antephora
Trail Camp

Duitsepos

Huilboom

Huilboom
Trail Camp

Otjomapenda
Shelter

Geelhout

Otjizongombe
Shelter

Groot

Bernabé de la
Bat Rest Camp

Kleine
Waterberg

Otjiwarongo

or good-quality handicrafts, take a look at the **Tsumeb Arts and Crafts Cen-**
-e (Mon–Fri 8.30am–1pm and 2.30–5pm; Sat 8.30am–1pm) nearby at 18
lain Street; it's run by an educational trust supporting Namibian craftsmen.
  Lake Otjikoto ⓮ ("deep hole" in Herero) lies just off the main route to
.tosha's Namutoni Gate, 24 km (15 miles) northwest of Tsumeb on the B1.
ormed when the roof of an enormous underground cavern collapsed, leav-
ig a steep-sided dolomite sinkhole some 90 metres (290 yards) deep, it's a
ompelling sight and well worth the detour. Otjikoto and nearby Lake Guinas
re the only known habitats of the little cichlid fish *Pseudocrenilabrus philan-*
er, a species of mouthbreeding tilapia; it occurs in a remarkable range of
olours from dark green to bright yellow and blue, perhaps because initially it
ad no natural predators in the lake and camouflage was unnecessary.
  Our final stop along this northern route is the farming town of **Groot-**
ontein ⓯, 60 km (37 miles) southeast of Tsumeb on the C42. Mainly used by
isitors as a jumping-off point for the Caprivi Strip, it does, however, boast
ne sight worth stopping for – the iron-and-nickel **Hoba Meteorite**, at 50 tonnes
he largest in the world. Having blazed to earth some 30,000–80,000 years ago,
: was discovered in 1920 by a local farmer and is now a national monument. It
es just 20 km (12 miles) west of Grootfontein on the B8 (entry fee).

Waterberg Plateau Park

You'll have to retrace your steps south again to reach central Namibia's jewel,
he **Waterberg Plateau Park ⓰**. An island of red sandstone cliffs lushly
hatched with green rising majestically above the surrounding savannah, the park
vas proclaimed in 1972 as a sanctuary and breeding-ground for threatened

Maps:
Area 170
Park 174

BELOW: cheetah at
Mount Etjo Safari
Lodge, near
Otjiwarongo.

Maps:
Area 170
Park 174

*Going to market –
the traditional way.*

BELOW:
Lake Otjikoto
was created
when the roof
of an underground
cave collapsed.

species such as white rhino, roan and sable antelope and tsessebe. The schem
has been very successful, with some species now being translocated to othe
areas. Other animals you might spot here include leopard, brown hyena an
caracal, together with over 200 bird species, from the rare Ruppell's parrot an
black eagle to Namibia's only breeding colony of Cape vultures.

This is not a park for self-drive tours. Instead, you can explore the nine shor
nature walks which have been laid out around the camp area, or book yourse
onto one of the organised **game drives** which the park operates twice a day, vis
iting hides and waterholes. But perhaps the best way to experience the park'
diverse landscapes – from woodland and grassland to thick acacia bush – is b
joining one of the four-day organised **wilderness trails** which run in the dry sea
son (between April and November), where you follow game trails with a qual
ified guide, and learn about ecology and wildlife issues.

The **Bernabé de la Bat rest camp** offers accommodation in pink sandston
bungalows spread along the plateau's wooded slopes, along with a restaurant an
shops, a petrol station and swimming pool. To reach the park from Otjiwarongc
it's a 27-km (17-mile) drive south on the B1, followed by 58 km (36 miles
east on the C22, before turning north onto the D2512 for 17 km (10 miles).

East of Windhoek

Compared to the rest of the country, central Namibia's eastern section has rel
atively few tourist attractions. The main draw here is the region's tranquillit
and unspoiled scenery – striking camel-thorn savannah vegetation on re
Kalahari sand. It's best explored on a day trip from Windhoek, or as part o
a route south following the fringes of the Kalahari to **Mariental** or **Keet
manshoop** via the C15 and C17.

Little **Dordabis** ⓱ has a lovely setting in a valle
surrounded by rounded hills; it's also the centre o
Namibia's karakul industry, with plenty of farm
breeding the sheep and workshops offering rugs an
wall hangings for sale. The **Dorka Teppiche** weavin
workshops (call in advance; tel: 062 573581), at Pep
perkorrel farm on the D1458 are open to visitors as ar
Ibenstein Weavers (tel: 062 560047), about 3 km (
miles) south of Dordabis on the C15.

Other attractions include the **Arnhem Cave** ⓲, th
longest cave system in Namibia with a total length o
4.5 km (3 miles). An underground trail takes you pas
various kinds of mineral deposits and six bat specie
– including the giant leaf-nosed bat *(Hipposidero
commerssoni)*, the world's largest insectivorous bat
As the cave is dusty, old clothes and a good torch ar
required. There's a small rest camp here, too.

To get there, take the B6 from Windhoek to the air
port. Follow the D1458 southeast for 66 km (41 miles
before turning north on the D1506 for 11 km to a T
junction, when you should turn south onto the D180
for 4 km (2.5 miles).

Busy **Gobabis** ⓳, 200 km (124 miles) east o
Windhoek on the B6, is a thriving cattle-ranching cen
tre and – with the border at **Buitepos** ⓴ just 120 km
(190 miles) east – the main jumping-off point i
you're heading east to Botswana.

The Nama

The Nama form a subgroup of the indigenous Khoikhoi (or "Hottentots"as they were misnamed in the past; this word is now deemed derogatory and should not be used). Most Khoikhoi within the boundaries of Namibia belong to the Nama and Oorlam groups. Pushed continuously northwards by a rapidly-advancing white farming community, the Nama, led by the famous chief Jan Jonker Afrikaner, settled in the Windhoek area in the mid-19th century.

Certain distinctive features make the Khoikhoi easily recognisable. The women's small and slender hands and feet are the subject of traditional praise poems. High and prominent cheekbones combined with a tapering chin and markedly platyrrhine noses add to the general flatness of the facial profile. Faces are animated by beautiful dark-brown or black eyes which seem to be almond-shaped on account of a particular fold of the upper eyelid. In common with the Bushmen, the women in particular have an extraordinary accumulation of subcutaneous fat over the buttocks (steatopygia).

The present-day Nama population numbers around 90,000. As pastoral nomads, the Nama traditionally had little need of permanent structures – their beehive-shaped rush-mat houses were perfectly suited to their lifestyle. The concept of communal land ownership still prevails among most clans today, except for the Aonin or Topnaars, whose *!nara* fields are the property of individual lineages.

Nama tribes at the coast have always considered the sea an important source of food. Occasionally the people have taken to gardening and, in a small way, even to agriculture. Recently, communal agricultural projects have been established at Hoachanas, Gibeon, Berseba and other places.

While their decorative art is somewhat poorly developed, the Nama possess a natural talent for music and poetry; no visitor to a Nama village at Sesfontein valley will easily forget the soft, lilting sounds of reed-flutes on a moonlit night. The literary talents of the people, meanwhile, expresses itself in prose and verse. Numerous proverbs and riddles, tales and poems have been handed down orally from generation to generation, while several hundred folk-tales are known and still told – some with as many as 40 different versions.

Internecine quarrels in the past and wars against the advancing intruders brought great suffering to the Nama; under the South Africans their living space was gradually confined to a number of so-called reserves. In spite of their heroic resistance against colonialism and their strenuous efforts to preserve their identity, their culture has been greatly eroded. But their heroes still live on in impressive tales and praise poems of chiefs and other prominent personalities.

There are 14 clans in Namibia, living mostly in the southern and central parts of the country. Since independence in 1990, there has been a tendency towards greater cooperation between different clans, and a real opportunity for a renaissance of the Nama nation's unique cultural heritage. ❑

RIGHT: there are 14 Nama clans in Namibia, living mainly in the central and southern parts.

NORTHERN NAMIBIA

Map on page 182

The densely populated far north is Namibia's rural heartland, with traditional villages and kraals *surrounded by thick bush offering a fine contrast to the arid wilds of Bushmanland*

Windhoek

Namibia's four northernmost regions – Oshikoto, Ohangwena, Oshana and Omusati – constitute its cultural heartland. The traditional home of the Ovambo, Namibia's largest ethnic group (in fact, before Independence the area was officially known as Ovamboland), this is the most densely populated part of the country, with most people making a living as subsistence farmers growing crops of maize and millet and raising cattle and goats.

Beyond the isolated towns stretches a series of flat, scrubby plains, dotted here and there with feathery makalani palms, baobab trees and the odd clump of mopane forest. A string of small traditional villages, cattle *kraals*, roadside craft markets and *cuca* shops (grocers' stalls) complete the picture.

Crossing the line

The best time to visit the former Ovamboland is during May, just after the rainy season when the bush is looking splendidly verdant (this area receives the highest rainfall in the country). Summers (November–February), meanwhile, can be unpleasantly hot and sticky.

Heading north from **Tsumeb ❶**, you'll have to stop at tiny **Oshivelo ❷**, some 91 km (56 miles) away along the B1, in order to pass through the "Red Line", a veterinary control fence designed to block the movement of cattle (and therefore the transmission of cattle diseases such as foot and mouth) down into the ranching districts of Central Namibia.

To the west lies the **Andoni Plain**, which until the early 1960s was part of Etosha National Park and home to huge herds of zebra, gnu and oryx. These days, the game's been displaced by cattle and much of the bush by wide, flat fields sown with vegetables and grain; wildlife's definitely in short supply. Keep an eye out, nonetheless, for birds such as the pied crow, hornbill, stork and heron.

The road north is also lined for some of the way by a prominent pipeline, siphoning off water from the Culevai River drainage system which is the main source of water round here. Essentially, the system's a web of shallow watercourses known as *oshanas*, which fill up with water during the rainy season and then hold underground water all year round.

Just before you get to Ondangwa, you'll notice signs for the turnoff to **Olukonda** village ❸, some 10 km (6 miles) southeast on the D3606. It's home to northern Namibia's oldest building, a mission house built in the late 1870s by the Finnish missionary Martti Rauttanen. The locals called him Nakambale, or "the one with the hat", and the name stuck; today **Nakambale House** is a museum, and adjoins a rest camp offering accommodation in an historic mission

PRECEDING PAGES: the winding Kunene River once fed the Ruacana Falls.
LEFT: Ovambo pottery is renowned.
BELOW: carrying water home from the river.

cottage, various traditional Ovambo huts and in a campsite, too. Rauttanen i buried in the graveyard adjoining the little thatched-roof church.

If you're coming from Tsumeb, **Ondangwa** ❹ is the first sizeable tow you'll encounter on the B1. Before Independence this was Ovamboland's mai administrative centre and, while Oshakati's now taken over that role, the plac still hums with life. From here, it's just 60 km (37 miles) on the B1 to th Angolan border post at **Oshikango**.

Oshakati

From Ondangwa, the C46 leads northwest to Oshakati, Ovamboland's "cap ital". The closer you get, the more built-up the area becomes, and you'll notic a marked increase in the traffic on the road, too. Little **Ongwediva**, som 25km (15 miles) from Ondangwa, is a noted educational centre with a well respected Teacher's Training College; of more interest to visitors, though, i the **Oshana Environment and Art Association**'s shop in the main road, sel ing art from all over the northwest along with a good range of crafts such a jewellery, pottery and baskets.

You'll find good-quality crafts from all over the north in little Ongwediva.

Fast-growing **Oshakati** ❺ is set near a particularly large *oshana* whic habitually overflows its banks after good rains, damaging houses and othe infrastructure in the process – something to bear in mind if you're travellin during the rainy season. It's a big, busy town with a lively atmosphere, bu there's not really much worth stopping for here apart from the substantia covered market on the town's western boundary, which sells everything fror frogs caught in local *oshanas* to woven baskets and dried mopani worms.

The road now loops northwest through the Omusati Region (*omusati* mean

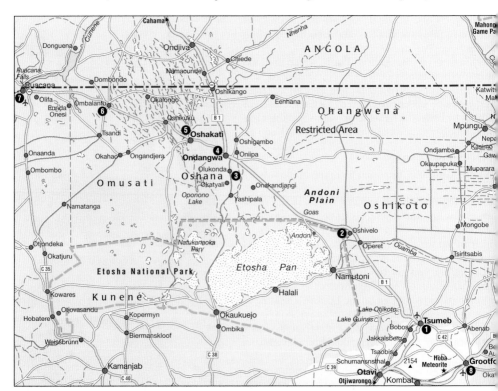

nopane" in Ovambo), and you'll notice these trees becoming more prolific the further west you go. About 110 km (68 miles) from Oshakati, you'll reach the dusty village of **Ombalantu** ❻, where the biggest attraction is an enormous baobab with a trunk containing a hollowed-out "room". It's been put to many different uses in the past, including stints as a church, school and even a post office! The tree's on the old South African Defence Force army base on the main road; ask for directions at any shop or petrol station.

uacana Falls

Heading further northwest, you'll pass the agricultural settlement of **Mahanene** about 40 km (25 miles) from Ombalantu before reaching the turn-off to sleepy **uacana** ❼ some 50 km (30 miles) further on. There's a petrol station and a shop here, but little activity – although you may sometimes see stately clusters of Himba clans people who have come east into town to stock up on goods before migrating back deep into the Kaokoveld.

From here, it's a scenic 25-km (16-mile) drive north across the Kunene River and up into Ovamboland's only mountain range for a view into Angola and the 85-metres (280-ft) high **Ruacana Falls**. Once a magnificent natural attraction, these are now dry except during the very wettest part of the rainy season (March–April), thanks to the construction of a major dam some 50 km (30 miles) upstream. To a lesser degree, the flow's also controlled by a weir just above the falls, built to divert water into the turbines of the 320-megawatt underground hydro-electric power plant stationed on the border.

If you're planning to head into the Kaokoveld from here, Ruacana is the last place to buy fuel before **Opuwo** *(see Northwestern Namibia, page 222)*.

Map
on page
182

TIP

The former Ovamboland is in a malarial area, so consult your pharmacist and start taking prophylactics before you travel here.

BELOW: baobab tree with built-in convenience.

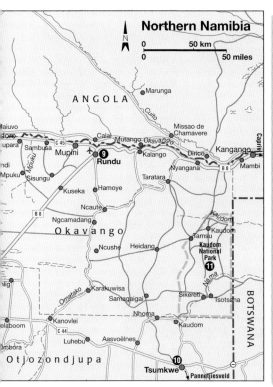

Northern Namibia

The Kavango region

Bordering Ovamboland to the northeast lies the lushly wooded and well watered Kavango area. This is Namibia's second most densely populated region, with most of its inhabitants living along the banks of the Okavango River and its floodplains in scattered villages of thatched, circular huts. The traditional way of life is still strong around here and, for many Western visitors, the Kavango region and the Caprivi further east probably represent the rural African experience as they always imagined it.

It's a 250-km (155-mile) drive on a good, tarred, almost dead-straight road northeast from the cattle-ranching town of **Grootfontein** ❽ to **Rundu**, the region's main centre. About halfway along you'll have to pass through the veterinary control fence again, marking the boundary between the big commercial cattle ranches of the central region and the subsistence farms of the north, most of which are communally owned. Across the line, the landscape becomes markedly more Third World, with patchy fields of millet and maize linking straggling rural hamlets. Roadside stalls also start to appear, selling wooden crafts and great piles of vegetables and fruit.

In a lovely setting high above the Okavango floodplain, with good views into Angola, busy **Rundu** ❾ has a wide range of places to stay spread out along the riverfront. Most lodges offer cruises and angling trips up and down the river, too, although water levels get very low just before the rains in January. This is a good place to stock up on fuel and supplies if you're planning to drive further east to the Caprivi (see page 203) and Botswana, and don't miss the chance to visit the **Mbangura Woodcarvers' Cooperative**, either – the handicrafts sold here (chiefly made from teak) are generally to a high standard.

BELOW:
well-stocked
handicrafts stall on
the road to Rundu.

East of Grootfontein, Central Namibia's fertile agricultural plains begin to shade into the hot and arid Kalahari region. This stretch of semi-desert – reaching all the way to the Botswana border – is still widely known by its old name, Bushmanland and, as the name implies, is home to a generous proportion of Namibia's Bushman (or San) peoples. Most of the communities living here are not nomadic any more, but settled in scattered villages; most scratch a living as subsistence farmers *(see Namibia's Peoples, page 63).*

Map on page 182

Bushmanland

The easiest way to get to Bushmanland's main town, **Tsumkwe** ⑩, is from Grootfontein. Bear in mind, however, that Tsumkwe is little more than a dusty crossroads, offering sparse supplies and without even a petrol station – so stock up before you go. To find it, head north on the B8 for 50 km (32 miles) before turning east onto the (gravel) C44. After 32 km (20 miles), you'll pass **Maroelaboom** police station; it's about another 200 km (125 miles) from here.

The **Omatako Valley Rest Camp** makes a good pit stop along the way – look out for signs about 88 km (55 miles) after you've turned east onto the C44. Run by the local San community, it has a good craft shop selling beads, necklaces, baskets as well as cold drinks. If you decide to check in for a stay, the camp can also arrange activities such as bush walks for game and bird spotting, and visits to local villages.

Tsumkwe's on the borders of the **Bushmanland Conservancy**, established in 1997 and run by a San development foundation keen to promote ecotourism as a way of preventing any further erosion of traditional San culture. Most hotels and lodges around Tsumkwe can arrange excursions with local guides into the

The area east of Twumkwe is home to the Ju'/hoan San.

BELOW: a traditional San (Bushman) hunt in progress.

Map on page 182

Game in Khaudom National Park includes the beautiful oryx antelope.

BELOW: you'll see plenty of roadside markets like these all over Kavango and Ovamboland.

conservancy, visiting villages to watch craft demonstrations and traditional dancing, or taking food-gathering trips into the bush.

Eastern Bushmanland is also characterised by the **Pannetjiesveld**, an area speckled with small pans around which modest amounts of game collect in summer, when the ground gets very dry. Visitors can expect to spot a good range of wildlife from lion, leopard, elephant and hyena to giraffe, kudu and roan antelope. During the rainy season, the area's often temporarily flooded and the bigger animals move further north – although the birdlife remains abundant. After good rains, you can expect to see great flocks of lesser flamingos and wood sandpipers on **Nyae Nyae**, the largest pan, and perhaps even rare wader species such as the great snipe.

If you're planning to explore beyond Tsumkwe, you will need to be completely self-reliant and be part of a group of at least two 4x4 vehicles (you can get to Tsumkwe in an ordinary saloon car, though). And, if you're planning to camp out around here, always sleep inside a tent – you're in a wilderness area, after all.

Khaudom National Park

Just north of Bushmanland on the Botswana border, the little-known **Khaudom National Park** ⓫ is a wild area of dry woodland savannah on stabilised Kalahari dunes, dotted with the occasional clay pan. Thanks to the *omurambas* (a Herero word meaning poorly-defined drainage lines) that crisscross the area, the vegetation's pretty dense, dominated by mangetti, Rhodesian teak and false mopane on the dunes, and acacia and umbrella-thorn elsewhere.

Game includes giraffe, kudu, oryx and steenbok, as well as some of the rarer antelope such as roan and tsessebe. As for predators, the park has a substantial lion population plus leopard, cheetah, black-backed jackal and spotted hyena. This is also Namibia's best park for spotting the elusive wild dog.

Khaudom's game isn't as abundant as that in Etosha, but there is a real sense that you're deep in the African wild. With this in mind, prepare yourself for pretty basic conditions. Water is available in each of the two camps, but there are no other supplies of any kind, so come well-equipped with food and fuel. Within the park, the roads are mainly sandy, so driving is slow.

Booking must be done in advance in Windhoek or you won't be admitted, and you must have two or more 4x4 vehicles per group.

The easiest way to reach the park is from Tsumkwe on the minor road leading north out of town, and signposted for Khaudom. Where the road splits, take the right fork for the park entrance and Sikereti camp, a total journey of about 60 km (37 miles).

Set amidst a grove of beautiful silver-leaf terminalia trees **Sikereti** has three basic rondavels and camping facilities, with no hot water, lights or electricity. **Khaudom** camp in the north, meanwhile, is set on the crest of a dune overlooking a water-hole; there are camping facilities and two rondavels here. Nothing is fenced, so don't leave any food outside that could tempt the larger wildlife. Bear in mind, too, that you'll have to depart early in the morning if you plan to reach Khaudom camp from Sikereti in one day. ❑

The Ovambo

Ovambo (or Ambo) is a collective name for a number of indigenous peoples living in Northern Namibia and Southern Angola who share a common origin and culture. Together they form by far the largest ethnic group within Namibia's boundaries, comprising about half of the total population.

Traditionally, the clan (*omuhoko*) was the most important political institution among the Ovambo. Four of the biggest clans live in the southern Kunene Province of Angola and eight in northern Namibia (the largest group, the Kwanyama – comprising 36 percent – is cut in two by the international boundary). Others are the Ndongo (29 percent), the Kwambi (12 percent), the Ngandjera (8 percent), and the Mbalantu (7 percent). Although each group speaks its own dialect, they are closely related to one another and there are no serious language difficulties between them.

Many Ovambo still adhere to a traditional economy based on a combination of agriculture and animal husbandry, supplemented by fishing in the shallow watercourses and pools. This way of life has been under pressure, however, ever since German colonial times, when an ever-increasing number of young men began to enter the labour market on farms, in towns and at industrial sites and mines. The introduction of the Western monetary system also brought about drastic changes to the traditional economy, with hundreds of small Ovambo-owned shops springing up across the land.

After the apartheid-system contract labour and pass laws were abolished, the southward migration of Ovambo people increased significantly. Today many Ovambo work in the larger towns as labourers, craftsmen, tradesmen and professionals.

The traditional social system reveals a close relationship with other central African Bantu cultures. A most striking feature is the predominance of matrilineal descent, a system which determines in particular the laws of inheritance and succession, as well as post-marital residency. In recent years, however, there has been a distinct shift towards a patrilineal society. External factors such as Christian doctrine, migrant labour, business enterprises undertaken by nuclear families and economic independence have all contributed to this change.

Traditionally each clan was headed by a hereditary chief or king, assisted by a council of headmen. Today, however, only three of the main clans are still ruled by chiefs-in-council; the rest have a system of senior headmen forming a council and administering their communities by joint action.

Regulating the land ownership system is one of the most important roles played by these officials. Personal ownership of the land is unknown here, and only life-long rights of utilisation may be granted by the chief via his headmen. After the death of the tenant, the right of utilisation reverts to the next higher authority and may be assigned to somebody else. Thus land never becomes private property and people are not permitted to acquire more than one district, ward or site at the same time. ❑

RIGHT: Ovambo family, heading home with lunch firmly in hand.

ETOSHA NATIONAL PARK

Set in high savannah in the north of the country, this is
one of the oldest and largest parks in Africa, and the best
for big game-spotting in an arid environment

Map
on page
192

Etosha National Park is the jewel in Namibia's wildlife crown. At first sight for the game viewer, however, it is a rather hollow jewel for – right in the centre of that part of the park open to the public – lies an enormous saline pan. Yet it is for this pan that Etosha is famous: 115 km (72 miles) long and up to 68 km (42 miles) wide, it covers an area of about 5,000 sq. km (1,930 sq. miles) and is as inhospitable as the most barren desert. Almost entirely devoid of vegetation, it gleams and shimmers in the noonday sun, creating the most fantastic mirages, inverting distant images and turning the black full stops of the male ostriches who stray onto its great white wastes into colons.

All this is good news for the game viewer, however, for almost all the animals are crammed around the rim of the pan (especially along its southern side), where a number of pumped and natural water-holes create a stage attracting a constantly-changing cast of players. For the enthusiastic visitor, rewarding watching is practically guaranteed.

PRECEDING PAGES:
dry winter
conditions make
game easy to spot.
LEFT: the park's
famed black rhino.
BELOW: a Beau
Geste-style fort
adorns the rest
camp at Namutoni.

A brief history

Etosha first gained official park status in 1907, when Governor von Lindequist of the German Colonial Government proclaimed Game Reserves 1, 2 and 3. Game Reserve No. 2 encompassed the Etosha Pan and Kaokoland from the Kunene River in the north to the Hoarusib River in the south, a total area of 93,240 sq. km (36,000 sq. miles). As such, it remained intact until 1947 when the Kaokoland portion was set aside for use and occupation by the Hereros. During the same year, 3,406 sq. km (1,315 sq. miles) was cut off from the Etosha portion and sectioned into farms, an area which became known as the Gagarus block.

It then became clear, however, that the reduced park area was too small to accommodate rare species such as mountain zebra and black-faced impala, migratory big game such as eland and elephant, and the influx of wildlife from adjacent areas. In accordance with the Elephant Commission of 1956, the boundaries of the park were extended towards the west to include unoccupied state land between the Hoanib and the Ugab Rivers.

This practically doubled the size of the park, safeguarded migration routes and created a corridor to the sea. The new park now extended from the Skeleton Coast in the west for nearly 500 km (300 miles) inland to the edge of the Etosha Pan in the east, a total surface area of 99,526 sq. km (38,427 sq. miles).

Unfortunately, the existence of what was effectively the largest game reserve in the world was

short-lived. As a result of the recommendations of the Odendaal Commission of 1963, the park area was drastically reduced, with total disregard for ecological boundaries. Solely for political reasons (that is, in order to accommodate South Africa's policy of separate homeland development or apartheid), 71,792 sq. km (27,719 sq. miles) were sacrificed to the land needs of Ovamboland, Kaokoland and Damaraland. By 1970 the park had been whittled down to its present size of 22,270 sq. km (8,600 sq. miles), a reduction of 77 percent – just a shadow of its former grandeur. From an ecological perspective, many wildlife experts feel it really should link up with the Skeleton Coast National Park.

The watchtower at Okaukuejo rest camp.

The pan and beyond

The park takes its name from the **Etosha Pan** ❶, the "great white place of dry water" which is the ultimate destination of channels draining from the catchment area in southern Angola. While the capacity of the Etosha Pan has been estimated at between 150–200 million cubic metres (195 and 260 million cubic yards), this quantity of water is almost never seen in the pan proper.

The pan can become partially flooded during the rainy season, but the water is too brackish for human or animal consumption; instead it supports a rich growth of blue-green algae. In a good rainy season, up to a million flamingos are lured to the pan to breed – a wonderful sight. When the water dries up very little vegetation grows on the pan, with the exception of occasional patches of a salt-loving grass, rich in protein, which provides good grazing for blue wildebeest, springbok and zebra during the dry winter months.

To the east of the pan is the treeless **Andoni Plain**, a typical grassland dom-

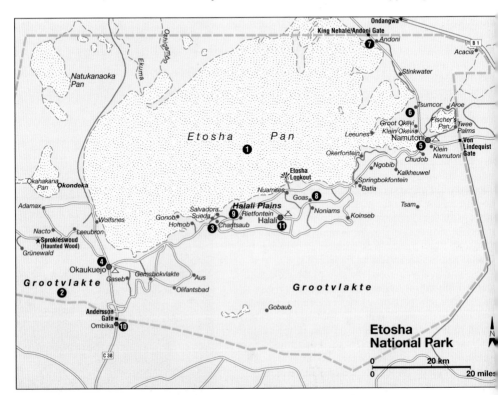

nated by the tall perennial grass, *Sporobolus spicatus*. Along the western and northwestern shore of the pan are the **Okondeka grasslands**, and between the Haunted Wood and the Charl Marais Dam is **Grootvlakte ❷**. These two grasslands are the main summer grazing areas for plains animals such as Burchell's zebra, blue wildebeest and springbok. The winter grazing areas, which sustain less palatable grasses, are the **Halali Plains**, extending from the water-holes known as **Charitsaub ❸** to **Nuamses** and **Gemsbokvlakte**.

The big game show

There are 114 mammal species in Etosha. Some (lion and steenbok, for example) can invariably be found in specific areas or home ranges, whereas others such as eland wander around in search of better grazing or browsing. Springbok, plains zebra, blue wildebeest and elephant, meanwhile, follow yearly migrational patterns depending on the availability of grazing and rainwater, which the animals prefer to fountain or borehole water.

When the rainy season begins in November, the animals seldom need to visit the water-holes along the tourist routes, congregating instead in large herds on the grass plains west of **Okaukuejo rest camp ❹** and in the area around **Fischer's Pan** near **Namutoni rest camp ❺**. Many young animals are born at this time of the year, but this is also when most of Etosha's 1,500 elephants leave the tourist section and move to the northern and southern areas. Some even leave the park altogether, depending on the availability of water.

Black rhino (for which the park is famed) occur mostly in the western and southwestern areas of the park and are generally seen in the vicinity of Okaukuejo either at night at the water-hole, or in the evenings and early

Map on page 192

TIP

When you stop to watch birds at a water-hole or along the road, keep an eye out, too, for camouflaged mammals hidden in shady places.

BELOW: male ostriches can be identified by their black plumage.

Giving Nature a Helping Hand

Experiments in recent years testify to the ingenuity Namibians have brought to solving wildlife management problems, each making a significant contribution to conservation in its own way.

Lions on the Pill: Fencing off an area to protect wildlife might seem like a solution to many conservation problems, but more often than not it actually creates just as many complications of its own. Migration routes are cut off, growing populations can no longer expand into unsettled areas, man-made water-holes affect game movements and the delicate balance of nature is upset.

In the case of the Etosha National Park, researchers found that fencing off the land led to a marked increase in the lion population and a significant decrease in the number of other predators. It was obvious that the lions had to be culled – but how?

Led by biologist Dr Hu Berry, the park's research team decided to experiment with the use of contraceptive implants in selected lionesses. Begun in 1981, the closely-monitored experiment was conducted on five prides in the Okaukuejo area. And a major undertaking it proved to be: before giving the lionesses an implant, each had to be darted with an immobilising drug and given a full "bush medical" which included weighing, the taking of temperature, blood and a pap smear, and the checking of teeth to determine age.

Not only was the experiment successful, it has subsequently been copied in other southern African reserves. It appears that contraception does not induce physical or behavioural changes amongst treated lionesses; once taken off the pill, they become pregnant within three months and go on to produce healthy cubs.

The AfriCat Foundation: As most of Namibia's cheetah and leopard populations are found outside fenced game reserves, farmers and local communities regularly lose livestock to predators. After years of research, this organisation – based at Okonjima in north-central Namibia – has devised ways of reducing, or at least minimising, stock losses through an educational campaign.

For example, Namibian farmers are being encouraged to trap "problem" animals on their farms, rather than shoot them. No cats are sold; instead, they are restored (if need be) to peak condition at Okonjima in large enclosures and then relocated to approved private game reserves in Namibia and South Africa. Relocation costs are met by the recipient. To date, some 260 cheetahs and 100 leopards have passed through the system.

More recently, in conjunction with the Namibian Ministry of Tourism and Environment, a leopard project has been initiated whereby leopards in the Okonjima area, fitted with radio collars, can be tracked to learn more about their movements.

A visit to the foundation's headquarters at Okonjima offers a chance to see not only these leopard on game drives, but lion and cheetah (in enclosures) as well. ❑

LEFT: biologist Dr Hu Berry prepares a darted Etosha lion for treatment.

mornings, as they browse in the cool of the day. Giraffe are widely distributed throughout Etosha but, being browsers, they avoid the plains unless it is to drink at a water-hole, when they make a particularly dramatic sight. Lion are distributed throughout the park with concentrations where prey is plentiful, along with both cheetah and the elusive leopard. Other large mammals to look out for in Etosha are Burchell's (or plains) zebra, blue wildebeest, gemsbok, kudu, eland, red hartebeest, roan antelope, springbok and the localised black-faced impala.

Smaller species

Less frequently seen species include the caracal with its characteristic tufted ears, the African wild cat, the aardwolf – a smaller distant relative of the hyena – and the spotted hyena, which can sometimes be heard howling or "laughing" at night. Also encountered are black-backed jackals, warthogs, honey badgers, squirrels and smaller antelope such as steenbok and grey duiker, along with the diminutive Damara dik-dik which can be seen especially in the Klein Namutoni area.

Of the 340 bird species which have been identified in the park, about one-third are migratory, such as the European bee-eater and several species of waders. During good rainy seasons large numbers of waterbirds and waders congregate on Fischer's Pan, including greater and lesser flamingos. Namibia's national bird, the dramatic crimson-breasted shrike, is fairly common in Etosha. It is also possible to spot, and ponder over the identification of, no less than 12 species of lark.

Of the 35 raptor species found in the park, 10 are migratory and come to

Map on page 192

A rare sight: an elusive leopard spotted near Klein Otavi water-hole.

BELOW: after the rains, Etosha is transformed into a nutrient-rich grazing-ground.

The lappet-faced vulture nests in the tops of acacia trees.

BELOW: many wildlife enthusiasts rate Okaukuejo as one of Africa's most exciting game-viewing water-holes.

Etosha only for the summer. These include the yellow-billed kite, steppe eagle, western red-footed kestrel and the booted eagle. The smallest bird of prey in the park is the pygmy falcon. The most common species of vulture are lappet-faced and white-backed vultures but examples of Cape, Egyptian, and hooded vultures can also be spotted by the observant birdwatcher. Other rare bird species found here include the black-tailed godwit, the goliath and purple heron, the dwarf bittern and the crowned crane.

Fruitful sites

The best game-viewing in Etosha is generally achieved by sitting quietly at water-holes and waiting to see what will turn up. This is especially true during the winter months (May–August) and before the rainy season (September–November), when the animals congregate around the watering points. If you arrive and the place is empty, don't just drive away – stop and have a good look around. It may just be that there is a predator lurking nearby, preventing the game from coming near the water. Look carefully in all the shady places where cats might lie up out of the sun, and scan the bigger trees for leopards.

As a general rule, most visitors arriving at water-holes park where they do not obstruct the views of others and turn off the engine. Not only is this quieter (especially if you have air conditioning), but it enables photographers to lean on the vehicle's open windows without the vibration from the engine blurring their pictures. Everybody has a much more enjoyable safari if each has his or her own pair of binoculars so that no-one becomes bored while the rest of the party discusses the finer points of a twitching lion's tail, or the tusks of a distant elephant only visible through a magnifying lens!

Map on page 192

The **Klein** and **Groot Okevi** water-holes just north of Namutoni are both frequented by black-faced impala, kudu, gemsbok, zebra, elephant and a great variety of birds, as well as predators such as leopard and cheetah. Further north is **Tsumcor** ❻, a favourite place for photographing elephants. Still further, on the Andoni Plain, is the **Andoni** water-hole ❼, where there are often many bird species. A new gateway to the park was opened here in 2003. East of Namutoni on the edge of Fischer's Pan are **Aroe**, frequented by elephant, springbok, blue wildebeest, kudu, zebra and giraffe, and **Twee Palms**, with its two landmark makalani palms, a favourite with photographers.

South of Namutoni lie **Chudob** and **Klein Namutoni**, both fed by artesian springs. Giraffe, black-faced impala and warthog can be observed at both of these water-holes. In the same vicinity is Bloubokdraai, where the Damara dik-dik can sometimes be seen at relatively close quarters. West of Namutoni is Kalkheuwel, where it is possible to get close to the game. During the dry season large numbers of animals come here to drink, including lion, gemsbok, giraffe and elephant.

Other water-holes

Other sites in this area include **Okerfontein**, on the edge of the pan, where cheetah and lion are sometimes seen; **Ngobib**, which attracts kudu, zebra and elephant; **Batia**, with its large herds of springbok, blue wildebeest and elephant; and **Goas** ❽, where you could see vast numbers of black-faced impala, blue wildebeest, red hartebeest, elephant and zebra, as well as lion and birds of prey.

Travelling west towards Okaukuejo is **Rietfontein** ❾, one of the best

Up to 10 million years ago, Etosha Pan was part of a vast inland lake, fed by the Kunene river. But when tectonic movements forced the river westward towards the sea, the lake slowly dried up.

BELOW: sunset at "the place of great white spaces".

One of Etosha's 114 mammal species, the ground squirrel.

BELOW: Etosha's birds include the dazzling little lilac-breasted roller.

known water-holes in the park. Many species, including leopard, are found here, as well as a wide variety of birds. **Charitsaub**, **Salvadora** and **Sueda** water-holes are situated close together further west and are a good bet for lion. Hundreds of springbok, zebra and gemsbok are often seen here too, but elephant only very rarely. Still further west is **Homob**, close to the pan and often frequented by both lion and elephant. There is also good game viewing at **Aus**, **Olifantsbad** and **Gemsbokvlakte**.

Furthest northwest of all is **Ozonjuitji m'Bari**, frequented by a variety of animals, but is rather far from camp. Here, the road travels through the well-known **Sprokieswoud** ("Haunted Wood"), the only place in the park where the wierdly-shaped African moringo is found growing in a flat area and as a dense forest. Moringos – endemic to Namibia and christened the "upside-down tree" by the Bushmen, normally grow on the slopes of hills and mountains. **Ombika ❿** lies south of Okaukuejo and close to the Andersson Gate; it's visited by a variety of game, especially lion.

Etosha's rest camps

Okaukuejo, the park's oldest and most popular rest camp and its administrative HQ, lies right in the centre of the park (most tourist maps show only the eastern sector, but in fact it stretches as far westwards as the C35 road at Otjovasandu). The accommodation here has recently been modernised and now offers a broad range of bungalows and rooms as well as a camping site, restaurant, shop, filling station internet café, and swimming-pool. It has a wonderful floodlit waterhole which is almost always active and can be exceptional at night, when black rhino can come almost within touching distance.

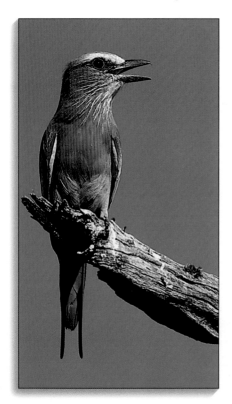

Namutoni's history goes back to 1851 when the explorers Sir Francis Galton and Charles Andersson camped near Namutoni Spring, a bowl-shaped limestone fountain in a marshy environment of tall reeds, once a drinking place for cattle. The first Fort Namutoni, built of unfired clay bricks, was completed in 1903 only to be razed to the ground the next year during the Herero uprising (the garrison of four soldiers and three ex-servicemen all escaped). In 1950 the rebuilt but dilapidated fort was declared a national monument; a few years later it was renovated according to the original design. First opened to tourists in 1958, the camp was greatly extended in 1983, when a shop, restaurant complex and 24 accommodation units were added. It also has a floodlit water-hole.

Opened in 1967, **Halali rest camp ⓫** is half-way between Okaukuejo and Namutoni. Here, attractions include the so-called **Tsumasa Trail** and the floodlit water-hole laid out on the dolomite hill closest to the rest camp. The grounds of the camp can be a very good place to see small animals and birds, which – because they are so used to seeing people – have become very tame and can easily be approached for pictures.

Although it may sound crazy, do take your binoculars to the water-holes at night. They really do enhance your night vision and help you to sort out what is a rock or a bush and what is a hyena. If you have a tripod, it is possible to achieve interesting effects by photographing animals in the floodlights on a timed exposure – some stay still, while those that move leave ghostly images on your film.

Recent years has also seen the opening of several private lodges and conservancies bordering Etosha. Foremost of these is the luxurious **Ongava Lodge and Tented Camp**, which lies on a privately managed 300 sq. km (166 sq. km) tract of acacia woodland abutting the southern park boundary near **Okaukuejo Rest Camp**. Managed by the highly regarded Wilderness Safaris, Ongava is open to lodge residents only, and guided game drives come with a high chance of sighting lion, giraffe, black-faced impala and both black and white rhino. Guided game drives out of Ongava also explore the road network within the national park, whose Andersson Gate lies about 15 minutes drive away.

Similar upmarket bases for exploring the eastern part of the nationals include the seriously luxurious **Mushara Lodge**, a new place situated 8 km from the Von Lindequist Gate. Nearby, the more mainstream **Mokuti Lodge** is set on a pedestrian-friendly private conservancy that harbours a good selection of antelope and other herbivores (including a misplaced herd of bontebok, a South African endemic), but no dangerous game. Another possible base for exploring the park is the 200 sq. km (77 sq. miles) **Onguma Game Reserve**, which opened in 2005 adjacent to the easterly Fischer's Pan, and offers an attractive combination of rustically comfortable accommodation and varied wildlife, including black rhino, lion, and more than 300 bird species. ❑

Map on page 204

BELOW: the hornbill is a common sight.

A RARE COLLECTION OF WINGED WONDERS

Namibia's diverse landscapes support a wide range of unusual bird life, from the biggest bird in the world to the tiny indigenous Damara tern

Namibia's a land of strong contrasts, ranging from the hyper-arid sand-sea desert of the southern Namib through arid savannah and deciduous woodlands, to tropical forests and wetlands associated with the Kavango and Zambezi Rivers in the north-east. In addition, currents along the Namib coast produce a rich marine environment, both in the open ocean, along sandy and rocky shores, and in protected lagoons. This diversity of habitats is reflected in the country's birdlife: to date, 620 of the 887 bird species listed for southern Africa have been recorded in Namibia. Of these, about 500 species breed locally, including some truly remarkable species.

BREEDS APART

One of the most striking sights of the coastal regions are the great flocks of greater and lesser flamingoes, whose honking can be heard all night when the tides are right for night-time foraging. Equally memorable, although very much smaller, is the sandgrouse, which occurs in large numbers in the Namib Desert. This bird has evolved a fascinating adaptation to its arid environment: the breast-feathers of the adult are specially modified to absorb and hold water. When it visits a water-hole to drink, it immerses its breast so that when it returns to the nest, the young chicks can release the stored moisture by nibbling the adult's feathers. The riverine forests of the inland wetland regions, meanwhile, support rare raptors such as the western banded snake eagle and the Pels fishing owl. But it is the ante-Namib – the transition zone between desert and the arid savannah – which supports Namibia's largest number of endemic species, including the stately Rüppell's korhaan *(pictured above)* and the elusive Herero chat.

△ **LITTLE DIPPER**
Red-knobbed coots *(Fulica cristata)* are a common sight on Namibia's dams and large sheets of open water.

▷ **HIGH LIFE**
The sizeable lappet-faced vulture *(Torgos tracheliotus)* a bushveld bird; it builds its nest right at the top of trees.

◁ **SMALL WONDER**
The tiny Damara tern *(Sterna balaenarum)* is endemic to th Namib coast and is an endangered species.

△ **NOW YOU SEE ME...**
The little Namaqua sandgrouse occurs in flocks of huge numbers throughout Namibia's desert landscapes.

▽ **POLLY FILLER**
The Cape parrot *(Poicephalus robustus)* measures about 36 cm (14 ins) and is a native of the riverine forests of Namibia's inland wetlands.

THE BIGGEST BIRD ON EARTH

The Namib Desert doesn't support a wide variety of birdlife, but what there is is memorable. The most striking desert-dweller is, of course, the ostrich, the world's biggest bird, which can often be spotted running elegantly across the gravel plains. Measuring up to 2.5 metres (8 ft) in height and weighing up to 135 kg (300 lb), the ostrich cannot fly, although it still has flight feathers; instead, it has evolved long, powerful legs as its main form of defence. One kick from an ostrich's two-toed, sharp-nailed foot is enough to kill a man. They can also run at up to 70 kph (45 mph) and can maintain speeds of 50 kph (30 mph) for up to 30 minutes. In the wild they occur in flocks of up to 40 birds and often travel in the company of herds of antelope such as springbok, oryx or wildebeest. Their long necks allow them to spot enemies from a great distance, and ostriches often serve as an early warning system for these other animals. True to myth, they may flatten their heads to the ground if approached. The females of the flock lay their eggs in a communal nest-scrape on the ground until a clutch of 15 to 20 eggs has accumulated. An ostrich egg is 15 cm (6 ins) long and weighs as much as 36 hen's eggs.

THE CAPRIVI

Thanks to a generous annual rainfall, this lush northeastern region supports a wide range of wildlife in some excellent, and little-known, national parks

Windhoek

Look at a map of Namibia and you are immediately struck by the strange panhandle of territory, the Caprivi Strip, sticking out to the northeast. Indeed, in order to keep themselves tidy, some maps detach the panhandle and print it elsewhere on the page so that its geographical eccentricity is not readily apparent. Like the straight lines that separate many African countries, the Caprivi Strip was the result of negotiations more than a century ago between colonial powers intent on getting the best deals for their various empires.

At the time, Germany had recently annexed Namibia (then South West Africa), and was seeking a trade route to the Zambezi in order – some say – to make an eventual link to Tanzania (then Tanganyika, and also in German hands). Britain was suspicious of her intentions and tried to block them by proclaiming the Protectorate of Bechuanaland (later to become Botswana), which included the Caprivi area. Eventually, both parties met at the Berlin Conference in 1890.

In a transaction more reminiscent of a Monopoly game than real life, Britain ceded control of both the Caprivi Strip and Heligoland (one of the North Frisian islands in the North Sea) in return for Zanzibar. The German Chancellor at the time, Baron von Caprivi, gave his name to the country's new acquisition, and this should have been the end of the story – except that Britain took it back, along with the rest of Namibia, during the First World War and governed it as part of Bechuanaland. Later, the Strip was administered by South Africa as part of South West Africa, and finally it became part of the Namibia that achieved independence in 1992.

Most people access the Caprivi area by driving up the B8 from **Grootfontein** to **Rundu** and then turning eastwards. About half-way up this road you leave behind the mainly white farming area with its large ranches, cross the veterinary fence erected to control cattle movements (and thus diseases) among livestock, and enter the sort of rural Africa more commonly seen in Botswana, Zimbabwe, Zambia or Angola. After driving hundreds of miles during which you will have barely seen a soul, suddenly there are villages of thatched rondavels by the roadside busy with people and animals. To reach the Caprivi proper, simply continue on the B8 from Rundu, which is tarred all the way to the border with Botswana at **Ngoma**.

LEFT: on the lookout for wildlife in the Linyati Swamps.
BELOW: Caprivi road after a thunderstorm.

Lush lands

The Caprivi is unlike anywhere else in Namibia. As distinct from the hot, dry desert areas, it is more tropical with warmer winters and the highest rainfall in the country. Some 450 km (270 miles) long and 100 km (60 miles) wide at its broadest, and less than

32 km (20 miles) at its narrowest, it is divided into three regions: the West Caprivi or Mukwe Area, the Caprivi Strip proper and Eastern Caprivi.

Much of the land in the neighbouring countries – Angola, Botswana, Zambia and Zimbabwe – immediately bordering the Caprivi is under some protection through conservation legislation. This, combined with the fact that there is an immensely rich variety of habitats – river systems, floodplains, riverine woodlands, and mopane and Kalahari woodlands – means that the wildlife in the Caprivi is equally rich. In a country where otherwise the only permanently flowing rivers are on its northern and southern frontiers, the presence of a constant supply of water is luxury indeed.

So flat and devoid of physical features is the region that 30 percent of the Eastern Caprivi can be flooded during the rains. One consequence of this is that you will find game in this region not found elsewhere in Namibia. Obvious water animals are hippo and crocodile but there are also antelope which are equally tied to water and more often thought of as being found in the neighbouring Okavango Delta such as red lechwe, sitatunga and reedbuck. Other game is also here in large numbers: no less than 60 percent of Namibia's elephants and buffalo use the area and there are calculated to be close to 6,000 elephant here; no respecters of international frontiers, they regularly move between the Caprivi and the four neighbouring countries. They are considered to be part of the much larger population of about 125,000 elephants that live in the region.

Winnowing grain. In the Caprivi, traditional rural life continues undisturbed.

A late start

Despite all this, it was only in the late 1990s that the Caprivi started developing as a tourist destination. Wilderness that had been a virtual war zone prior to

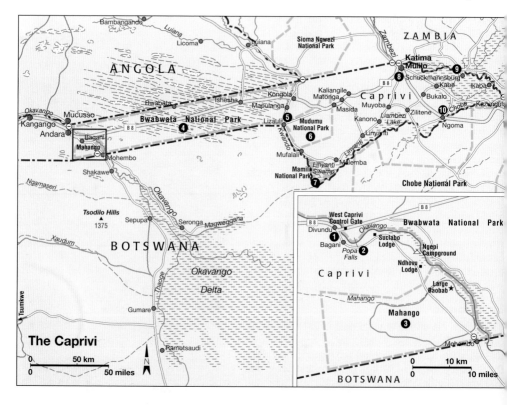

Map
on page
204

ndependence – when the former South African Defence Force was engaged n a war with independence-seeking guerillas based in Angola – and wildlife hat had been persecuted by both the military and the guerrillas now began to rehabilitate rapidly.

For the tourism industry this was a heaven-sent opportunity, and it wasn't ong before the first luxury lodges appeared in the far eastern end of the panhandle, where Zambia, Zimbabwe, Botswana and Namibia share a border. Western Caprivi has been slower to develop mainly because it abuts Angola, where a civil war has been raging for 25 years. Tourist accommodation around here is still rather more rustic and "no-frills" than the upmarket establishments at the other end of the strip.

Popa Falls

A little over 200 km (120 miles) from Rundu, you will reach **Divundu** ❶ where you leave the B8 and take the Botswana road towards **Mohembo** to reach **Popa Falls** ❷. A small reserve (25 hectares/63 acres) surrounds rapids, rather than a proper waterfall, where – thanks to a geological fault manifested here as a broad quartzite ledge – the Okavango River drops some 2.5 metres (8 ft) through a maze of islands.

Small it may be but its influence is immense; this is the start of the basin which is the Okavango, and after Popa Falls the river gradually spreads across the Kalahari to create the famous inland delta. The banks of the river are dominated by knob thorn acacia and other mature species, while the small islands, connected by bridges, are home to a wide variety of birds including: both pied and malachite kingfishers, swamp boubou, black crake and rock pratincole.

BELOW: roadside market, Katima Mulilo.

*Red-knobbed coot,
Mamili Reserve.*

BELOW: traditional
fishing methods
are still much in
evidence here.

Mahango National Park

If you continue along the Botswana road for 40 km (24 miles), you will reach **Mahango National Park ❸**, scheduled for incorporation into the yet-to-be-proclaimed Bwabwata National Park. It is hoped that this will eventually form part of the ambitious Kavango-Zambezi Transfrontier Park, along with a number of other abutting conservation areas in Namibia, Botswana, Angola, Zimbabwe and Zambia. Although small, Mahango is agreed by many to be one of Namibia's top reserves. Its tall riverine forest includes large baobabs, while the floodplains that flank the river are a good place to spot red lechwe and reedbuck. Sable and roan also do well here, and there are large numbers of elephant, buffalo, hippo and crocodile. Nevertheless, the sheer density of the vegetation, which is what the mammals find so attractive, can make game viewing a frustrating business.

The reserve is also particularly rich in birds, with more species recorded here than in any other of Namibia's parks. As you might expect, in the river and wetland areas there are many birds which are attracted to water including: plovers, kingfishers, fish eagles, egrets, cranes and storks. African skimmers, vagrant to South Africa and considered to be threatened in Namibia, nest on sandbanks in the river. These black and white birds fly along with the lower mandible of their bill, which extends beyond the upper mandible, just under the surface ready to snap up any small fish that should come their way. There are also numerous woodland species, too, including several raptors, and both Meyer's and Cape parrots.

Two road loops in the reserve run from the main road which runs through the middle of the park. The more productive eastern road will lead you towards the river and is negotiable by a two wheel drive saloon car, while the western one can only be driven in a 4x4.

Map on page 204

If you return to the B8 you cross the Okavango and pass through the checkpoint, before continuing along the Caprivi Strip. Between here and the Kwando River to the east, the road passes through the soon-to-be gazetted **Bwabwata National Park ❹**. Although declared a reserve area in 1968, it was taken over by the South African Defence Force shortly afterwards and the army remained in control for about 20 years. During this time little was done for conservation and the area was at best neglected and at worst abused – especially by ivory poachers.

The only access into the park is at the eastern, Kwando River end. This is a good area for elephants as well as other mammal species such as giraffe, sable, roan, eland, tsessebe and kudu. Lion, cheetah, hyena and wild dog may also be seen here, along with some exciting birds, including crested guinea fowl.

Mudumu National Park

Heading south towards the Kwando River, a right turn off the B8 onto the D3511 will lead you past signs for the **Lizauli Traditional Village ❺**, a living open-air museum. Here, you can shop for locally-made handicrafts and learn about traditional Caprivian fishing and farming methods, music, basket-making and traditional medicine on an informal tour.

From here it's just a short drive to the northern boundary of one of Namibia's newest national parks, Mudumu. Both this and its equally new neighbour, Mamili National Park, require a 4x4 vehicle to explore them, and both are still in the development stages as far as facilities for visitors are concerned.

Mudumu National Park ❻ is mainly a woodland park with some wetland where it flanks the Kwando River. Since being gazetted, the amount of game in the park has increased and now there are substantial numbers of impala, zebra

BELOW: elephants and hippos sharing a water-hole at Mahango Game Reserve.

The Kavango

For more than 400 km (240 miles) the Okavango River forms the border between Namibia and Angola. Both sides of the wide floodplains here are home to the Kavango people, Namibia's second-largest ethnic group. Many of those living on the Namibian side of the river were originally based in Angola, but fled south in the 1970s to escape that country's civil war. As a result, the Kavango population almost doubled in size.

Between them, the five main Kavango clans speak four different dialects. The Kwangari in the western region and their immediate neighbours, the Mbunza, speak a common language. Shishambyu and RuGciriku are also closely related, but the adjacent ThiMbukushu in the east has far less affinity with the rest of the dialects.

Traditionally, the Kavango have made their living by fishing and by cultivating sorghum, millet and maize on the fertile ground. Today,

however, thousands of young Kavango people are finding work as labourers on farms, in mines and in urban centres. Another important local industry is woodcarving for tourists and the commercial market. The main technique used here is hewing with the aid of an *adze* (an instrument like an axe, with the blade at right angles to the handle); knives are only used for the fine touches. Unfortunately, most of the work is produced with the mass market in mind, but here and there a genuine work of art can be found.

Like most other groups in northern Namibia, the Kavango social organisation is based on the matrilineal system of relationship. This penetrates all spheres of social life, in particular family law, the law of inheritance and succession, the marriage system, the political structure and the traditional religious system.

At present, however, the region is in a state of transformation from the old traditional order to new forms of economic, social and political life. Christian missions have played an important part in this transition phase, a key role having been undertaken by the Catholic Congregation of the Oblates of the Virgin Mary, now deeply rooted in Kavango society. German, and later Finnish, missionaries pioneered work in the fields of education, health, agriculture and commerce here. For many years they were the dominant development agency until government bodies took over much of their work.

Numerous institutions and enterprises all over the region bear witness to the development programme carried out by the government. There are now about 100 schools, including a number of secondary schools. At Rundu a government hospital with three operating theatres, modern sterilisation facilities, a well-equipped X-ray section and a steam laundry were erected a few years ago. The leper and tuberculosis hospital at Mashare can accommodate over 400 patients.

In addition, where until relatively recently vehicles had a difficult drive along deep sandy tracks – parts of which could only be negotiated by a four-wheel-drive – there are now well-constructed roads. ❏

LEFT: Bringing home the shopping near Rundu, in the Kavango region.

nd kudu as well as slowly growing populations of sable, roan and tsessebe. redators tend to be rare here, although wild dog are seen from time to time. The voodland is mixed – some areas are mopane while others close to the river, consist of various figs, acacias and sausage trees. Walking tours are available, too.

Map on page 204

Mamili National Park

If anything, **Mamili National Park** ❼ – in the very south of the eastern Caprivi, at the change of direction where the Kwando River becomes the Linyanti – is even less developed than Mudumu, with no facilities provided at the various camping sites. Access to the park is only by 4x4 vehicles and, again, walking is allowed. Adjoining the Okavango Delta and based around two large wooded islands, Lupala and Nkasa, the area is actually very similar to the Delta in its maze of channels, islands, lagoons and peninsulas. When flooded, about 80 percent of the park is covered by water but in the dry season there are oxbow lakes, great floodplains and large reed beds.

Katimia Mulilo's Caprivi Arts Centre is a good place to find high-quality curios.

This is the largest protected wetland in Namibia, so game is not as abundant here as it is in some of the country's other parks (but then nor are other tourists). This is, however, an excellent area for mammals, with large herds of elephants, sitatunga, lechwe and reed buck. Both lions and hyenas are regularly seen, too, and it's also home to one of the largest concentrations of buffalo in Namibia – over a thousand animals.

Mamili is wonderful for birds, too. Some 70 percent of Namibia's species can be spotted here, including rare wattled cranes which nest in the park, three species of coucal – Senegal, coppery-tailed and black – chirping cisticola and slaty egret. Geese and ducks abound when the park is flooded, while summer migrants include

BELOW: this vegetable garden at a Katima mission-school is watered by the Zambezi.

Map on page 204

squacco herons, yellow-billed kites and several roller species. The loop road through the area will return you to the B8 from where you can reach **Katima Mulilo ❽**, the Caprivi's regional capital. Set on the bank of the Zambezi, Katima was established by the British in 1935 to replace the original German headquarters in the area at **Schuckmannsburg ❾**, further east along the river. It's a thriving place with a distinct frontier feel, bolstered by the fact that you can cross the border into Zambia from here, over a newly opened bridge. Local landmarks include a giant baobab painstakingly hollowed out and fitted with a toilet by a former regional commissioner; it stands behind the Caprivi Regional Council building.

Katima is the hub from where the growing number of tourist lodges in the area are supplied, and to which various safari operators are drawn when they leave the bush. It's a good place to pick up supplies (especially as it has a colourful market), get car repairs carried out and change money, but bear in mind it is also reputed to be the only town in the world where elephants have priority!

South of Katima is **Liambezi Lake** which now rarely holds water. The water level in the Zambezi appears to have passed through a number of phases during the last century; for about the first 24 years, for instance, the average flow at Victoria Falls was 750 cubic metres (2,460 cubic feet) a second. By 1946 this had almost doubled to almost 1,400 cubic metres (4,592 cubic feet), a flow which lasted until 1982 when the volume fell to 750 cubic metres (2,460 cubic feet) once more. The significance of all this is that Liambezi Lake finally filled with water at some time in the 1950s – the only previous record was from Selous, who recorded seeing it full in 1879 – and became a very important feature of the eastern Caprivi, supporting a huge fishing industry. But by 1982 the flows into the lake had stopped, fishing collapsed, and within a few years it had been taken into cultivation and grassland for cattle. If it is to flood again, this is likely to be through the Chobe River which, when the Zambezi is high, will reverse its flow to fill the lake once more.

BELOW: village celebration, west Caprivi.
RIGHT: grinding corn at Lizauli Traditional Village.

To the border

From Katima, the tar road continues for a further 70 km (40 miles) to the border post at **Ngoma ❿**. Once over the border in Botswana, you can take a gravel road through Chobe National Park to Kasane. From here you can travel south into the rest of Botswana, or cross into Zimbabwe and follow the mighty Zambezi to see it plummet over the magnificent Victoria Falls.

In January 2000, tragedy struck the Caprivi Strip when three French tourists and a number of medical aid workers were killed by Angolan guerrillas in separate attacks at Bagani, close to the Angolan border. In the months before the killings, anti-government Unita rebels from Angola had begun crossing into western Caprivi on a regular basis, stealing cattle and goods, burning houses and attacking Namibian citizens – actions widely seen as reprisals for the Namibian government's decision to allow Angolan government troops to attack Unita from Namibian soil.

After these attacks, the Namibian government advised tourists against going to the Caprivi. Today it's once again considered safe to travel in the region. ☐

NORTHWEST NAMIBIA

Map on page 216

Some of the country's most dramatic scenery can be found in this empty land, where ancient cultures, petrified forests and desert elephants enliven one of Africa's last true wildernesses

nland from the desert plain of the Skeleton Coast rises an austere and rugged wilderness, one of the last real wildernesses in Africa. Although it falls within the Kunene and Erongo regions, it's still commonly referred by its old names, **Kaokoland** (for the northern region) and **Damaraland** or the south). Home to a unique flora and fauna as well as some hauntgly beautiful scenery, this wilderness is the least-populated part of Namibia. amaraland's the ancestral home of the Damara people *(see page 220)*, while the far north live the Himba, semi-nomadic pasturalists whose lives cene around their cattleherds.

As the rock paintings in Damaraland's Twyfelfontein valley illustrate, ildlife has survived in this parched land for thousands of years. Today, rare esert elephants and black rhino forage alongside scattered sand-rivers such the Hoanib and the Hoarusib, while nomadic herds of game including ıdu, oryx and Hartmann's mountain zebra roam the north and the east, here the vegetation's more dense. A rich and varied birdlife – from endemic ıecies such as the Herero Chat and Ruppell's korhaan to the ostrich – and host of curious plants such as the commiphora and the *Welwitschia mirabilis* sort of underground tree) also eke out an existence in these seemingly ırren wastes.

Although most of the main sights in southern amaraland are accessible in an ordinary saloon ır, a 4x4 wheel drive is essential in Kaokoland and northern Damaraland too, if you plan to explore vay from the main highway. In Kaokoland you ıould always travel in convoy with a minimum of vo 4x4 vehicles and aim to be totally self-suffient, carrying extra fuel and water, comprehensive ıaps and a GPS navigation aid (although roads may ε marked on the map, in practise some simply ɔn't exist).

Given these conditions, by far the safest and most ıteresting way to experience the area is to travel ith a specialist tour operator and knowledgeable ıide, who can give an insight into Kaokoland's ,scinating plants, wildlife and cultures.

outhern Damaraland

ondescript **Khorixas ❶**, the former administrave capital of Damaraland, is 131 km (81 miles) ıe west of Outjo on the C39 and well placed as a ase for exploring the south and for stocking up on ıpplies. Otherwise, there's not much to see here, though the **Khorixas Community Craft Centre** a Save the Rhino Trust-backed project – at the ıtrance to the town is definitely worth a visit if ɔu're interested in good-quality crafts.

PRECEDING PAGES: rock formations, southern Damaraland. **LEFT:** young Himba mother and baby. **BELOW:** the dramatic Spitzkoppe.

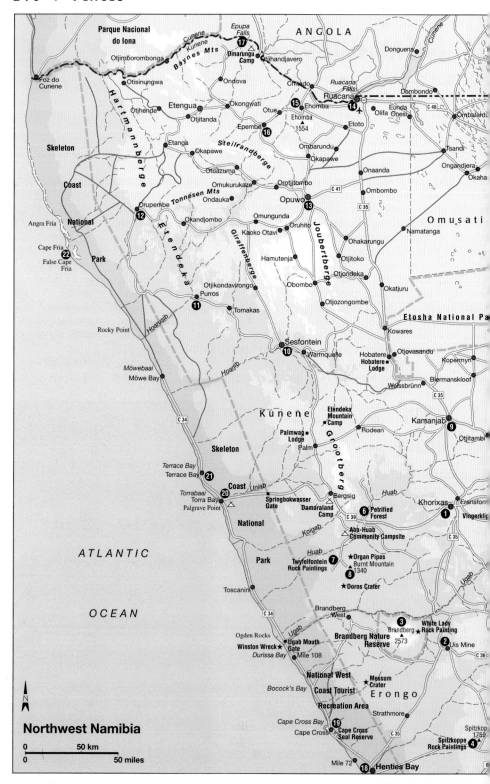

Northwest Namibia

0 _____ 50 km
0 _____ 50 miles

Follow the C35 south towards sleepy **Uis Mine ②**, which initially evolved around a small tin mine (now closed). Just beyond the town – some 105 km (65 miles) from Khorixas – turn west onto the D2359 and follow it for 28 km (17 miles) to the **Brandberg ③**, an oval-shaped massif which towers above the surrounding plains. Around 120 million years ago there was a volcano here, set in a rocky plateau. Gradual erosion of the plateau's own lava-layers has exposed this giant chunk of weather-resistant granite, whose highest point, the **Königstein** (2,573 metres/8,440 ft), is the highest in Namibia.

For thousands of years, the Brandberg's caves and overhangs were used as shelters by the nomadic San (Bushmen). The richest seam of rock art sites is to the northeast near the **Tsisab Ravine**, where you can see a painted frieze featuring the so-called "White Lady of the Brandberg" – a sweaty three-hour return walk, so avoid setting out in the heat of the day. This celebrated 40 cm (16 inch) tall humanoid painting was first described in the 1950s by the French archaeologist Abbe Henri Breuil, who theorised that the white pigment indicated that the figure (which he thought was female) depicted a person of Mediterranean origin. Breuil's rather fanciful ideas were then popularised by apartheid theorists as proof of an ancient European influence in the region. The 'white lady' theory is now thoroughly discredited by rock art experts, who recognise the figure to be a male hunter or shaman – and to be no more European in origin than are the elephants and other animals painted in white pigment elsewhere in Namibia.

There are at least 17 other rock-painting sites within a 1-km (1-mile) radius of the White Lady, most of which depict big game such as lions, giraffes and ostriches. Guides from the local community can be hired if you want to explore the area more thoroughly.

South of Uis is the dramatic **Spitzkoppe ④**, a pyramid-shaped mountain known as the "Matterhorn of Namibia" which offers several more rock-art sites and some good walking trails to boot. To reach it from Uis, take the C36 Omaruru road for 1 km (1 mile) before turning south on the D1930 for 76 km (47 miles), followed by the D3716. Near the site, the Spitzkoppe Community Project (initiated by a group of local Damara) has established a small camp-site, with guides for hire.

Around Khorixas

Just east of Khorixas is another famous local landmark, a slender 35-metre (115-ft) high monolith known as the **Vingerklip ⑤** ("rock finger" in Afrikaans). Take the C39 for 46 km (29 miles), followed by the D2743 for about 21 km (13 miles) to reach this spectacular limestone pinnacle, poking up from the surrounding flat-topped terraces like something from a science fiction movie set. It's a favourite haunt of rock kestrels, too.

The equally odd-looking **Petrified Forest ⑥** – a collection of fossilised logs that have been estimated to be between 240 and 300 million years old – lies about 42 km (26 miles) west of Khorixas along the C39. Remnants of at least 50 trees can be seen, some partially buried in the surrounding sandstone.

Map on page 216

Khorixas' towering **Vingerklip** *is a noted local landmark.*

BELOW: these rocky "Organ Pipes" can be seen near Twyfelfontein.

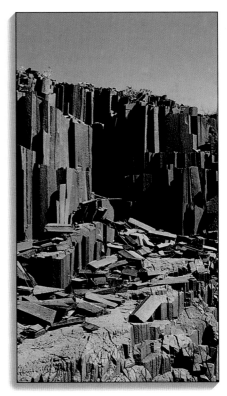

TIP

You need a permit
from the MET (Ministry
of Environment and
Tourism) office in
Windhoek (tel: 061
236 975) if you want
to visit the spectacular
Doros Crater near
Twyfelfontein.

BELOW: a few of the
fossilised logs that
make up the
Petrified Forest.

A guided tour takes about an hour (the site's open daily; small entrance fee).
The biggest attraction around here, though, is the boulder-strewn hillside
known as **Twyfelfontein ❼** (open 8am–5pm; entrance fee), lying just southwest of the Petrified Forest. Home to a superb collection of San rock art –
more than 2,000 rock engravings and paintings depicting animals, animal
spoor and people, some dating back to before 3300 BC – it's considered one of
the richest rock-art sites in Africa. Local guides will lead visitors along the two
trails that run uphill from the parking lot, past the 'Doubtful Spring' after which
Twyfelfontein is named, to a hillside scattered with about a dozen engraved or
painted panels. Named after two of the more striking engravings on display,
the Dancing Kudu and Lion Man Trails each take about one hour to walk, inclusive of stops to admire the artwork and the views, and they could be covered
together in about 90 minutes. Climatically, the most comfortable time to visit is
early morning, shortly after the gates open, but this is also when the site is
busiest – for a more peaceful perusal, try visiting at around 4pm.

To reach Twyfelfontein, follow the C39 from Khorixas for 73 km (45
miles) before turning onto the D3254 for 36 km (22 miles). There's a community-run camp-site at nearby **Aba-Huab**, and several new lodges in the
pipeline, too.

Other attractions worth visiting around here are the **Organ Pipes**, a mass
of perpendicular dolerite slabs thought to be between 130 and 150 million
years old (they're about 10 km or 6 miles east of Twyfelfontein on the
D3254), and nearby **Burnt Mountain ❽**. This range is pretty uninspiring
when the sun is high but turns into a glowing kaleidoscope of colour – red,
orange, grey and purple – when its shales reflect the early morning and late

afternoon light. Southeast of Twyfelfontein, meanwhile, are the equally dramatic **Doros** and **Messum Craters**, both of which can only be reached with a 4x4 drive.

Map on page 216

Northern Damaraland

The further north you travel in Damaraland, the more the route begins to take on an expeditionary feel. The scenery becomes more rugged and austere, sand dunes encroach upon the road, the sun blazes down and one can travel for miles without seeing a single soul. However, several large blocks of land around here have been reserved by the government for tourism (each allocated to different operators) and, although development is controlled, these are reasonably well-supplied with private lodges and camps. Prior booking is required for the community owned (but privately managed) **Damaraland Camp**, Palmway Rhino Camp, and the **Etendeka Mountain Camp**, all of which have a collection point for those arriving by saloon car. **Palmwag Lodge**, meanwhile, is open to casual visitors *(see Travel Tips, page 268)*.

The main draw around here is the wildlife, especially the desert-adapted elephants and black rhinos, although the latter are seldom seen except by visitors to palmway Rhino Camp. Most camps offer game drives and guided walks into the heart of the terracotta-coloured mountains where you could also spot gemsbok, kudu, springbok, mountain zebra and a splendid range of birds including the black eagle. If you're determined to see a desert rhino, tracking trips leave daily from Palmway Rhino Camp

From Palmwag, it's 118 km (73 miles) to little **Kamanjab ⑨**, near the western approach to Etosha. It's a useful place to stock up on fuel and supplies,

One of Damaraland's greatest assets is its wealth of San (Bushmen) paintings.

BELOW: Himba camp, Kaokoland.

The Damara

The Damara form only about 7.5 percent of Namibia's 1.6 million-strong population, but they are one of the oldest ethnic groups in the country. The existence of a negroid group of hunter-gatherers in this region, speaking the dialects of the Central Khoisan, has for a long time aroused special interest both among scientists and the general public. A number of hypotheses about their origin and ancient history have been postulated, but the mystery is still far from being solved.

Traditionally, the Damara community has consisted of a number of subdivisions *(haoti)*. These are clusters of clans and extended families which were formerly concentrated in specific areas. In pre-colonial times, the Damara populated an extensive area from the Khuiseb River (southeast of present-day Walvis Bay) up towards the Swakop River; in the central parts from Rehoboth and Hochanas to the Khomas Highlands, west of

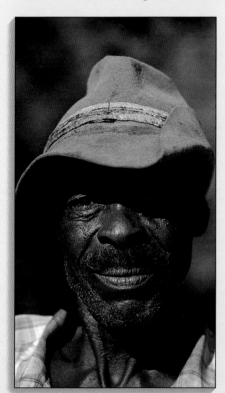

Windhoek; and especially in the area where they are presently concentrated – northeast of the Namib around Outjo, Kamanjab, Khorixas and Brandberg.

About two centuries ago, the Damara began to be ousted from their traditional areas by advancing Nama and Herero, the latter hunting them down and either killing them or carrying them off as slaves. Finally, at the request of the Rhenish Missionary Society, the Herero chief Zeraua ceded the Okombahe area to some Damara in 1870. Later, several other reserves were created by the colonial authorities, such as Otjimbingwe and Sesfontein. During the 1960s, the government bought 223 farms from European settlers and in 1973 proclaimed an area of 11.6 million acres (4.7 million hectares) as so-called Damaraland, with an administrative centre established at Khorixas.

Within the boundaries of this territory live only a quarter of the total Damara population. The same percentage may be found in the district of Windhoek, and the remainder is distributed throughout the north-central area.

Towards the end of the 18th century the Damara first came into contact with European travellers, who usually described them as hunter-gatherers. There is, however, ample archaeological evidence to suggest that not only had some clans been keeping small herds of stock for centuries, they were also small scale gardeners, growing mainly tobacco and pumpkins.

In line with their predilection for small stock farming and cattle breeding, livestock production has become an important source of income for the Damara. Today, however, many work on farms, in the urban centres and on mines. The number of independent commercial enterprises – general dealers, bottle stores, restaurants, petrol stations, itinerant traders – is on the increase. Hundreds of teachers, clerics and officials form a modern intelligentsia, among them some of Namibia's most eloquent politicians. In short, the Damara have succeeded in liberating themselves from their former dependency and have acquired a highly respected position among the people of Namibia. ❏

LEFT: a friendly Damara smile. The Damara are one of Namibia's most ancient ethnic groups.

although there's not much else to stop for and only one place to stay. Fortunately, there are a number of lodges and guest farms in the vicinity, among them Hobatere and Huab Lodges which are both on large private reserves *(see Travel Tips, pages 266 & 268).*

Map on page 216

From Palmwag, it's 91 km (56 miles) on the D3706 to Damaraland's northern boundary and the sprawling Herero settlement of **Sesfontein ⑩**. Scattered with picturesque fan palms *(Hyphaene petersiana)* which give it the appearance of a desert oasis – especially after a long, dusty drive – it was a strategic military outpost for the German colonial government. The main monument from that period, **Fort Sesfontein** (1896) has now been renovated and turned into a hotel.

Kaokoland

Beyond Sesfontein lies **Kaokoland**, a vast, empty and inhospitable area stretching west to the Skeleton Coast, east to Etosha and all the way north to the Kunene river on the Angolan border – a total of about 49,000 sq. kilometres (19,000 sq. miles). Travelling overland here is a slow business (there are only about five driveable roads) and should never be attempted alone or without a plentiful supply of food and water, and a satellite navigation system. If you plan to do this trip, seek advice first.

Himba jewellery featuring beaten wire beads pressed into a leather surround.

It's wiser to sign up for an organised 4x4 tour; you could find yourself heading northwest along the D3707 to the camp-site at **Purros ⑪**, on the tree-lined banks of the Hoarusib River. Set up to provide employment for the local Himbas as well as accommodation for visitors, you can arrange escorted visits to Himba villages from here, and guides for your own game drives.

BELOW: mounted Himba, with briefcase.

Map on page 216

Ancient culture

Unlike Namibia's other indigenous peoples, the **Himba** (a subsect of the Herero nation) still live exactly as they have since they migrated down from Angola and settled in this remote area some 300 years ago. It's a timeless lifestyle that requires no Western trappings or even running water – livestock (cattle and goats) constitutes wealth for this pastoral society, so the territory of each clan has to be large enough to allow them to move their herds enormous distances, following the few straggling pastures which spring up after the rains.

As they roam this huge wilderness, the Himba construct rough "camps" to sleep in, from which they can also gather roots and hunt game. When they leave to find better grazing for their goats and cattle, household items get left behind, which they will use on their return. In a telling example of how their culture is now, having abruptly to adapt to the outside world after centuries of isolation, there have been several unfortunate incidents in the last few years where Himba camps have been denuded by unwitting tourists, who thought them abandoned.

Sensitivity towards the Himba way of life is an essential part of a Kaokoland journey. Always gain permission before you enter any of the semi-permanent Himba settlements, for instance, and ask first before you take photographs (expect to pay, too). Gifts of tobacco and mealie-meal (cornmeal), however, are usually appreciated.

Purros is about half-way to **Orupembe** ⑫, some 208 km (129 miles) from Sesfontein across the wide, flat **Giribes Plains**. You'll see scattered herds of springbok as you travel, along with the odd "fairy circle" – small round patches of earth where no vegetation grows, possibly due to toxic chemicals in the soil left behind by *Euphorbia* bushes that have long since died.

At Orupembe, the road turns east with a slow descent through rocky terrain and the dramatic Tonnesen and Giraffen mountain passes. It's about 108 km (67 miles) to a camp-site at **Onganga** on the upper reaches of the Hoarusib River, before a further 84-km (52-mile) drive through the small settlement of **Kaoko Otavi** and a north turn onto the D3705 to **Opuwo** ⑬, the only real town in Kaokoland. (If you're coming from Kamanjab, it's some 254 km or 158 miles on the C35 and C41.) A dusty, somewhat shambolic place with a real frontier atmosphere, Opuwo's a good place to stock up on food and fuel. There's a large Himba settlement on its perimeter, and it's not unusual to mingle with local clanspeople in their striking traditional dress – hair coiffed with mud into intricate styles, bodies shining with red ochre – as you shop at the supermarket.

If you'd prefer a self-drive 4x4 tour, you could try the circular four-day route heading north from Opuwo to Ruacana and back via Epupa Falls in the west – although it must be stressed once again that it is vital to travel with a minimum of two vehicles, to be completely self-sufficient and to carry fuel and water.

From Opuwo, take the C41 east to the C35 (the main road north to Ruacana), a journey of 142 km (88 miles). Fill up with fuel in **Ruacana** ⑭; you

BELOW: view from Damaraland's Grootberg Pass after good rains.

Map
on page
204

won't have another chance until you get back to Opuwo. Now take the C46 west for a few kilometres before continuing on the D3700 for 55 km (34 miles), a picturesque drive following the Kunene river to **Swartbooisdrift**, where there's accommodation at Kunene River Lodge and good camping spots. West of Swartbooisdrift the road is atrocious, so continue south on the D3702 for 20 km (12 miles) to **Ehomba** , followed by the D3702 for 10 km (6 miles) before joining the D3701 for 31 km (19 miles) to the tiny Himba settlements of **Epembe** and **Otjiveze**. Head northwest on the D3700 for 31 km (19 miles) to **Okongwati**, continuing north for 73 km (45 miles) to **Epupa Falls**. The Baynes Mountains, Kaokoland's highest peaks, rise to the west.

A series of falls thundering into a palm and baobab-fringed gorge surrounded by desert, Epupa's a stunning sight. Unfortunately, the entire Kunene river valley (including the falls) has been proposed by the Namibian and Angolan governments for a giant hydro-electric dam project. If it goes ahead, much of the Himba territory would be drowned and the people displaced. Sacred ancestral grave and fire sites would be destroyed and a unique desert wetland ecosystem wiped out.

From Epupa, retrace your steps along the same route to Otjiveze and then continue south for a further 73 km (45 miles) back to Opuwo.

Another option is to explore the western Kaokoveld, travelling down to Orupembe through the two long, barren but hauntingly beautiful valleys (**Hartmann's** and the **Marienfluss**) that run north to south from the western end of the Kunene River. Trips can be organised through specialist tour operators, or by booking into the superbly isolated Serra Cafema Lodge, a fly-in tented camp on the dune-fringed banks of the Kunene. ❑

BELOW: a stretch of the lovely Epupa Falls, now under threat from a proposed dam development.

THE SKELETON COAST

Map
on page
216

*The most haunting and evocative of all Namibia's attractions,
this treacherous stretch of wild Atlantic shore is backed
by a bone-bleaching desert heaped high with giant dunes*

Windhoek

Situated in the remote northwestern corner of Namibia, the Skeleton Coast
is arguably one of the loneliest stretches of coastline in Africa, and certainly among its most fascinating and untouched wilderness areas. Once
an area for seafarers to fear and shun thanks to its treacherous shoreline flanked
by bone-bleaching desert wastes – where ship-wrecked sailors would almost certainly perish for lack of fresh water – it is now prized as a place of beauty and
tranquillity, as well as solitude.

A journey up the Skeleton Coast will probably start at **Swakopmund** on the
southern tip of the **National West Coast Tourist Recreation Area**, which
extends for 200 km (120 miles) from the Swakop River to the Ugab River in
the north. During the hot summer months, many Namibians escape from the
heat of the interior to the cooler coastal resorts; Swakopmund's one of the
most popular, attracting thousands of holidaymakers over the peak Christmas
season. It's not hard to see why – this pretty little place has retained much of
its colonial character, thanks to the high proportion of houses built in the
Jugendstil (Art Nouveau) style so popular in Germany at the turn of the last
century. The town's called after the Swakop River that flows into the Atlantic
just south of the town – although the Namas who first settled in the area called
the river *Tsoaxoub*, a rather coarse reference to its
muddy appearance when, in flood, it carries vast
amounts of brown desert sand to the sea.

PRECEDING PAGES:
the Skeleton Coast
is a ships'
graveyard.
LEFT: the lagoon at
Sandwich Bay is a
flamingo haven.
BELOW: ghost crabs
like the solitude.

Heading north

The coastline directly north of Swakopmund is managed as a tourist area and has extensive facilities
(spaced at regular intervals) for camping and caravanning. Seen outside the holiday season, these sites
seem not just empty, but bleak and inhospitable –
yet once the locals pour in over the Christmas period,
they take on an entirely different atmosphere. In fact,
Mile Four is considered to be one of the biggest
caravan parks in southern Africa.

Thirty-two kilometres (19 miles) north of Swaopmund on the C34 is **Wlotzkasbaken**, a rather strange
village of small bungalows and chalets used by the
keenest fishermen. Fresh water has to be delivered
and pumped to the individual water towers which
stand on spidery lattice legs beside each dwelling like
enormous ornate candlesticks. Some 35 km (22 miles)
further north on the same road you come to **Henties
Bay ⑱**, the last place to obtain fuel before heading
still further north. It's famed for some of the best fishing opportunities available along Namibia's coast.

One of the most intriguing forms of plantlife to
occur in deserts is the lichen, a complex symbiosis of
fungus and an alga. The gravel plains, rocky outcrops

and mountain slopes along the Skeleton Coast are home to over a hundred species – inspect the ginger lichen fields beside the road and you should be able to spot several different kinds. Normally hard and brittle, lichens come to life or "bloom" when water is sprinkled over them, moving visibly and becoming soft and leathery to the touch. Like other desert vegetation, lichens are dependent on fog for their survival, although they can manage without moisture for long periods of time. Visitors should take note, however, that vehicles must stay on the established roads, as their wheels destroy the lichens and leave unsightly, virtually permanent, tracks behind.

Fur seals and fishing boats

Most of the Namib's plants have extremely deep root systems, to soak up what little water's available.

Cape Cross ⑲ is some 53 km (32 miles) north of Henties Bay. This is the home of Namibia's largest breeding colony of Cape fur seals, an estimated 120,000–200,000 animals – which helps to explain the powerful smell (if you close your eyes they sound like an enormous flock of bleating ewes and lambs). Unlike some seal species, Cape fur seals suckle their young for almost a whole year, only weaning last year's pup in order to make room for this year's. Around mid-October the bulls, great maned beasts weighing almost 360 kg (800 lbs), arrive to stake out their territories and defend them against intruders. By early December the young pups are born and the seals mate almost immediately afterwards although the fertilised egg remains dormant for about three months before starting to develop. The area's now a reserve (open 10am–5pm daily; entrance fee).

BELOW: the Cape fur seal colony at Cape Cross.

Cape Cross is also of historical interest. In 1486 the first European to set foot on the Namibian coast, the Portuguese navigator Diego Cão, erected a stone cross at the site that was later to become known as Cape Cross. Two replicas of

the cross can be seen today. The first, erected by German soldiers in 1893 – after the original was taken to Germany – stands on a hillside overlooking the bay. The other is a faithful replica of the original and was unveiled in 1980 on the very spot where Diego Cão planted his cross.

Just before you reach the entrance to the national park you will see a sign pointing west to the first of the famous Skeleton Coast wrecks – that of the **Winston**, a fishing boat which broke up here after running aground in 1970.

Map on page 216

The Skeleton Coast National Park

The **Skeleton Coast National Park**, a narrow tract of coastline about 30–40 km (20–25 miles) wide and 500 km (300 miles) long between the Ugab River and the Kunene River on the frontier with Angola, was proclaimed a nature reserve in 1971. Nowadays the infrastructure is kept to a minimum and the number of visitors is limited, for the special qualities of the area can only be retained by minimising human impact as far as possible.

In the southern third, tourism is restricted to two angling resorts, **Torra Bay** ⓴, a caravan and camping site, and **Terrace Bay** ㉑, a small rest camp with cooking facilities or meals if you prefer. Both resorts have boundaries within which visitors must remain. Both are reached via the main coastal road from Swakopmund, passing through the **Ugab Mouth gate**, or from the interior via the **Springbokwasser gate** in Damaraland. Travellers must be in possession of a permit issued in Windhoek and may not leave the main roads except in the demarcated fishing areas.

If you have not booked accommodation in either of the resorts, you can obtain a permit at one of the gates but you will only receive permission to use the C34

BELOW: black-backed jackals fighting over dead fur seal pup.

Famous Shipwrecks

Countless ships have come to grief along Namibia's coastline, but few of the wrecks have remained intact. Thanks to relentless pounding by the steel-grey Atlantic Ocean breakers and sand-blasting by the prevailing southwest wind, little more remains than twisted chunks of rusting metal, broken masts, scattered planks and a vast array of flotsam and jetsam strewn all the way up the coast.

Some of the wrecks date back to the days when Portuguese explorers and the ships of the Dutch East India Company sailed around the Cape en route to India. Their vessels not only fell victim to gales, but to the Benguela Current, too, with its sea-fogs, heavy swell and deadly cross-currents. They also had to contend with a remarkably treacherous coastline, dotted with reefs, unexpected shoals and sand dunes that stretch into the sea.

It was an aircraft mishap that gave the Skeleton Coast its descriptive and appropriate name. When a Swiss pilot, Carl Nauer, disappeared along the Namibian coast in 1933, the journalist, Sam Davis, covering the accident for Reuters and the *Cape Argus*, suggested that Nauer's bones might one day be found on the "Skeleton Coast", the graveyard of ships and men.

The shipwreck which best personifies the loneliness of Namibia's coastline, however, is that of the *Eduard Bohlen*, a steamer that ran aground in September 1909 at Conception Bay, 100 km (60 miles) south of Walvis Bay. Its rusting remains can still be seen partly buried in the sand, several hundred metres inland from the present shoreline.

The best-known wreck is that of the *Dunedin Star*, a British cargo ship which ran aground late on the night of 29 November 1942, about 40 km (25 miles) south of the Kunene Mouth. The story of the rescue of the 21 passengers and crew of 85, covered at the time by maritime reporter John Marsh and subsequently published in his book entitled *Skeleton Coast*, reads as an excruciating series of disasters. One rescue boat, the *Sir Charles Elliott*, ran on the rocks, two crew members losing their lives in their attempts to swim to safety. A Ventura bomber involved in the rescue took a nosedive into the sea, the three airmen escaping from the fuselage when it drifted ashore. In the end, the castaways only reached Windhoek on Christmas Eve. All that can be seen today is the rusting remains of a fuel tank, part of the fated ship's cargo.

One reasonably well-preserved wreck is that of the *Montrose*, which met its fate in June 1973. It's still lying on the beach at Terrace Bay, partially buried in the sand. North of Möwe Bay, meanwhile, lie the burnt-out remains of the fishing boat *Karimona*, wrecked in September 1971. Lastly, the rusting hull of the *Benguela Eagle*, which ran aground in June 1973, is embedded in the sand 25 km (16 miles) north of the Ugab River mouth near the shattered remains of the *Girdleness*, wrecked in November 1975 on the rocks south of the Ugab. ❑

LEFT: all washed up on the Skeleton Coast – wrecks are a common sight around here.

and D3245 roads between that and the other, and you must enter the gate before 3pm to allow time to drive through before sunset.

Map on page 216

Into the desert

The Skeleton Coast is part of the northern Namib Desert which extends from the Kunene River in the north to Cape Cross in the south. A narrow band of dunes stretches along the coast, seldom reaching further than 20 km (12 miles) inland, except in the far north. Saltpans occur sporadically all the way up the coast, the largest of which are the **Cape Cross saltpan** and the **Cape Frio brine-pan complex** in the far north. East of the sand desert are flat, wide gravel plains with scattered inselbergs and further east again is the escarpment, defined in the north by the Otjihipa Mountains.

The coast is pleasantly cool throughout the year, except on those days during the winter months when bergwinds blow and temperatures, higher than those in summer, are often recorded. Inland temperatures rise sharply during the day.

The landscape of the national park is probably little different from what it was 10,000, 10 million or even 100 million years ago. The richly-coloured volcanic rock is interspersed with mica-schist, gneiss and granite. Towards the coast, outcrops of granitic and gneissic rocks have ghost-like, honeycomb patterns, caused by the salts contained in the coastal fog that penetrate inland during the night.

While part of the interest of the park lies in its sweeping landscapes, unchanging for many kilometres, part, too, is in the detail and for this reason you must leave your vehicle and go on foot. Long hiking trips are not practicable because of the lack of water but guided walks over a number of days are conducted by

Droughts in the interior cause lions to move down the river courses to the coast.

BELOW: the curiously shaped Bogenfels Rock is a local landmark.

Map on page 216

The white clay "temples" of the Hoarusib Canyon, just inland from the coast.

BELOW: breeding cormorants.

Nature Conservation officials along the course of the Ugab River, which marks the southern border of the park. All of the river valleys running through the park repay even an hour's stroll and it is clear from the tracks that many animals use these valleys both for living in and as highways.

While road access will only allow you to visit the south of the park, it is now possible to reach the interior of what is a true wilderness area by flying in to the recently-established camp in the only concession area in the north of the Skeleton Coast. Small groups stay here and travel out from the camp with expert guides to see such things as the roaring dunes, Rocky Point, Agate Mountain and the remarkable white clay "temples" of the **Hoarusib Canyon**, impressive formations of yellowish-white sedimentary clay thought to be the result of the damming up of the river beyond the dunes, between 20,000 and 50,000 years ago. There is also a colony of 40,000 seals at **Cape Fria ㉒** to visit in a more natural setting than those at Cape Cross.

Dunes on the move

Wherever you are on the Skeleton Coast, dunes are a living and integral part of the landscape. A typical dune formation is the crescent-shaped **barchan**, which is formed by the prevailing southwest wind and moves in a northeasterly direction with speeds averaging between 2–3 metres (6–10 ft) a year. These are best seen where they march across the 3245 road as it leaves the coast.

It is not difficult to find the tracks of black-backed jackal and brown hyena which roam the beaches along the coast, keeping them clean of dead seals, birds and fish. The most commonly seen larger mammals are springbok and gemsbok, both of which are ideally suited to an arid environment. In years when good rains occur and there is sufficient ground cover, their numbers increase and even zebra will move in from the interior, followed by beasts of prey such as spotted hyena, lion and leopard. Droughts in the interior have, in the past, caused lions to move down the river courses to the coast where they have been observed to feed on the carcasses of Cape fur seals. This is also the only place in the world where elephant, black rhino, giraffe and lions occur in a desert environment. The "desert elephants", for example, are known to travel between feeding-grounds and water-holes as much as 70 km (45 miles) apart.

Contrasting sharply with the apparent barrenness of the desert is the immense richness of the adjacent ocean. The Benguela Current flows northwards from the Antarctic laden with oxygen and a rich variety of zoo and phytoplankton, driven to the shore by west winds. The upwelling of the current causes it to rise to the surface. Exposed to the sun, a plankton "bloom" is produced which feeds large schools of pilchards and anchovies, on which seals, cormorants, gannets and many other marine creatures feed. In rough seas the plankton washes onto the beach in large quantities of bubbling, yellow froth, drying as a dull green coating on the pebbles and sand. Plenty and paucity, beauty and death, old rocks and new dunes – part of the intrigue of the Skeleton Coast is that it is full of such remarkable paradoxes. ❑

THE LIVING DUNES OF THE NAMIB DESERT

This vast, sandy region may look remote and desolate, but in fact it's teeming with life, from plants, insects and reptiles to large mammals

The Namib is one of the most ancient deserts in the world. Although there is some debate about exactly how old it is, it's generally accepted that this narrow coastal tract between the Atlantic and southwestern Africa's Great Western Escarpment has been at least semi-arid, and in places totally arid, for around 50 to 80 million years. The great sea of sprawling sand dunes that cascade down to the very edge of the Atlantic, however, only date back some five million years. This was when the Atlantic's icy Benguela current – which prevents rainfall from the west and thus plays a major role in maintaining the Namib's arid conditions – became fully established, giving rise to the present southern dune field which stretches between Lüderitz and Swakopmund.

SOMETHING IN THE AIR

Although (as with most deserts) the Namib receives minimal amounts of rain, the coastal region has an alternative source of moisture: fog. The freezing cold waters of the Benguela current, along with the south Atlantic's anticyclone pressure system, act together on the scorching heat of the desert to produce the swirling fogs which are so typical of the Namib coastline. Natural obstacles such as rocky outcrops cause the fog to condense and droplets to form, thus creating the possibility for plant and animal life to exist in this seemingly inhospitable terrain.

▷ **THE EYES HAVE IT**
Leaving its burrow at night, the web-footed Palmato gecko (*Palmatogecko rangei*) hunts termites, moths and other small insects.

▷ **GRASSED UP**
This dune grass species sends out roots up to 20 metres (66 ft) long to take advantage of the fog water in the top surface millimetre of sand. It flowers every summer.

△ **HARDY SURVIVOR**
This curious-looking plant is a species of Trichocaulon. Coastal fog water, which has been trapped in cracks and crevices in rocks, provides it with nourishment.

△ **KINGS OF THE DESERT**
Namibia's rare coastal desert lions live by scavenging carcasses thrown up by the sea and by hunting fur seals.

△ **IN THE TRANSITION ZONE**
The Herero chat is endemic to the escarpment area of the Namib, between the desert and the arid savannah.

AN AGE-OLD NAMIB RECIPE

Rock paintings like the one pictured above (from the Brandberg on the edge of the Namib) are evidence that man has roamed Namibia's deserts for at least several hundred thousand years. These desert-dwellers managed to survive not just by hunting small mammals but thanks to various hardy plants that became staple foods. Take the *!nara* plant, for example, a relative of the cucumber and endemic to the Namib. Each year, the female plants (some of which live for centuries) produce dozens of melons which are avidly consumed by any creature that can break through the tough, prickly skin. Following a method devised by their forefathers, the Topnaar Nama people who live along the banks of the Kuiseb River in the central Namib scoop out the fleshy centres of the *!naras* before cooking them, straining off the seeds and frying them on clean sand. The flesh is also spread out to dry after which it can be rolled up and eaten – a readily portable snack. The plant itself, meanwhile, provides shelter and food for a host of other organisms such as mice, lizards and insects.

△ SURVIVAL OF THE FITTEST
The *Hoodia gordonii* is well-adapted to desert conditions: its waxy leaves reduce transpiration, while a slow growth rate helps it cope with infrequent moisture.

◁ CHANGING LANDSCAPES
The striking clay "castles" of the Hoarusib Canyon are one of the highlights of a tour of the Skeleton Coast Park Concession Area.

THE NAMIB

Thanks to the severity of its climate, the Namib has been able to preserve itself in a near-pristine state for 80 million years, although it is also surprisingly accessible to visitors

Maps:
Area 242
Town 240

Beguiled by photographs of its wonderful apricot dunes at sunrise, the Namib Desert epitomises Namibia for many visitors; this is what they come to see. And despite its apparent remoteness, it is surprisingly accessible – either by light aircraft from Windhoek, or by road via Okahandja through southern Damaraland, past Karibib and Usakos to the coast.

Namibians calculate the vast distances between destinations in their country in hours rather than miles, and those in the know will tell you it is a three-and-a-half-hour drive from Windhoek to the most popular jumping-off point for a Namib exploration – the resort of **Swakopmund ❶**, a small slice of Bavaria perched on the desert's northern edge.

Swakopmund

Founded in 1893 by the *Schutztruppe* captain Curt von François, who aimed to establish a harbour that could compete with the British-controlled Walvis Bay, Swakopmund has retained much of its German character and continental atmosphere. There's a good sprinkling of *Jugendstil* (German Art Nouveau) buildings which merit a closer look, although if you want some more in-depth historical background then a visit to the **Swakopmund Museum ❹** is a good starting point. Founded in 1951 by an itinerant German dentist, Dr Alfons Weber, it provides a comprehensive perspective of the town and its surroundings and possesses considerable historical and ethnological collections (on the beachfront by the Strand Hotel; open daily, 10am–1pm and 2–5pm; entrance fee).

Close by in Strand Street is the **Kaiserliches Bezirkgericht ❸**, a stately mansion originally built as a magistrate's court but now serving as the holiday residence of Namibia's President. It is backed by municipal gardens which are home to a 21-metre (69-ft) high stone lighthouse as well as an imposing **Marine Memorial ❻**, dedicated to the German soldiers sent in to suppress the Herero uprising in 1904.

Heading away from the beach, **Daniel Tjongarero Street** is due east across Tobias Hanyeko Street and lined with historical buildings. Then there's the **old railway station ❹** in nearby Theo-Ben Gurabib Street, an excellent example of Wilhelmenian-style architecture; it's now part of the Swakopmund Hotel and Casino complex.

Situated right on the corner of Theo-Ben Gurabib and Tobias Hanyeko Streets, the **Kristall (Crystal) Gallery** (open Mon–Sat 9am–5pm; entrance fee) houses a superb collection of semi-precious stones and other geological wonders from all around Namibia. The gallery's centrepiece is a remarkable 500-million-year-old quartzite crystal that stands

LEFT: at Sossusvlei, the ground is baked into crazy-paving patterns.
BELOW: 4x4s can damage the Namib's dunes.

twice as tall as a person – indeed, weighing in at more than 14,000kg (30,000 lb), it is credibly claimed to be the largest such formation in the world.

In terms of shopping, eating out, and entertainment, Swakopmund is – after Windhoek – the best equipped town in Namibia, with an excellent selection of supermarkets and other shops, restaurants, delicatessens, banks, internet cafés and tour operators concentrated on and around the main drag through the town centre, Sam Nujoma Avenue. At the heart of this urban bustle, abutting the venerable Hansa Hotel on the corner of Sam Nujoma Avenue and Roon Street, an upmarket mall (simply called The Arcade) houses several good art and craft shops, the top-notch Swakopmund Buchhandlung (Bookshop), several coffee shops, and even a modern cinema complex showing recent western releases.

The **National Marine Aquarium** Ⓔ on the southern outskirts of town is well worth a visit, especially on those afternoons when a diver descends into the main tank to feed the sharks (open Tues–Sun 10am–4pm; closed Mondays; shark-feeding at 3pm every Tues, Sat and Sun; entrance fee). A very different but equally engaging animal collection is housed by the **Living Desert Snake Park** (open Mon–Fri 8.30am–5pm, Sat 8.30am–1pm, closed Sun, feeding time 10am Sat only; entrance fee) on San Nujoma Drive immediately east of the city centre. Privately owned and managed, this herpetological zoo includes specimens of several species associated with the sandy and rocky terrain of the surrounding Namib, including the spectacular horned adder, the sidewinderlike southern dune adder, and the beady-eyed Namaqua chameleon.

Aside from being an attractive resort town, Swakopmund is now entrenched as Namibia's main centre for adventure tourism. Indeed, a good half-dozen reputable local operators scattered now offer visitors a wide range of day trips and

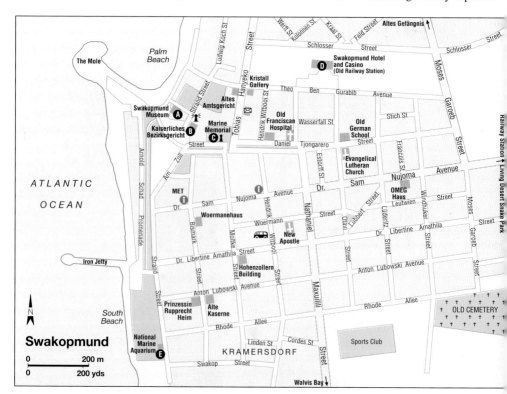

activities – skydiving, quad-biking, sand-boarding, dolphin cruises and deep sea fishing, as well as township tours, nature drives into the brooding Namib dunes, or kayak excursions through choppy seas to the seal and penguin colonies around Walvis Bay – in short, enough variety to keep the most active traveller busy for days!

Driving south from Swakopmund, the road crosses the Swakop River by way of the longest bridge in Namibia (688 m/2,250 ft) to **Walvis Bay ❷**, which lies a mere 30 km (19 miles) from Swakopmund and, with a population estimated at around 45–50,000, is probably the second-largest town in Namibia. The Portuguese explorer Bartholomeu Diaz, who later pioneered a sea-route around Africa's southern tip, anchored here on 8 December 1487. However, thanks to the absence of fresh water supplies in the area, nearly three centuries were to pass before the European powers started to take an interest in this splendid natural harbour.

Passing into British hands in 1878, from the early 1920s Walvis Bay was officially deemed to belong to South Africa, despite – confusingly – being administered as an integral part of Namibia. In 1977 it was formally transferred to South Africa's Cape Provincial Administration before finally becoming wholly Namibian more than 15 years later in 1994, some time after the rest of the country had become independent.

Declared a Ramsar Site in 1995, Walvis Bay's **lagoon** offers some excellent opportunities for birdwatching – indeed, it's considered to be one of the most important wetlands in southern Africa, supporting, among others, almost half of the region's flamingo population. The sight of thousands of these graceful birds feeding in the shallow waters – or better still, flying overhead like thin sticks

Map on page 242

Ballooning over the desert at sunrise is a popular excursion.

BELOW: Schülstrasse's German-style houses, Swakopmund.

with black and pink wings – is quite breathtaking. A motorboat or canoe trip on the lagoon will not only provide good birdwatching, but may also reveal seals and dolphins too.

The lagoon can also be explored by road, heading southwest from the town centre along an extension of Nangolo Mbumba Drive. Almost immediately upon exiting the town, this road is flanked by a shallow lagoon on one side and tall dunes on the other, with a rich marine birdlife dominated by large flocks of great white pelican, the localised Damara tern, and a profusion of waders. Continue southward for another 10 km (6 miles), turning right at the salt-processing plant, and you'll reach a car park (popular with local fisherman), from where a very sandy track (suitable to experienced 4x4 drivers only) leads to Pelican Point, the site of a lighthouse and a colony of around 100 Cape fur seals.

More birdlife can be seen at Sandwich Harbour, which is situated almost on the **Tropic of Capricorn** about 40 km (25 miles) south of Walvis. This wetland plays host to a considerable number of migratory birds en route from their nesting

The Welwitschia mirabilis, *one of the Namib's most extraordinary plants.*

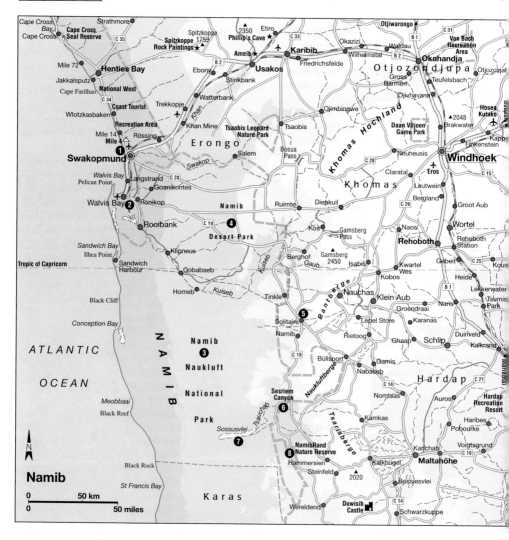

Map on page 242

rounds in the northern hemisphere to the warmer climes of the Cape's west coast. In a good year, up to 50,000 wintering birds can be found here, while the occasional brown hyena, jackal or even oryx may also be seen along the shoreline.

This lagoon can only be reached by four-wheel-drive vehicle and a special permit is required, obtainable from Namibia Wildlife Resorts offices in Swakopmund and Windhoek as well as their rest camps. No vehicles are allowed beyond the northern fence of the lagoon, and visitors wishing to explore the area must do so on foot. Great care must be taken that vehicles do not get stuck.

Birders may be lucky enough to spot the rare Gray's Lark in the Kuiseb Canyon area; it's endemic to the Namib's gravel plains.

The Namib-Naukluft National Park

Not only is the **Namib-Naukluft National Park ❸** the third-largest game park in Africa (it covers almost 5 million hectares), but it protects a surprising amount of wildlife and a whole sweep of landscapes, from the apricot ripples of the dune Namib to the rocky mountains of the Naukluft range.

The park's oldest and most northerly section, known as the **Namib Desert Park ❹**, stretches between the Swakop and Kuiseb Rivers. It's often simply called the "gravel desert", and it's easy to see why; the flat, rock-strewn landscape slopes gently away into the horizon with only the occasional isolated *inselberg* (from the German for island-mountain) breaking the monotony.

A popular half-day trip into this section from either Swakopmund or Walvis Bay is **Welwitschia Drive** (permit required) along the Swakop River, where you can see some fine examples of the remarkable *Welwitschia mirabilis* plant. First described in 1852 by a German botanist, Dr Friedrich Welwitsch, the oldest plant on the route is estimated to be close on 1,000 years old. Another botanical curiosity are the large fields of lichen, a remarkable form of plant life con-

BELOW:
sand dune-riding near Sossusvlei.

sisting of both algae and fungi, which derive their moisture from sea fog
You'll also drive past a curious collection of rock mounds in the bed of th
Swakop River which are known as the **Mountains of the Moon**, along with
series of stark black dolerite dykes running like the plated spines of dinosau
along the ridges of the mountains.

The Kuiseb Canyon

Another of the park's main attractions lies about 140 km (84 miles) to the ea
and south of Walvis Bay – the **Kuiseb River** and its **canyon**, a remarkab
geological phenomenon. It's actually a canyon within a canyon, formed som
20 million years ago – the original river course gradually silted up with i
own sediment, eventually forcing the water to cut a new route.

Following the Kuiseb's course upstream brings you to a viewpoint at **Car**
Cliff offering a spectacular panorama of the escarpment and the river valley. Yc
may spot baboon around here, along with klipspringer antelope, mountain zeb
and oryx. Predators include the black-backed jackal and the elusive leopar

A second canyon, the **Gaub**, lies nearby on a tributary of the Kuiseb, and
like the latter a well-wooded and generally dry river bed, although here th
underground river nourishes large trees such as the camel thorn, the false ebor
tree, the shepherd's tree and the ana. Consequently, this is also a good place
find birds and insects, and to stop for picnics.

The Solitaire area

Immediately south of the Kuiseb stretches much of the most atmospheric se
tion of the park, the **Dune Namib**. In spite of its desolate appearance, th

The little web-footed gecko is one inhabitant of the Namib's dunes; it feeds on crickets and beetles.

BELOW: unusual souvenir shop, Namib-Naukluft National Park.

"IT COULD BE A DIAMOND... "

August Stauch was quite content with life. He had a fi
position with the German railway company Lenz & C
and his pretty wife, Ida, tended lovingly to him and th
two children. If only it wasn't for the asthma… when
firm won a contract from the German Colonial Railw
Building and Operating Company to build a line far away
German South West Africa, he was an obvious choice fo
posting. The colony's dry, sunny climate would certair
be good for his asthma, and it was only a two-ye
contract. Accordingly, Stauch sadly took leave of his fam
and set out, landing at Windhoek in May 1907.

Stauch's main task as railway inspector was to ke
part of the new track being built between Lüderitz and A
free of sand from the shifting dunes. One day, in April 19
an unusual stone stuck to the oiled shovel of a work
Zacharias Lewala, who ran to his foreman: "Must g
Mister little *klippe* (stone). Is *miskien diamant* (is may
diamond!) The foreman stuck the stone in his pocket a
later told Stauch the tale, laughing. But Stauch didn't lau
instead, he tried to cut the crystal in his pocket-watch w
the stone – and succeeded. Lewala's find turned out to
part of one of the world's richest alluvial diamond fiel
which today is still a mainstay of Namibia's economy.

emains one of the most accessible of all the world's sandy deserts. The roads
1 the area can generally be used by two-wheel-drive saloon cars, although the
oing may be slow. Daytime temperatures are extremely high throughout the
ear and ample supplies of water should be carried as a precaution, particu-
irly if you intend clambering to the top of a huge dune.

Over millions of years, the Orange River has carried vast quantities of sand
rom its origins high up in the Lesotho Highlands down to the Atlantic Ocean.
he Benguela Current has then transported the sand northwards from the river's
iouth and deposited it on the shore to create these coastal dunes, and from
ere it's been vigorously driven northeast by the wind. Currently, this "march-
1g" of the dunes continues at a rate of 20 metres (60 ft) a year.

There are a variety of dune shapes in the Namib, but all have gentle slopes on
1eir windward (exposed) sides and steep leeward (sheltered) sides. Some of the
unes can be more than 300 metres (1,000 ft) high, making them the highest
nywhere in the world. To reach them, drive south from the Kuiseb and Gaub
'anyons across the Tropic of Capricorn for about 66 km (40 miles) to the tiny
ettlement of **Solitaire ❺** on the C14. From here, a further 70-km (44-mile)
rive southwards along route 36 will bring you to the **Sesriem Canyon ❻**,
·here the Tsauchab River has cut a spectacular gorge some 40 metres (120 ft)
eep into layers of schist and gravel deposited millions of years ago. It's a
elightful spot which acquired its evocative name because early settlers required
x lengths of leather thongs (*rieme* in Afrikaans) to haul water from the canyon
elow in order to water their teams of oxen.

A fairly steep but manageable path leads into the canyon where the con-
omerate layers are clearly visible; you can also see from the material caught

Map on page 242

BELOW: view over
the Namib-Naukluft
National Park
towards the
Heinrich Mountains.

high up on the walls of the gorge that it fills right up after heavy rain. There is a camp-site here and several lodges nearby, some of which offer the possibility of ballooning over the desert at dawn.

The heart of the Namib

An hour and a half's drive (60 km/37 miles) deeper west into the desert brings you to **Sossusvlei** ❼, a huge clay-pan surrounded by massive dunes – the very highest dunes of the desert in fact. Saloon cars can travel to within 4 km (2½ miles) of the *vlei* ("pan" in Afrikaans), while 4x4 drive vehicles can continue up to the parking area by the pan itself. You can choose to walk to Sossusvlei or one of the other pans nearby such as Hidden Vlei or Dead Vlei.

This, truly, is the heart of the Namib. The yellow and grey-buff hues of the pan contrast sharply with the brick-red dunes, providing spectacular opportunities for photography, especially at dawn and dusk when the low sun creates a symphony of colour, light and shadow. These are enhanced even further if the pan is flooded, which generally only happens once or twice every decade, most recently in early 2006. Occasionally, the graceful shape of an oryx, standing on the crest of a dune, can be seen etched against the skyline – not as a favour to photographers, but as one of the strategies used by this desert antelope to catch the slightest breeze and reduce its body temperature.

The Naukluft Mountains

Jutting out from the desert area on the western edge of the main escarpment is a small range known as the Naukluft Mountains. This and a corridor of land to the west linking the mountains to the desert below used to be known as the Naukluft Park, but in 1979 were incorporated into the bigger Namib Desert Park to create the Namib Naukluft National Park we know today.

Originally intended as a sanctuary for the indigenous Hartmann's mountain zebra, the area has permanent water and supports a wide range of elusive mammals and birds. The area can only be explored on foot and two circular day trails – the Olive and the Waterkloof – start at the camp-site, each requiring about six hours of fairly strenuous walking and climbing. A third, the Naukluft Trail, is a tough seven-day affair but well worth the effort if you want to explore what is one of Namibia's most exciting landscapes.

The Naukluft area is best reached from the C1 between Solitaire and Maltahöhe with a turn-off on the D854. Accommodation-wise, there are a limited number of camp-sites which must be booked in advance in Windhoek.

Bordering the park to the west is the **NamibRand Nature Reserve** ❽, one of the largest private reserves in southern Africa. Offering a good range of desert landscapes and game, it's home to several upmarket lodges and small camps where guests can take advantage of expert guides – a nice way to round off a self-drive tour of the park and a fascinating corner of Namibia.

SOUTHERN NAMIBIA

The wide plains of Namibia's "Deep South" may seem arid and inhospitable, but they're home to some intriguing sights – from towns swallowed by desert dunes to the mighty Fish River Canyon

Map on page 250

S tretched between the Namib Desert in the west and the dry Kalahari in the east, southern Namibia's flat, wide-open expanses are characterised by stony outcrops peppered with quiver trees and low, table-top mountains. Often neglected as a tourist destination because it lacks northern Namibia's wealth of big game, the region nevertheless contains a range of unusual sights, including one of the world's least-visited geological wonders.

Windhoek

The quickest way to reach the south is to take the B1 from Windhoek. At first the road passes through bush interspersed with large trees and you may even see baboons crossing the road between the capital and **Rehoboth ❶**, 87 km (52 miles) to the south. Although it's bypassed by the main highway, Rehoboth has an interesting history as the stronghold of the Baster community who farm the area. A mixed-race group – the progeny of Cape Dutch settlers and the indigenous Khoikhoi – the Basters found themselves rejected by both communities. Eventually, many of them banded together and migrated northwest away from South Africa, settling around the little mission station of Rehoboth in 1870. Throughout the last century, they made many attempts to obtain home rule for their community and did, in fact, finally obtain a measure of independence when Namibia was under South African control – although, ironically, this was granted in order to strengthen the divisions within the country in the name of apartheid.

PRECEDING PAGES: the Fish River Canyon, Namibia's answer to the Grand Canyon. **LEFT:** quiver trees are a kind of aloe. **BELOW:** Duwisib Castle near Maltahöhe.

Hardap Game Park

After you cross the Oanob River to the south of Rehoboth, the taller trees disappear. Shortly afterwards, you also leave the Auas Mountains behind – the last obvious topographical feature until you reach **Mariental ❷**, 174 km (105 miles) further south. Just before Mariental, the road drops off the central highland plateau; a right turn along Route 93 here will take you to **Hardap Dam ❸**, the largest reservoir in Namibia with a surface area of some 25 sq. km (10 sq. miles). The lake here is a haven for freshwater anglers, while the aquarium adjacent to the tourist office houses a number of different fish species from Namibia's major rivers.

For game-viewers, an early morning or late afternoon drive in the **game park** on the southern and western side of the dam is rewarding. Along with black rhino (re-introduced at the end of the last century and Namibia's southernmost population), the game includes red hartebeest, kudu, eland, oryx, springbok and Hartmann's mountain zebra. The dam is one of Namibia's only two white pelican breeding sites, but it also attracts plenty of other birds, from red-knobbed coot and squacco heron to osprey, fish eagles and cormorants.

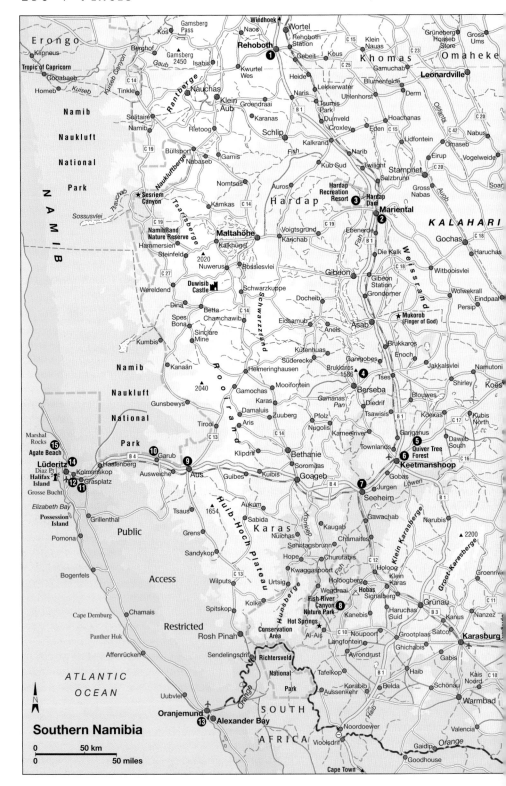

Southern Namibia

0   50 km

0   50 miles

Mariental itself is a typically dry and dusty Southern African everytown, equipped with a few small hotels, filling stations, supermarkets and restaurants– even a Wimpy. Superficially, it is an improbable setting for a flood, but that is exactly what happened here in March 2006, when the sluice gates to nearby Hardap Dam were opened too late after heavy rains, and the town was submerged waist-high in water, causing millions of dollars of damage.

To the northeast of Mariental, a clutch of newish game ranches set on the western fringe of the Kalahari makes for a convenient first stop out of Windhoek en route to the far south. The most established of these is the Intu Africa Kalahari Game Reserve, which offers accommodation in three small camps as well as guided game drives into an 180 sq. km (70 sq. miles) enclosure where grazers such as giraffe, various dry-country antelope and Burchell's zebra cohabit with small predators such as suricate, bat-eared fox and black-backed jackal. Similar but smarter, the new Bagatelle Lodge has accommodation set on the crest of a dune and a similar range of wildlife to Intu Africa, supplemented by recently re-introduced cheetah.

As you continue south along the B1 towards Keetmanshoop, you'll see the imposing sandstone mass of the Weissrand escarpment dominating the scenery to the east. Formed by the incision of the Fish River between 5 and 15 million years ago, the escarpment has been cut back at an estimated rate of 4 km (2.5 miles) every million years, and has actually retreated some 40 km (25 miles) from the river during this time.

Still further south beyond blink-and-you'll-miss-it **Asab**, is the extinct volcano of **Brukkaros** ❹ to the right of the road, towering to an altitude of 1,586 metres (5,203 ft) above the surrounding plains and with a crater of 600 metres (2,000 ft)

Map on page 250

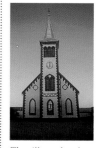

The village church at Rehoboth.

BELOW:
Keetmanshoop, with the Rhenish Mission church in the background.

across. With its distinctive conical shape, Brukkaros is a reminder of the last major volcanic upheavals which shook Namibia some 80 million years ago. If you're interested in exploring the crater on foot, turn off the B1 onto Main Road 98, signposted for the former mission station of **Berseba**. Just before you reach the village, there's a turn-off to the right (the D3904) which leads to the mountain. From the end of the road it's a 30-minute walk to the crater's floor and then about an hour's fairly steep climb up to the old observation station perched on the edge of the rim, offering superb views down to the plains below. Make sure you have sufficient water, a snack, stout walking shoes and a hat before setting off.

An unusual forest

Back on the B1, turn left a few miles north of Keetmanshoop onto the C16 to Aroab, and then left again less than a mile further on to the C17 (signposted for Koës) to reach the **Quiver Tree Forest ❺** some 12 km (8 miles) to the east. The quiver – which grows up to 7 metres (23 ft) high – is one of four Namibian aloes to be classified as a tree; around 250 such trees grow amongst the rocky outcrops here and the grove has been declared a national monument. Close by is **Giants' Playground**, a series of huge rock totems strewn across the landscape like piles of oversized tin cans. Known locally as the *Vratteveld*, these outcrops are erosional remnants of molten lava dating back some 180 million years.

The transport hub of **Keetmanshoop ❻** is a good starting-point from which to explore Namibia's southernmost reaches. Situated some 480 km (298 miles) south of Windhoek, the town dates back to 1866 when a small settlement was established here by missionary Johan Schroeder and named in honour of the then president of the Rhenish Missionary Society, Johann Keetman. The town's old-

BELOW:
wild horses in the desert near Garub.

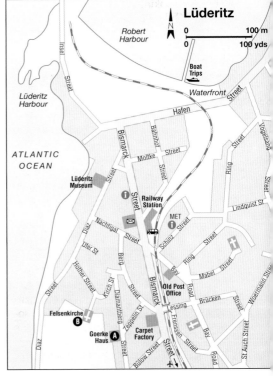

Map on page 250

est building is the imposing Rhenish Mission Church, erected in 1895 to replace an earlier structure which was destroyed by floods. Today it is used as the **Keetmanshoop Museum** and hung with memorabilia; its gardens are dotted with wagons along with a replica of a Nama hut (open Mon–Fri 7.30am–12.30pm, 1.30–4.30pm; closed weekends; free).

The town is also an important centre for Namibia's Karakul sheep-breeding industry *(see page 172)*.

The Fish River Canyon

The world's second-biggest canyon (after Arizona's Grand Canyon) lies an easy day trip from Keetmanshoop. To reach this magnificent site – one of Africa's great natural wonders – head southwest on the B4 towards Lüderitz, turn left at **Seeheim ❼** onto the gravel C12 and head south. If you're travelling during the rainy season, ask at the town's main hotel about the state of the road, as it sometimes floods.

A right turn onto the D601 south of **Holoog**, a left onto the D324 and a right onto the C10 will take you to the **Fish River Canyon Park ❽**, some 161 km (100 miles) long and up to 549 metres (1,800 ft) deep, whose entrance is at Hobas camp-site. The site boasts modern toilet facilities, a shop and swimming pool.

From Hobas you can drive to several observation-points along the eastern rim which offer awe-inspiring views over the rocks and riverbed far below. Access to the bottom of the canyon – a conservation area – is not allowed unless you have obtained the necessary permit (day visitors can get hold of one at either the Hobas or the Ai-Ais entrance gate). If you're interested in hiking the entire canyon, bear in mind it's quite a challenge; every day between May and September intrepid walkers who have made the necessary advance booking set off from the northern-most viewpoint to hike the 85 km (53 miles) to Ai-Ais, a four or five-day trek.

Into the forbidden territory

From Hobas a gravel road winds through the mountains for about 70 km (43 miles) to the **Ai-Ais Hot Springs**. For the final 10 km (6 miles,) the road twists down through a wonderful ravine between piles of loose and shattered buff and dark brown rocks; the sudden greenness around the Ai-Ais spring at the bottom comes as a real surprise. Although rather strenuous, an ascent of the hills overlooking Ai-Ais is rewarded with spectacular views of the rest camp down below, and the inhospitable canyonlands stretching away to the west.

West of the Fish River, the Hunsberg Mountains form part of the Fish River Canyon conservation area but, because of its rugged terrain, the area is not open to the public – a pity, because as well as offering beautiful scenery, it is the habitat of several rare botanical species. It is the intention in future to manage the area as a trans-frontier park – one of the so-called "Peace Parks" – in conjunction with the South African National Parks Board's planned developments for the Richtersveld National Park just south of the Orange River.

Signpost reminding motorists that the Sperrgebiet is a restricted area.

BELOW: enjoying the views at Fish River Canyon

When you're exploring the Lüderitz peninsula, stick to hard-surface roads and avoid loose sand and the area's seemingly negotiable salt pans.

BELOW: petroglyphs in the Sperrgebiet area. Access to the archaeological treasures of this vast tract of land is strictly controlled.

Back on the main road (the B4) between Seeheim and Lüderitz, you will cross the Fish River just as the northernmost signs of the canyon begin to show. Continuing further west, Diamond Area I (also known as the **Sperrgebiet**, or "forbidden territory"), is entered a few miles beyond **Aus** ❾. As the name suggests, this area is strictly controlled and it is illegal to leave the road until you get to Lüderitz. Stretching between the Orange River in the south and 26 northern latitude, Diamond Area I extends about 100 km (60 miles) inland from the Atlantic. Jointly owned by the Namibian Government and De Beers, NAMDEB, as it is known, has the exclusive mining rights to this diamond-rich area.

Ghost towns and wild horses

Except for an area of about 1,600 sq. km (600 sq. miles) near Lüderitz, the section of Diamond Area I north of the main road now forms part of the **Namib-Naukluft National Park**, the largest conservation area in Africa and the fourth largest park in the world *(see page 241)*.

As you approach **Garub** ❿, keep an eye out for **the wild horses of the Namib** which are usually seen in this vicinity; a pumping-station is maintained to provide water for them. During the German Colonial period a contingent of troops was stationed at Garub and it's thought that the horses are the offspring of animals abandoned when the Germans retreated ahead of the advancing South African forces in 1915. Their numbers fluctuate from year to year, but during favourable conditions more than 100 horses roam the inhospitable desert.

A once-stately house at **Grasplatz** ⓫ serves as a reminder of the hectic period following the discovery of diamonds here in 1908 *(see page 242)*. A few miles further west, forlorn **Kolmanskop** ⓬ rises like a ghost town out of a sea of

sand. Once the centre of the flourishing diamond mining industry, today it's a mere shadow of a more glorious era. Abandoned in 1956, nature has since reclaimed most of the town and sand has swept through broken windows and open doors, although towards the end of the 20th century some buildings such as the casino, the skittle alley and the retail shop were restored. The town can be visited only on guided tours, after a permit has been obtained from Lüderitz Safaris and Tours in Lüderitz (tel: 063 202719).

Today, the equivalent diamond-rush town is **Oranjemund** ⓭ (Orange Mouth) about 8 km (5 miles) from the mouth of the Orange River near the South African border. This became the focus of Namibia's diamond industry following the discovery of diamonds here in 1928. The 100-km (60-mile) stretch of coastline north of the town was once considered the world's richest alluvial diamond field, but it's now nearing the end of its lifespan and production is expected to wind down within the next 15 years. For obvious reasons, strict security measures are in force and this mining town, which appears from maps to be accessible only by air, is not open to tourists.

Lüderitz and around

From Kolmanskop, it's just 9 km (5½ miles) to the sleepy old fishing port of **Lüderitz** ⓮, huddled amongst granite outcrops and tall dunes of Namib sand. Don't miss a visit to the town's most striking German colonial building, the pale blue **Goerke Haus** Ⓐ in Zeppelin Street, perched above the town on the slopes of Diamantberg. Although not typical of the local art nouveau architectural style, it's rich in the detail of this period (opening times are limited to Mon–Fri 2–4pm; Sat and Sun 4–5pm; closed public holidays; entrance fee).

The nearby **Felsenkirche** Ⓑ (Evangelical Lutheran Church), consecrated in 1912, is especially worth visiting during the late afternoon, when the stained-glass windows are beautifully illuminated by the setting sun. The altar window was donated by Kaiser Wilhelm II himself.

The Lüderitz Peninsula is characterised by numerous bays, lagoons and unspoilt stretches of beach which are accessible by car or, if one has the time and energy, on foot. At **Diaz Point**, 22 km (14 miles) outside Lüderitz, a replica of the cross erected by Bartolomeu Diaz on 25 July 1488 serves as a reminder of the 15th-century Portuguese explorations. Fur seals can be seen on the rocks offshore here, while a varied marine birdlife includes the rare black oystercatcher, migrant waders such as turnstone and whimbrel, and various gulls and terns. As an alternative (weather permitting), it's worth taking a boat trip via Dias Point to **Halifax Island** where you can get close-up views of the jackass penguin colony.

The **beach** ⓯ at **Agate Bay**, 8 km (5 miles) north of town, is popular with bathers, but the chances of finding any agates are slim. Another popular beach for swimming and picnicking is **Grosse Bucht** at the peninsula's southern point, while at the nearby **Sturmvogelbucht** the remains of an old Norwegian whaling station can be seen rusting away. ❑

Maps:
Area 250
Town 252

One of Namibia's best-known desert plants, the hoodia, in full flower.

BELOW: quiver tree, Fish River Canyon.

Travel Tips

TRAVEL TIPS

T RANSPORT

GETTING THERE
AND GETTING AROUND

GETTING THERE

By Air

There are only two direct services between Namibia and Europe: Air Namibia and LTU. In addition, regional services to neighbouring countries provide convenient connections with international flights to and from other Southern African capitals.

The country's national airline, Air Namibia, operates 2–3 direct return flights a week between Windhoek and Frankfurt . The journey takes 10 hours.

From Johannesburg, South African Airways (SAA) operates a few return flights per week to several European capitals, with easy onward connections to Windhoek, while LTU and Lufthansa both fly return to Frankfurt.

From the UK, SAA and British Airways fly to South Africa, from where you can pick up a regional flight to Windhoek. It is also possible to fly directly from the US with SAA to South Africa, and then connect to Windhoek.

The cheapest flights between Johannesburg and Windhoek are operated by an excellent online booking agency: see www.kulula.com or tel: +27 11 921 0111.
NB reconfirmation of return flights is essential.

For £5–15 you can make your flight carbon-neutral at either www.climatecare.org or www.carbonneutral.com.

Airports

All international flights land at **Hosea Kutako International Airport**, which lies about 45 km (28 miles) east of Windhoek, and is also the arrival and departure point for most scheduled regional and domestic flights to/from the capital. **Eros Airport** (5 km/3 miles) from the city centre serves domestic and some regional charter routes.

Airline Offices

Air Namibia
Independence Avenue
Gustav Voigts Centre
Windhoek
Tel: 061 298 2552
Fax: 061 221382
Email: reservations@airnamibia.co.uk or info@airnamibia.de;
www.airnamibia.com.na
British Airways/Comair
Independence Avenue
Sanlam Building, Windhoek
Tel: 061 248528
Fax: 061 248529
www.ba.com
LTU
MacAdam Street, Windhoek
Tel: 061 375900
Fax: 061 375902
www.ltu.de
Lufthansa
Independence Avenue
Sanlam Building, Windhoek
Tel: 061 226662
Fax: 061 227923
www.lufthansa.com
South African Airways (SAA)
Carl List Building
corner of Independence Avenue and Fidel Castro Street
Windhoek
Tel: 061 273340
Fax: 061 235200
www.flysaa.com
TAAG (Angolan airline)
Independence Avenue
Sanlam Building, Windhoek
Tel: 061 226625
Fax: 061 227724
Email: airline@taag.co.uk
www.angola.org.uk/taag.htm

By Sea

Passenger liners call very infrequently at Walvis Bay en route between Southampton and Cape Town, Durban and Mauritius.

It is virtually impossible to obtain a passage on any other vessels and there is very little chance of arranging a "working" passage.

By Rail

The only cross-border rail service between Namibia and its neighbours is with South Africa. Scheduled Transnet passenger trains run from Johannesburg and Cape Town to Upington, where travellers transfer to the twice-weekly TransNamib passenger train service to Windhoek's main train station.

Passenger trains do not have dining saloons. Some trains have a catering/refreshment car for part of the journey only, so check when booking your ticket as you may need to take your own food and drink. Sleeping berths are provided for first- and second-class passengers. First- and second-class coupés accommodate two and three passengers, while first- and second-class compartments sleep four and six passengers respectively. You can provide your own bedding (sleeping bag) or buy bedding tickets when you make the reservation or on the train.

For more details contact **TransNamib**, tel: 061 298 2077, fax: 061 298 2654, www.transnamib.com.na.

By Bus/Coach

The main approaches from South Africa are tarred: Johannesburg to Windhoek via Upington and

Ariamsvlei (1,971 km/1,225 miles), and Cape Town to Windhoek via Springbok and Noordoewer (1,493 km/928 miles). It is also possible to take the asphalt Trans-Kalahari Highway from Johannesburg via Botswana to Buitepos on the border, just east of Gobabis, which is much quicker than travelling via Upington.

There is a service between Namibia, Zimbabwe and South Africa on luxury coaches with air-conditioning and reclining seats. Intercape-Mainliner operates a Windhoek–Johannesburg service (19 hours) which departs three times a week via Gobabis and Botswana, and four times a week via Keetmanshoop and Upington. Coaches run between Windhoek and Cape Town (16 hours) twice weekly, and there is a once-weekly return to Victoria Falls in Zimbabwe. Tickets must be pre-paid and reservations can be made at the **Intercape**-Mainliner Depot, 2 Galilei Street, Windhoek, tel: 061 227847 or fax: 061 228285. You can also book online through the South African head office (tel: 0860 287287 or 021 3804400) or make an online booking at www.intercape.co.za.

Ekonoliner operates between Walvis Bay and Cape Town, but passengers can board in Windhoek, from where the journey takes just under 18 hours. Central reservations: Ekono Bus Service, tel: 061 205935; fax: 061 206505.

GETTING AROUND

Out and About

Namibia's road network is well developed by African standards. All the main towns have direct links on tar roads, and the gravel roads are also in reasonably good condition (you will, however, need a 4x4 vehicle when driving in remote areas such as Kaokoland, Bushmanland and parts of the Kavango region as there are no developed gravel roads at all here).

Take great care in the rainy season, when gravel roads can be slippery. This is also when those riverbeds that are normally dry (the *omuramba*) come down in flood; they can be dangerous to cross. Also bear in mind that on gravel roads your average driving speed should not exceed 80 kph (50 mph), and estimate driving times accordingly.

All roads in Namibia are numbered and clearly signed en route. Detailed topographical maps

(1: 250 000 and 1: 50 000) are very useful when travelling off the beaten track – in Kaokoland, for example. 1: 1000 000 scale maps of regions and districts are also available, as are geological maps of Namibia. Both can be bought at the Office of the Surveyor General in Windhoek, at the corner of Robert Mugabe and Lazarett Street.

By Air

Air Namibia, the country's national airline, operates regular flights from Windhoek to Swakopmund, Lüderitz, Oranjemund, Keetmanshoop, Tsumeb, Okaukuejo (Etosha National Park), Ondangwa, Rundu and Katima Mulilo. All of these flights return to Windhoek on the same day.

All destinations in Namibia can be reached by charter flights. Here is a list of some fly-in safari operators:

Atlantic Aviation
PO Box: 465 Swakopmund
Tel: 064 404749
Fax: 064 405832
Email: info@flyinnamibia.com
www.flyinnamibia.com
www.natron.net/tour/aviation

Namib Wilderness Safaris
PO Box 6850, Windhoek
Tel: 061 225178
Fax: 061 239455
Email: info@nts.com.na

Skeleton Coast Fly-in Safaris
PO Box 2195, Windhoek
Tel: 061 224248
Fax: 061 225713
Email: info@skeletoncoastsafaris.com
www.skeletoncoastsafaris.com

By Train

Although the domestic rail service operated by TransNamib is primarily goods-oriented, passenger services are available on all routes. Passenger trains run on Tuesday, Friday and Sunday in both directions between Windhoek Station (on the corner of Bahnhof Street and Mandume Ndomufayo Avenue) and Walvis Bay. The journey takes approximately 11 hours.

Passenger trains are scheduled in both directions between Windhoek and Tsumeb on Friday and Sunday (19 hours). Services also operate between Otjiwarongo and Grootfontein; Otjiwarongo and Outjo; and Windhoek and Gobabis. No catering facilities are provided, but first and second-class passengers can purchase bedding tickets either when making their reservation or on board the train.

TransNamib
Tel: 061 298 2030
Fax: 061 298 2277
www.transnamib.com
Regular fixed-departure rail safaris between Cape Town and Windhoek, typically taking 7–14 days in total, are offered by the companies listed below. An advantage of this sort of trip is that much of your travel is done by night, leaving the days free to explore places of interest, but it is obviously less flexible than a self-drive holiday.

Desert Express
Private Bag 13204, Windhoek
Tel: 061 298 2600
Fax: 061 298 2601
Email: dx@transnamib.com.na
www.desertexpress.com.na

BELOW: camping in style

Shongololo Express
PO Box 330, Tableview 7439
South Africa
Tel: (27) 21 556 0271
or 11 781 4616.
Fax: (27) 21 557 1034
Email: info@shongololo.com or
desheike@netactive.co.za
www.shongololo.com

Rovos Rail
PO Box 2837, Pretoria, South Africa
Tel: (27) 12 323 6052
Fax: (27) 12 323 0843
Email: reservations@rovos.co.za
www.rovos.co.za

By Bus/Coach

Intercape-Mainliner (tel: 061 227847;
fax: 061 228285) operates a luxury
bus service between Windhoek and
Walvis Bay four times a week. Stops
along the five-hour journey include
Okahandja, Karibib, Usakos and
Swakopmund. Intercape-Mainliner
also operates a shuttle service from
Windhoek to the airport. The schedule
is available at most hotels.

The Intercape-Mainliner service
between Windhoek and
Johannesburg operates four times
weekly via Keetmanshoop and
Upington, and three times per week
via Gobabis and Botswana.

Ekonoliner (tel: 061 229780; fax:
061 228264) operates a weekly luxury
bus service between Walvis Bay and
Cape Town (Friday departures; returns
Monday). Stops in Namibia include
Swakopmund, Arandis, Usakos,
Karibib, Okahandja, Windhoek,
Rehoboth, Mariental, Keetmanshoop

Restrictions on Travel

Entry into Diamond Areas 1 and 2
is strictly prohibited and visitors
travelling between Aus and
Lüderitz are not permitted to leave
the road.

Day permits to travel through
the Skeleton Coast Park can be
obtained from the reservation
office in Windhoek and the tourist
offices at Swakopmund and
Okaukuejo only and are not issued
at the gates. Day visitors are not
permitted to call at Torra Bay and
Terrace Bay and must reach the
park gates before 3pm.

Although the Caprivi Game
Reserve is a declared
conservation area, travellers may
not leave the main road. Control
points are manned by officials of
the Directorate of Veterinary
Services at Bagani in the west and
at Kongola in the east.

and Grünau. It is best to carefully
check the timetable of both services
since some of the stops are made in
the small hours of the morning.

Taxis

Taxis cruising the streets of Windhoek
and other larger towns are a familiar
sight, but operate mainly between the
town centre and suburbs.
Radio Taxis, tel: 223098
Taxi Prime Radio, tel: 272307 or 081
127 7575
Taxi Express, tel: 239739
Taxi Services Hovy, tel: 237273
(operating from the taxi rank behind
the bus terminal).

Some of these taxis also do airport
transfers. Beware of taxis operating
illegally, because they have no
passenger liability insurance.

City Tours

The following companies offer city
tours: **Swakopmund Historical
Tours** (tel: 461647); **Pack
Safaris** in Windhoek (tel: 061
231603; www.packsafari.com).

Driving

Although drivers' licences from
certain foreign countries are in theory
accepted in Namibia, visitors are
advised to obtain International
Driving Permits before their
departure. Only visitors from South
Africa are unlikely to encounter
problems if they do not.

Driving is on the left-hand side of
the road and the wearing of seat belts
by the driver and front-seat passenger
is compulsory. The maximum
permissible alcohol level for drivers is
0.16 percent. On major roads the
maximum speed limit is 120 kph (75
mph) and in urban areas 60 kph (37
mph), unless a lower speed is
indicated. The recommended speed
limit on gravel roads is between 80
and 100 kph (50–62 mph), depending
on the condition of the road.

Tourist attractions are generally
well signposted and most are
accessible by sedan car. A word of
warning though: although roads in
Kaokoland have been classified as
district roads, most are impassable
to cars and not signposted. The
"salt" roads in Swakopmund and
northwards along the coast are also
particularly treacherous when wet
and special caution is advisable.

Travelling at night in the rural
areas can be hazardous – keep a
sharp eye out for kudu and warthog,
which frequently graze in the road
between dusk and dawn. Guinea fowl,

too, are are in the habit of leaping out
in front of vehicles. Stray livestock is
a menace in the northern parts of the
country, while gravel roads passing
through farmland are often unfenced,
so keep your eyes peeled for roving
stock. Watch out also for the wild
horses of the Namib west of Aus,
especially at night when they seek the
warmth of the tarred road.

Petrol and diesel are available
along all major tourist routes, as
well as in some state-owned rest
camps. In Damaraland fuel is only
available at Khorixas, Uis,
Sesfontein and Palmwag, and in
Kaokoland only at Opuwa. Between
Rundu and Katima Mulilo the
availability of fuel is reliable. There
are no filling stations along the
three passes linking Windhoek and
Swakopmund/Walvis Bay.

Insurance

Whenever hiring a vehicle, insurance
and collision damage waiver (CDW) is
necessary. In most cases the CDW
covers only 80 percent and the rest
must be paid by the driver in the case
of an accident. Most accidents
happen because people drive too fast
on gravel roads.

Car Hire (Windhoek)

Advanced 4x4 Car Hire
Tel: 061 246832
www.advancedcarhire.com
African Car Hire
Tel: 061 223246
www.africarhire.de
Avis Car Hire
Aviation Road,
Tel: 061 233 166
www.avis.co.za
Britz Car Hire
Tel: 061 250654
www.britz.co.za
Budget Car Hire
Windhoek Airport
Tel: 061 228 720
www.budget.co.uk
Odyssey Car Hire
Tel: 061 223269
www.odysseycarhire.com
Pegasus Car & Camper Hire
Tel: 061 251451
www.pegasuscar-namibia.com

Camping Car Rental (Windhoek)

Asco Car Hire
Tel/fax: 061 377200
www.ascocarhire.com
Car, 4x4,and camping rental.
Camping Car Hire
36 Joule Street
Southern Industrial Area
Tel:061 237 756
www.africa-adventure.org/c/campingcar
Vehicle and camping equipment
rental specialist.

A CCOMMODATION

HOTELS, YOUTH HOSTELS, BED & BREAKFAST

Where to Stay

Visitors to Namibia are increasingly well catered for when it comes to accommodation. Indeed, there is no better indicator of how greatly the country's tourist industry has expanded over the past decade-and-a-half since independence than the immense increase in the number, variety and overall quality of lodgings. There are smart business-style hotels in the cities and swish yet organic bush lodges in the game reserves, down-to-earth small-town guesthouses and rural guest farms, and even well-equipped state-run campsites and self-catering resorts in the national parks. Standards are generally high, and rates are very reasonable by international standards, this despite a significant post-independence swing away from the budget-oriented South African self-drive market to a truly cosmopolitan clientele.

It is advisable to book hotel and lodge accommodation in advance, ideally through a reputable tour operator, particularly if you are travelling during the peak international tourist seasons, which runs from July to February but experiences something of a lull in October and November. If you prefer a more spontaneous approach, you're unlikely to ever experience a problem finding a room in Windhoek, and should also be able to improvise in larger towns, especially out of season, but do bear in mind that the distances between rural lodges are often daunting – you wouldn't want to pitch up in the Sesriem-Sossusvlei region, for instance, and end up having to drive from door-to-door looking for a vacant room, so do at least make a phone booking a day or two ahead.

For campsites and self-catering accommodation, advance reservations are essential during Namibian and South African summer holidays (early December to mid-January), and on most weekends and public holidays, especially around Easter. At other times of year, campsites and self-catering resorts are seldom fully booked. During the peak summer season, accommodation is restricted to three nights at each of the camps in the Etosha National Park and to 10 nights at each of the following rest camps: Ai-Ais, Gross Barmen and Daan Viljoen. Visitors should note that no refund will be made if a reservation is cancelled or altered less than 10 days prior to the first date indicated on the reservation advice.

Note that all accommodation and campsites in the national parks and other state-owned reserves and resorts (several of which are listed in the pages that follow) are managed by **Namibia Wildlife Resorts**. The main booking office in Windhoek can be contacted during the opening hours of 8am–5pm Mon–Fri (tel: 061 285 7200; fax: 061 224900; email: reservation@nwr.com.na) or you can book online at www.nwr.com.na.

Travellers who want a true taste of the Namibian rural way of life can contact the **Namibian Community Based Tourism Association** (NACOBTA – tel/fax: 061 255977; email: nacobta@iafrica.com.na; www.nacobta.com.na), a non-profit organisation that manages a selection of community-run tourism projects and campsites supporting the development of rural communities.

ACCOMMODATION LISTINGS

WINDHOEK AND ENVIRONS

City Centre

The accommodation listed below all lies within the city centre or easy walking distance of it.

Hotel Heinitzburg
22 Heinitzburg Street
PO Box 458
Tel: 061 249597
Fax: 061 249598
Email: heinitz@mweb.co.na
www.heitzenburg.com
Part of the prestigious Relais and Chateaux Group, this stalwart hotel fringing the city centre is dripping with character, housed as it is in a century-old castle, complete with turrets and watchtower. It's on a hill, too, so lots of scope for photographing the sunset. Excellent food and wine with friendly service. **$$$$**

Kalahari Sands Hotel and Casino
Gustav Voigts Centre,
Independence Avenue
PO Box 2254
Tel: 061 280 0000
Fax: 061 222260
www.suninternational.com/resorts/Kalahari
Email: ksands@sunint.co.za
Four-star 173-room high-rise hotel in the city centre above an excellent shopping mall. With a pool, gym and spa facilities. Restaurant with à la carte menu. **$$$$**

Hotel Fürstenhof
Frans Indongo Street
PO Box 316
Tel: 061 237380
Fax: 061 228751
Email: fursten@united-hospitality.com
www.united-hospitality.com.
A few minutes walk from Independence Ave. Good value traditional hotel with a pool; serves French and German cuisine accompanied by good wine list. **$$-$$$**

The Hilltop House
12 Lessing Street, Windhoek
Tel: 061 249116
Fax: 061 247818
Email: hilltop@iafrica.com.na
www.thehilltophouse.com
Upmarket, friendly owner-managed B&B, with attentive service, rooms that rate among the most comfortable in Namibia, and great views over suburban Windhoek just 10 minutes walk from the city centre. Has five comfortable en-suite double rooms with TV. There's a pool, too, and the choice of eating in-house or letting the receptionist to book you into the restaurant of your choice. **$-$**

Olive Grove Guesthouse
20 Promenaden Road
PO Box 90590
Tel: 061 239199
Fax: 061 234971
Email: info@olivegrove.com.na
www.olivegrove.com.na
Peaceful, elegantly furnished new hillside guesthouse situated just ten minutes walk from the city centre. The rooms are large and airy, while facilities include a plunge pool, sauna, a highly rated restaurant and excellent breakfasts. **$$**

Villa Verdi Guesthouse
4 Verdi Street
PO Box 6784
Tel: 061 221994
Fax: 061 222574
Email: villaverdi@leadinglodges.com
www.leadinglodges.com
Elegant hotel with good facilities and spectacular views of the Auas Mountains. **$$**

Suburban

Hotels listed below lie some distance from central Windhoek or on the city outskirts

Windhoek Country Club and Resort
Western Bypass
PO Box 30777
Tel: 061 2055911
Fax: 061 252797
Email: windhoek@legacyhotels.co.za
www.legacyhotels.co.za
This large luxury hotel is ideal for golfers, with an 18 hole course attached, and must rank among the top two or three addresses in town when it comes to service and facilities, but it's also rather characterless and isolated for those who want to explore the city. **$$$$**

Hotel Safari & Safari Court
Aviation Road
PO Box 3900
Tel: 061 240240
Fax: 061 235652
Email: reservations@safarihotel.com.na
www.safarihotel.com.na
Located near Eros Airport, these four- and three-star hotels stand on the same grounds and have a joint capacity of 430 rooms, making it probably the largest hotel complex in the country. As with the country club above, it has all the facilities you'd expect at this price range, but comes across as rather bland. The restaurant serves Namibian game. **$$-$$$**

Arebbusch Travel Lodge
PO Box 80160, Olympia
Tel: 061 252255
Fax: 061 251670
Email: atl@mweb.com.na
www.arebbusch.com
Reminiscent of a nationals park rest camp (albeit without the game), this pleasant and affordable lodge lies in large acacia-studded grounds abutting the Arebbusch River. Accommodation is in en-suite chalets or rooms with a small, well-equipped kitchen, TV, direct-dial telephone and air conditioning. The lodge also has a good restaurant and pool, and a popular campsite. **$-$$**

Windhoek Environs

The hotels listed below all have rural settings outside Windhoek and would form a convenient alternative to staying in the city itself.

PRICE CATEGORIES

Based on B&B rate for twin or double room.
$$$$ = above US$225 (N$1500)
$$$ = US$150–225 (N$1000–1500)
$$ = US$75–150 (N$500–1000)
$ = under US$75 (N$100)

Eningu Clayhouse Lodge
PO Box 21783, Windhoek
Tel: 061 226979
Fax: 061 226999
Email: logufa@mweb.com.na
www.natron.net/tour/eningu
Situated on Pepperkorrell Farm near Dordabis, about 45 minutes drive southeast of Hosea Kutako International airport, this is a super alternative to staying in the city, with spacious rooms and original décor on the edge of the Kalahari and a good selection of facilities and activities (including a swimming pool). **$$$**

Eagles Rock Leisure Lodge
PO Box 6176
Tel: 061 257166
Fax: 061 257122
Situated in the Khomas Hochland Mountains some 40 km (25 miles) west of Windhoek, this rustic lodge offers a warm, welcoming atmosphere, good cuisine, plenty of activities, and service in Italian and German as well as English. **$-$$**

Okapuka Ranch
PO Box 5955
Tel: 061 257175
Fax: 061 234690
Email: okapuka@iafrica.com.na
www.natron.net/Okapuka
Situated 30 minutes drive north of Windhoek (a good springboard for trips to Etosha and Caprivi) this pleasant private game ranch harbours a good selection of game, and facilities include walking trails, horse-riding, tennis courts and a swimming pool. **$$$**

Auas Game Lodge
PO Box 80887
Tel: 061 240043
Fax: 061 248633
Cell phone: 081 127 0043
Email: auas@iafrica.com.na
www.auas-lodge.com
Relatively near to the international airport, this is a good place to stay over before leaving on a tour or leaving the country after a visit, with plenty of game around as well as good walking opportunities. Family-friendly. **$–$**

Airport Lodge
PO Box 5913
Tel: 061 231491
Fax: 061 236709
Email: airportl@mweb.com.na
www.natron.net/tour/airport/main.html
Award-winning small lodge set halfway between the city centre and Hosea Kutako Airport (free minibus transfers to both), offering accommodation in comfortable thatched bungalows with attractive décor and a pool. **$$**

Heja Game Lodge
PO Box 588
Tel: 061 257 151
Fax: 061 257 148
Cell phone: 081 124 1345
Email: heja@namib.com
This well stocked game lodge has a pleasant setting in the hills east of Windhoek, along the road to Hosea Kutako Airport. Comfortable rooms and decent meals; facilities include horse-riding, game drives, a swimming pool and inexpensive airport transfers. **$$**

Daan Viljoen Game Park
Bookings through Namibia Wildlife Resorts (see page 261)
Set 20 km (12 miles) west of Windhoek, this small game park is serviced by a self-catering resort with bungalows (using communal kitchen and washing facilities), a restaurant and kiosk, a swimming pool, walking trails, a varied birdlife, and a camping/caravan site. **$–$$**

CENTRAL NAMIBIA

OKAHANDJA AND ENVIRONS

Oropoko Lodge
PO Box 726
Tel: 062 503871
Fax: 062 503842
oropoko@iafrica.com.na
www.oropoko.com
Situated about 60 km (37 miles) northwest of town, this upmarket hilltop lodge has a good view over the central bushveld and a surrounding 110 sq. km (24 sq. miles) game sanctuary inhabited by introduced rhino, giraffe and antelope. Spacious rooms, good food, large swimming pool, game drives and hunting. **$$–$$$**

Okahandja Lodge and Campsite
Tel: 062 504299
Fax: 062 502551
Email: okalodge@africaonline.com.na
www.okahandjalodge.com
Situated alongside a camelthorn-fringed watercourse 2 km (1.2 miles) north of the town centre, this good value lodge has 24 clean, functional thatched rooms, large grounds centred on a swimming pool, and a rich indigenous birdlife. An inexpensive campsite is attached. **$$**

Moringa Guest Farm
PO Box 65
Tel: 062 501106
Fax: 062 503872
Email: moringa@iway.na
www.moringasafaris.com
Longstanding family-run guesthouse offering homely accommodation, game drives and walks on a 200 sq. km (72 sq. miles) game farm stocked with giraffe, cheetah and various naturally occurring antelope and small predators. Named after an endemic baobab-like tree that's common on the property. **$$**

Sylvanette Guesthouse
311 Hoogenhout St
Tel: 062 505550
Fax: 062 505560
Email: sylvanette@iway.na
www.sylvanette.com
Centrally located guesthouse offering clean, friendly, unpretentious accommodation at very reasonable rates. **$–$$**

Gross Barmen Resort
Bookings through Namibia Wildlife Resorts (see page 261)
Set on a hot springs resort and small dam about 25 km (15½ miles) southwest of Okahandja, this government-style resort offers accommodation in bungalows, camping and caravan sites, as well as a restaurant, shop, walking trails, thermal pool and swimming pool. **$–$$**

Von Bach Recreation Resort
Bookings through Namibia Wildlife Resorts (see page 261)
Situated about 10 km (6 miles) south of Okahandja, this lies in a small game reserve surrounding the dam that supplied most of Windhoek's water. Huts (bedding excluded), communal washing facilities, camp/caravan sites. **$**

Karibib

Etusis Lodge (south of Karibib)
PO Box 5
Tel: 064 550826
Fax: 064 550961
Email: etusis@iway.na
www.etusis.com
Accommodation set in beautiful surroundings on a well stocked game farm in the shadow of the Otjipareta Mountains south of Karibib. Comfortable rooms with en-suite toilet and shower. **$–$$**

Hotel Erongo Blick
Park Street
PO Box 67
Tel/fax: 064 550009
A simple hotel, set in the town centre, with a pool and sauna. **$**

Usakos

Ameib Ranch & Campsite
PO Box 266, Usakos
Tel: 064 530803
Fax: 064 530934
Simple but comfortable accommodation on a farm known for its superb rock formations, prehistoric rock art and (mostly captive) wildlife. Camping available. **$$**

Usakos Hotel
Bahnhof Street
Tel: 064 530259
Fax: 064 530267
A plain, clean hotel with simple restaurant. **$**

Omaruru

Epako Game Lodge
PO Box 108
Tel: 064 570551/2
Fax: 064 570553
Relatively luxurious lodge with a lovely setting on a dry riverbank in as well-stocked 110 sq km (24 sq. miles) game farm 22km (17½ miles) north of town. Rooms are air-conditioned and the food has a strong French influence. **$$–$**

Erongo Wilderness Lodge
PO Box 581
Tel: 064 570537
Fax: 064 570 536
info@erongowilderness.com
www.erongowilderness.com
Set about 15 km (9 miles) out of town, on a rocky hill offering panoramic views, this exclusive tented camp is a walker's paradise and the surrounding country supports plenty of indigenous small wildlife. **$–$$**

Omaruru Game Lodge
PO Box 208
Tel: 064 570044
Fax: 064 570134
Email: omlodge@iafrica.com.na
www.omaruru-game-lodge.com
Situated about 15 km (9 miles) northeast of Omaruru, this is a fine Swiss-owned lodge with thatched bungalows, good food, and a wide variety of introduced game kept in semi-captivity. **$$–$**

Hotel Staebe
Monument Street
Tel: 064 570035
Fax: 064 570450
Email: staebe@iafrica.com.na
Clean, efficient German-run hotel in town centre, overlooking the Omaruru watercourse, with swimming pool and campsite **$–$**

Central Hotel
Wilhelm Zeraua Road
PO Box 29
Tel: 064 570030
Fax: 064 570481
Small, traditional hotel. **$**

Omaruru Rest Camp & Caravan Park
Tel: 064 570516
Email: jdg@iway.com
Well-run municipal camp offering inexpensive hutted accommodation and campsites on the northern outskirts of town. **$–$$**

OTJIWARONGO AND ENVIRONS

Okonjima Lodge
Tel: 067 304563/4
Fax: 067 304565
Email: okonjima@iway.na
www.okonjima.com
Home to the multiple award-winning Africat Foundation, the world's largest leopard and cheetah rescue and release programme, Okonjima consists of two separate lodges (main and bush camp) and a new exclusive

villa, all of which offer an intimate atmosphere, rustically luxurious accommodation and superb cuisine, as well as a busy activity schedule embracing open vehicle expeditions to habituated leopard and rehabilitated cheetah. **$$$$**

Otjibamba Lodge
PO Box 510
Tel: 067 303133
Fax: 067 304561
Email: bamba@iway.na
www.otjibamba.com
Situated in a private game ranch just 4 km (2½ miles) south of Otjiwarongo along the B1 towards Windhoek, this popular owner-managed lodge makes for a convenient overnight stop en route to or from Etosha, with spacious rooms and a fine restaurant overlooking a waterhole. **$$**

Out Of Africa Town Lodge
Long Street
Tel: 067 312230
Fax: 067 302236
Email: oatlodge@iway.na
www.out-of-afrika.com
Functional suburban hotel offering comfortable rooms, decent food and good facilities (air-con, TV in rooms, swimming pool) at highly competitive rates. **$**

Outjo

Hotel Onduri
Etosha Road
PO Box 14
Tel: 067 313405

Fax: 067 313408
Simple, centrally located and rather bland town hotel with air-conditioned rooms. **$$**

Etosha Garden Hotel
6 Otavi Street
PO Box 31
Tel: 067 313130
Fax: 067 313419
Email: egh@mweb.com.na
Good service in green suburban setting, with swimming pool and a fine restaurant attached. **$–$$**

Ombinda Country Lodge & Campsite
PO Box 326
Tel: 067 313181
Fax: 067 313478
Email: afrideca@mweb.com.na
www.namibialodges.com
Situated on the eastern outskirts of town, this privatised and refurbished former government rest camp offers accommodation in rustic wood cabins or bungalows set in large grounds with a swimming pool, tennis courts and a decent restaurant. **$–$$**

Otavi

Khorab Safari Lodge & Campsite
Tel: 067 234352
Fax: 067 234520
Email: khorab@iafrica.com.na
www.resafrica.net/khorablodge
Situated alongside the B1, 3 km (1.9 miles) south of Otavi, this rustic family-run lodge is far more attractive than any of the limited

options in town, offering comfortable thatched accommodation, good service and food complemented by a lengthy wine list. Campsites are available. **$$**

Otavi Garden Hotel
PO Box 11
Tel: 067 234336
Fax: 067 234333
Very basic hotel with a combination of en-suite rooms and ones using shared bathrooms, fairly run-down but acceptable. **$**

Tsumeb

Minen Hotel
Post Street
PO Box 244
Tel: 067 221071
Fax: 067 221750
Email: minen@mweb.com.na
www.namibweb.com/minenhotel
Centrally located opposite a small park, this place has a relaxing outdoor area, several different types of rooms, a swimming pool, and a very good kitchen. **$–$$**

Hotel Makalani
4th Road
PO Box 24
Tel: 067 221051
Fax: 067 221575
Email: makalani@mweb.com.na
www.makalanihotel.com
Simple, clean, comfortable hotel. **$–$**

Grootfontein

The Stone House
10 Toenessen St
Tel/fax: 067 242842
Email: boet@mweb.com.na
Pleasant new suburban guesthouse with just three luxury rooms, all with air-con, satellite TV, mini-bar and use of swimming pool and internet facilities. **$$**

Meteor Inn
Okavango Road
Tel: 067 242078
Fax: 067 243072
Email: meteor@iway.na
An adequate countrified town hotel with basic facilities and rooms laid out around a courtyard. **$**

Roy's Camp
Tel/Fax: 067 240302
Email: royscamp@iway.na
This pleasant camp, which lies 55 km (34 miles) north of Grootfontein along the B8 towards Rundu (just past the Tsumkwe turn-off), has rustic bungalows and camping sites, as well as a swimming pool, restaurant and bar. There's good birding in the area, and a pleasant walking trail where

you are likely to see antelope. Visits to a nearby Bushman encampment can be arranged. **$**

Waterberg Plateau Park
Waterberg Wilderness Lodge
Tel: 067 687018
Fax: 067 687020
Email: wwl@natron.net
www.natron.net/tour/wwl
Situated on the farm Otjosongombe, which has been in the same family for almost a century and comprises the only private land on the Waterberg Plateau, this highly regarded and very exclusive lodge offers guests the opportunity for guided walks into a stretch of untrammelled bush teeming with big game

(including buffalo and rhino), colourful birds and great views. **$$$$**

Bernabe de la Bat Rest Camp
Bookings through Namibia Wildlife Resorts (see page 261)
Set within the park, on the wooded slopes of the escarpment, this attractive government rest camp offers accommodation in bungalows, camping sites, and decent facilities including a shop, a restaurant and a swimming pool. Guided game drives leave the camp daily, while a network of self-guided walking trails offers an opportunity to soak up the scenery and superb birdlife. **$–$$**

Gobabis

Gobabis Hotel
Corner of Heroes Lane and Mark Street
PO Box 942
Tel: 062 562568
Fax: 062 562641
Simple accommodation with a pool and beer garden. **$**

Arnhem Restcamp & Camping
Tel: 061 581885
Email: arnhem@mweb.com.na.
Situated at the Arnhem Caves, between Windhoek and Gobabis, this pleasant and affordable camp has a few thatched huts, a field kitchen, camping sites, ablution blocks and a swimming pool. **$**

NORTHERN NAMIBIA

Ondangwa

Pandu Ondangwa Hotel
Tel: 065 241900
Fax: 065 241919
Email: gm-ondangwa@united-hospitality.com
www.united-hospitality.com
Formerly the Cresta, this reasonably priced four-star hotel is situated southeast of the town centre some 6 km (4 miles) from Ondangwa airport. The 90 air-conditioned rooms come with coffee and tea making facilities, satellite television and direct-dial telephone. Facilities include a business centre, swimming pool and à la carte restaurant. **$$**

Punyu International Hotel
PO Box 247
Tel: 065 240009
Fax: 065 240660
A simple but pleasant hotel in the town centre. All rooms have TV, telephone and air conditioning. **$**

Oshakati

Oshakati Country Lodge
Robert Mugabe Avenue
PO Box 15200
Tel: 065 222380
Fax: 065 222384
Email: countryhotel@mweb.com.na

www.namibialodges.com
Relatively new lodge with 50 rooms built around a lush courtyard with swimming pool, and thatched dining and sitting area. All rooms have telephone, TV, air conditioning and mini-bar. **$$**

Oshandira Lodge
PO Box 958
Tel: 065 220443
Fax: 065 221189
Email: oshandira@iway.na
Situated alongside the airport, this comfortable hotel 17 air-conditioned rooms with telephone and TV. Has a green setting and a good restaurant. **$**

Santorini Inn
Main Street
Private Bag 5569
Tel: 065 220457
Fax: 065 220506
Email: anita@santorini-inn.com
www.santorini-inn.com
Different types of rooms with air-conditioning and telephone. Hotel has squash court and à la carte restaurant. **$$**

Continental Hotel
PO Box 6
Tel: 065 220170
Fax: 065 221233
Wide range of rooms. Clean with en-suite bathrooms and all are air-conditioned. **$**

RUNDU AND ENVIRONS

Hakusembe Lodge
PO Box 1327
Tel: 067 220604
Fax: 067 221623
Cell: 081 124 5421
Email: hakusembe@mweb.com.na
About ten chalets very close to the Okavango River some 15km (9 miles) west of Rundu. Good watersport, fishing and birding. **$$$**

Shamvura Camp
Tel: 066 256179
Fax: 066 258297
Email: shamvura@iway.na
www.orusovo.com/shamvura
Situated on a high sand dune overlooking a knobthorn-lined stretch of the Okavango River about 120km (74½ miles) east of Rundu, this wonderfully isolated self-catering camp is popular with game fishermen and offers some excellent birding, canoeing and rambling. Camping sites are available. **$$**

N'Kwazi Lodge
PO Box 1623
Tel: 066 686006/7
Fax: 066 686008
Cell phone: 081 242 4897
Gas-lit wooden chalets in a pleasant setting near the river some 20km (12 miles)

northeast of Rundu. Activities include birdwatching, riding, fishing and traditional dancing. **$$**

Kavango River Lodge
PO Box 634
Tel: 067 255244
Fax: 067 255013
Email: kavlodge@tsu.namib.com
With a superb location in central Rundu overlooking the Okavango River and the Angolan floodplain on the opposite bank, this popular resort consists of 14 self-catering bungalows with all facilities. There's a good on-site restaurant. **$**

Khaudom National Park
Khaudom and Sikereti Camps
Bookings through Namibia Wildlife Resorts (see page 261)
Communal washing facilities. Bring your own gas light and stove, as well as bedding and bath towels. Camping available. **$**

ETOSHA AND ENVIRONS

Etosha National Park
Okaukuejo, Halali & Namutoni Rest Camps
Bookings through Namibia Wildlife Resorts (see page 261)
Respectively situated in the

west, centre and east of the public sector of the park, all three of these camps offer self-catering accommodation in modest bungalows and camping facilities, as well as a shop, restaurant, filling station and swimming pool. Okaukuejo also has an internet café. **$-$$**

East of Etosha

Mushara Lodge & Villa Mushara
PO Box 1814, Tsumeb
Tel: 067 229106
Fax: 067 229107
Email: mushara@iafrica.com.na
www.musharalodge.com
Situated about 8 km (5 miles) from the Von Lindequist entrance gate, this superb upmarket lodge consists of two stylishly decorated 140 sq. km (54 sq. miles) villas with all mod cons (from CD player with ceiling speakers and a small library of Africa-related books to private plunge pools and a choice of indoor or outdoor showers) as well as ten twin en-suite bungalows. It's well positioned for game drives in eastern Etosha and the grounds protect an exciting selection of acacia-dwelling birds. Other attractions include a swimming pool, a large thatched dining and sitting area, and excellent food. **$$$-$$$$**

Mokuti Lodge
PO Box 403
Tel: 067 229084
Fax: 067 229091
mokuti.reservation@olfitra.com.na
www.namibsunhotels.com.na
Situated at the Von Lindequist entrance gate to Etosha National Park, Mokuti Lodge has African

charm while meeting international standards. All 100+ chalets have air conditioning, en-suite bathrooms, TV, direct-dial telephone. Good restaurant and a swimming pool, too. **$-$$**

Onguma Safari Camps
Tel: 061 232009
Fax: 061 222574
Email: oguma@visionsofafrica.com.na
www.ongumanamibia.com
Situated on the eastern border of Etosha, only five minute's drive from the Von Lindequist entrance gate and abutting Fischer's Pan, this private reserve protects a similar range of species to the adjacent national park and offers wide variety of accommodation, ranging from a well-equipped campsite to a luxury tented camp. **$-$$$**

Etosha Aoba Lodge
PO Box 469, Tsumeb
Tel: 067 229100
Fax: 067 299101
Email: aoba@tsunamib.com
Thatched bungalows in a pleasant setting in the bush. Comfortable and good value for money. **$$**

South of Etosha

Ongava Game Reserve
PO Box 6850, Windhoek
Tel: 061 274500
Fax: 061 239455
Email: info@nts.com.na
www.wilderness-safaris.com
Situated immediately south of the Andersson entrance gate, this 30 sq. km (11.5 sq. miles) private reserve, managed by Wilderness Safaris, harbours a similar selection of game to Etosha, and is particularly noted for its excellent lion and rhino (black and white) sightings. A trio of exclusive lodges is scattered around the reserve, with a total of 24 double units, all of which blend well with the environment. near The most sumptuous (and expensive) lodge is Little Ongava, which consists of just three tented units with private plunge pool built on a dolomite hill, chalets are all thatched and have en-suite bathrooms. Activities include guided

game drives within the private reserve and into the adjacent national park, as well as rhino-tracking walks. **$$$-$$$$**

Naua Naua Lodge
PO Box 347, Outjo
Tel/fax: 061 252299
Email: nauanaua@namibnet.com
www.nauanaua.com
This has a beautiful setting amongst hills and bushveld about 30 km (19 miles) from Etosha's Andersson Gate. Bungalows are very comfortable. The lodge takes a maximum of 17 guests. **$$$**

Western Etosha border

Hobatere Lodge
PO Box 110, Kamanjab
Tel: 067 330261
Fax: 061 221919
Email: hobatere@mweb.com.na
www.africa-adventure.org/h/hobatere
Situated 80km (50 miles) north of Kamanjab on the Etosha border, this consists of 12 twin-roomed en-suite bungalows, plus a pool, viewing hide, treehouse, and shop. Spending a night in a treehouse gives a new dimension to game-viewing. Can organise guided walks, game drives and night drives, and birding excursions. **$$$$**

Kavita Lion Lodge
PO Box 118, Kamanjab
Tel: 067 330224
Fax: 067 330269
Email: kavita@iway.com.na
www.kavitalion.com
A lodge with a comfortable, informal atmosphere, with the chance to learn about the Afri-Leo Foundation which is based here on the western Etosha border. Has 5 twin-bedded rooms and a pool. Can organise game drives, bush walks, birding trails, and pre-arranged visits to Himba homesteads. **$$$**

CAPRIVI

Divundu/Bagani area

Ndhovu Safari Lodge
PO Box 5035, Divundu

Tel: 066 259901
Fax: 066 259153
Email: reservations@resdes.com.na
www.ndhovu.com
Situated close to the Popa Falls, this consists of 8 luxury tented units with en-suite bathrooms. Plenty of wildlife and birds in the vicinity. Activities include game drives to Mahungu National Park, fishing trips, bird walks and sunset cruises. **$-$$$**

Suclabo Okavango Lodge
PO Box 894, Rundu
Tel: 066 259005
Fax: 061 375333
Email: wts@leadinglodges.com
www.leadinglodges.com
Situated between Popa Falls and the Mahangu Game Reserve, this lodge offers 11 chalets with en-suite facilities. Good views of the Okavango River, and activities include boat trips to nearby hippo and croc pools. **$-$$**

Mahangu Safari Lodge
PO Box 5200 Divundu
Tel: 066 259037
Fax: 066 259115
Email: eden@mweb.com.na
www.mahangu.com.na
Thatched bungalows set in a beautiful garden overlooking the Okavango River near Mahangu National Park. **$-$$**

Popa Falls Camp
Bookings through Namibia Wildlife Resorts (see page 261)
Communal washing and kitchen facilities; shop with a few basic commodities. No electricity, but gas lighting is supplied. **$-$$**

Kongola and Mudumu Environs

Lianshulu Lodge
PO Box 90391, Windhoek
Tel: 061 254317
Fax: 061 254980
Email: lianshul@mweb.com.na
www.lianshuli.com.na
Luxury thatched bungalows accommodating up to 22 guests overlooking the Kwando River about 40 km (25 miles) south of Kongola in Mudumu National Park, opposite Botswana. **$$-$$**

Namushasha Country Lodge
PO Box 6597, Windhoek
Tel: 061 374750
Fax: 061 256598
Email: afrideca@mweb.com.na
www.namibialodges.com
Very well situated overlooking a hippo pool on the Kwando River south of Kongola, this recently renovated luxury lodge arranges good guided game drives, boat trips and horse-riding. A 4 km (2½ miles) nature walk offers the opportunity to see many of the 400 bird species recorded in the vicinity. **$–$$**

Mazambala Island Lodge
PO Box 1935, Katima Mulilo
Tel/fax: 066 250405

Email: mazambala@mweb.com.na
Very rustic chalets on the Kwando River south of Kongola. Plenty of wildlife around, including buffalo, elephant, lion, red lechwe and an immense variety of birds. **$$**

Katima Mulilo

Zambezi Lodge and Campsite
PO Box 198, Katima Mulilo
Tel: 066 253149
Fax: 066 253631
Email: katima@iafrica.com.na
www.namibsunhotels.com.na
Hotel-like lodge (with campsite attached) in Katima Mulilo on the banks of the Zambezi River – good overnight stop. **$$–$$$**

Zambezi-Chobe Confluence

Ichingo Chobe River Lodge
PO Box 1856 Ngewze
Tel: 0267 6250143
Fax: 0267 6250223
With a beautiful setting on Impalila Island overlooking the Chobe River, this luxurious lodge consists of eight tented units with balcony. Activities include boat trips, and superb guided bird walks. **$$–$$$**

King's Den Lodge
P O Box 198, Katima Mulilo
Tel/fax: 0267 6250814
Email: kingsden@botsnet.bw
www.namibsunhotels.com.na
King's Den is on the eastern Caprivi, opposite Kasikili Island on the

Chobe River, overlooking the game-rich plains of Botswana's Chobe National Park. **$$–$$**

Impalila Island Lodge
PO Box 70378, Bryanston 2021
South Africa
Tel: (27) 11 7067207
Fax: (27) 11 4638251
Email: res@islandsinafrica.com
www.islandsinafrica.com
This superior lodge on the island's northwestern shore has 8 double chalets offering rooms with a view over the Zambezi rapids, but it's best known for its activities. Can arrange fly-fishing and birding trips, along with guided walks, mokoro trips and guided motor-boat trips. Good food, too. **$$$–$$$$**

NORTHWEST NAMIBIA

KHORIXAS AND ENVIRONS

Vingerklip Lodge
PO Box 443, Outjo
Tel: 067 290318
Fax: 067 290319
Email: vingerkl@mweb.com.na
www.vingerklip.com.na
This medium-sized lodge consists of 22 room comfortable bungalows attractively located next to the striking finger-like rock formation for which it is named. The panoramic views are complemented by good food, a swimming pool and low-key activities such as walking and birding. **$$$**

Bambatsi Holiday Ranch
PO Box 120, Outjo
Tel: 067 313897
Fax: 067 313331
Email: bambatsi@natron.net
Situated on the C38 midway between Outjo and Khorixas, this eight bungalow guest farm is well positioned for visits to Vingerklip, Twyfelfontein and the petrified forest, while on-site facilities include a swimming pool, horse-riding, game viewing, tennis court and mountain bikes. **$$$**

Khorixas Lodge & Rest Camp
PO Box 2
Tel: 067 331196
Fax: 067 331388
Email: khorixas@mweb.com.na
www.nwr.com.na
A large, well-run, functional self-catering resort and campsite, 4 km (2½ miles) out of town and well placed for visits to the Brandberg and other rock art sites. Has 38 clean but basic bungalows, as well as a swimming pool, shop and restaurant. **$$**

White Lady B&B
Tel/fax: 064 504102
Email: whitelady@iway.na
http://whitelady.webz-i.com
Situated in Uis, the closest town to the Brandberg, this new B&B offers clean thatched en-suite accommodation set around a sparkling pool, as well as a campsite with plunge pool and birdwatching hide. **$$**

Brandberg Rest Camp
PO Box 35, Uis
Tel/fax 064 504038
Email: brandberg@iml-net.com.na
Simple clean accommodation and campsites situated close to the base of a massif known for its superb prehistoric rock art. Facilities include a restaurant, swimming pool

and tennis court. **$**

Twyfelfontein & Environs

Mowani Mountain Camp
Tel: 061 232009
Fax: 061 222574
Email: mowani@visionsofafrica.com.na
www.mowani.com
Stylish, top-of-the-range tented camp whose location is ideal for exploring the rock engravings at Twyfelfontein. **$$$$**

Twyfelfontein Country Lodge
PO Box 6597, Windhoek
Tel: 061 374750
Fax: 061 256598
Email: afrideca@mweb.com.na
www.namibialodges.com
This popular, comfortable lodge has a scenic setting at the base of a golden cliff just 5 km (3 miles) from the Twyfelfontein rock art site. Good buffet meals, a swimming pool set amidst the rocks, and a range of guided activities in the surrounding countryside. **$$$**

Aba Huab Campsite
PO Box 131 Khorixas
Community-run campsite set on an acacia-fringed dry watercourse about 10 km (6 miles) from Twyfelfontein. Facilities are limited to a bar and ablution block. **$**

Damaraland

Palmwag Rhino Camp
PO Box 6850, Windhoek
Tel: 061 274500
Fax: 061 239455
Email: info@nts.com.na
www.wilderness-safaris.com
Run in collaboration with the Save The Rhino Trust, this superlative exclusive bush camp is the only permanent encampment in the vast private Palmwag concession, and game drives offer a great opportunity to se a wide selection of typical desert wildlife. Rhino-tracking walks are led by experienced guides every morning, and come with a high chance of seeing this desert population of this endangered creature. **$$$$**

Damaraland Camp
PO Box 6850, Windhoek
Tel: 061 274500
Fax: 061 239455
Email: info@nts.com.na
www.wilderness-safaris.com
No creature comforts are lacking in this spectacular wilderness location, which lies in the heart of the territory inhabited by the legendary desert-dwelling elephants of Damaraland. Accommodation is in 8 large twin-bedded tents

with en-suite bathrooms; there's also a plunge-pool and a shop. The lodge can organise game drives, walking, birdwatching and star-gazing. **$$$$**

Huab Lodge
PO Box 180, Outjo
Tel: 061 224712
Fax: 061 224217
Email: info@huab.com
www.huab.com
Award-winning lodge situated on a private reserve halfway between Khorixas and Kamanjab with superb guiding, and imaginative cuisine. Offers 8 comfortable thatched bungalows set near a dry river bed, with a pool and a thermal spring. Activities include horse-riding, game drives, guided walks and birding. **$$$$**

Palmwag Lodge and Campsite
PO Box 339, Swakopmund
Tel: 064 404459
Fax: 064 404664
Email: travel@palmwag.com.na
www.Palmwag.com
One of Namibia's oldest lodges, set amongst an oasis-like stand of makalani palms fed by a subterranean river in what is otherwise a rather dry region. Regularly visited by desert elephants and other wildlife, this 42-room lodge also has a campsite, a restaurant, a snack bar and two swimming pools. Activities include game-drives, walking trails, rhino-tracking and birding. **$$$–$$$$**

Sesfontein

Fort Sesfontein Lodge
PO Box 7, Kamanjab
Tel: 065 275534
Fax: 065 275533
Email: fort.sesfontein@mweb.com.na

PRICE CATEGORIES

Based on B&B rate for twin or double room.
$$$$ = above US$225 (N$1500)
$$$ = US$150–225 (N$1000–1500)
$$ = US$75–150 (N$500–1000)
$ = under US$75 (N$100)

www.fort-sesfontein.com
Charming Beau Geste style fort in tropical gardens. Has 10 double rooms, 3 family suites, a campsite, pool and restaurant. Offers guided day tours too. **$$$**

Opuwo and environs
Omarunga Camp Epupa
Tel: 061 234342
Fax: 061 233872
Situated within walking distance of the Epupa Falls, 180 km (112 miles) northwest of Opuwa, this consists of 10 luxury en-suite tents as well as 6 campsites for equipped campers. Can arrange guided walks and visits to Himba homesteads. **$$**

Ruacana Eha Lodge
Tel: 065 270031
Fax: 065 270095
Email: info@ruacanaehalodge.com.na
www.ruacanaehalodge.com.na
Situated in Ruacana about 50 km (31 miles) northeast of Opuwa, this is a comfortable modern lodge with 21 en-suite rooms, a good restaurant, a swimming pool and a gym. Activities include Himba village visits and guided walks. The adjacent campsite has cheap hutted accommodation using common ablution blocks. **$–$$**

Ohakane Lodge
PO Box 8, Opuwo
Tel: 065 273031
Fax: 065 273025
Email: ohakane@iafrica.com.na
www.natron.net
Good rooms, swimming pool and restaurant in the middle of Opuwo, 'capital' of the Himba. **$–$$**

SKELETON COAST

Skeleton Coast Camp
PO Box 6850, Windhoek
Tel: 061 274500
Fax: 061 239455
Email: info@nts.com.na
www.wilderness-safaris.com
The only accommodation set within Skeleton Cast National Park, this luxurious and exclusive six-room lodge, managed by Wilderness Safaris, caters to fly-in clients only, and a stay of at least four days is

recommended to see the area properly. Wildlife includes desert-adapted elephant, brown hyena, cheetah and various antelope and dry-country birds. Spectacular scenic excursions are also offered, as are visits to some of the shipwrecks that gave the Skeleton Coast its name. **$$$$**

Serra Cafema Camp
PO Box 6850, Windhoek
Tel: 061 274500
Fax: 061 239455
Email: info@nts.com.na
www.wilderness-safaris.com
With its remote but pretty location on a Himba concession bordering the Kunene River east of the park boundary, this new Wilderness camp is often visited in conjunction with Skeleton Coast Camp. The dunes that rise from the riverbank make for spectacular setting, and activities include quad biking in the dunes, game and birdwatching drives in the Hartmann Valley, and visits to local Himba communities. **$$$$**

Terrace Bay Restcamp
Bookings through Namibia Wildlife Resorts (see page 261)
Formerly the quarters of a mining company, this remote resort (almost 300 km/186 miles north of the nearest town, Henties Bay) has well-equipped bungalows and restaurant set along the rocky Atlantic coastline. **$$**

Torra Bay Campsites
Bookings through Namibia Wildlife Resorts (see page 261)
Very basic camp/caravan sites 100 km (62 miles) south of Terrace Bay, open from 1 December to 31 January. A shop and filling station are open during the December school holidays only, when water and firewood are on sale. **$**

Henties Bay, Cape Cross and Environs

Cape Cross Lodge
Tel: 064 694012
Fax: 064 694013
Email: bookings@capecross.org
www.capecross.org
Luxurious and wonderfully

isolated oceanfront lodge situated 4 km (2½ miles) from the Cape Coast seal colony and 50 km (31 miles) north of Henties Bay. Day visitors to Cape Cross are welcome to drop in for a meal. **$$$–$$$$**

Hotel De Duine
34 Duine Road
PO Box 1, Henties Bay
Tel: 064 500001
Fax: 064 500724
Email: afrideca@mweb.com.na
www.namibialodges.com
Cell phone: 081 127 2371
A reliable beachfront hotel with a friendly service. Comfortable rooms with direct-dial telephone and en-suite bathrooms. Good meals. **$–$**

Mile 72, Mile 108 and Jakkalsputz Campsites
Bookings through Namibia Wildlife Resorts (see page 261)
These campsites are almost exclusively used by anglers; the facilities are very basic. Toilets are provided and hot showers are available for a small fee. During the Namibian December school holidays a shop/kiosk is manned at all camps and fuel is obtainable at Mile 72 and Mile 108.

THE NAMIB

Swakopmund
Swakopmund Hotel and Entertainment Centre
2 Theo-Ben Gurabib Street
PO Box 616
Tel: 064 4105200
Fax: 064 4105360
Email: swakopmund@legacyhotels.co.za
www.legacyhotels.co.za
This four-star hotel includes the old railway station (reception and small bar). The 90 en-suite rooms are very well equipped with tea/coffee makers, TV, phone, mini-bar, air conditioning and safe. Good restaurant. Also casino. **$$$**

Hansa Hotel
3 Hendrik Witbooi Street
PO Box 44
Tel: 064 414200
Fax: 064 414299
Email: reservations@hansahotel.com.na
www.hansahotel.com.na

A centrally located, award-winning 50-room hotel which celebrated its centenary in 2005, its vintage reflected by its the superb period architecture and characterful, stylish décor. Efficient, friendly service. Superb kitchen. Nice, intimate bar with fireplace. **$$$**

The Burning Shore
Tel: 064 207568
Fax: 064 209836
Email: burningshore@mweb.com.na
www.burningshore.com

This plush 12-room lodge, situated 15 km (9 miles) south of town along the road to Walvis Bay, is one of the smartest options in the area – and its popularity is likely to be boosted after having made international headlines in 2006 when it was booked out for several weeks by Brad Pitt and Angelina Jolie. **$$$**

Sam's Giardino
89 Anton Lubowski Ave
Tel: 064 403210
Fax: 064 403500
Email: samsart@iafrica.com.na
www.giardino.com

A must for gourmets and wine-lovers, this comfortable and affordable 10-room guesthouse is justifiably renowned for its fine kitchen, which reflects the nationality of the enthusiastic Swiss owner-manager, and a cellar stocked with a handpicked selection of the finest Cape wines. **$$**

Strand Hotel
PO Box 20
Tel: 064 400315
Fax: 064 404942
Email: strand.reservations@olfitra.com.na

Two-star beachfront hotel close to the beach and town centre. Some of the 45 rooms have a sea-view. Two restaurants. **$$**

Hotel Europa Hof
39 Bismarck Street
PO Box 1333
Tel: 064 405061
Fax: 064 402391
Email: europa@iml-net.com.na
www.europahof.com

This centrally located hotel combines traditional German architecture (Fachwerk) with comfortable rooms and a highly rated

seafood restaurant. **$$**

The Stiltz
Tel/fax: 064 400771
Cell: 081 1272111
info@thestiltz.in.na
www.thestiltz.in.na

This attractive new lodge consists of eight stilted wooden bungalows (best view from #7) linked by a raised walkway in the coastal scrub overlooking the bird-rich Swakop Lagoon within walking distance of the town centre. No restaurant. **$$**

Swakopmund Municipal Restcamp
Private Bag 5017
Tel: 064 4104333/4
Fax: 064 4104212
Email: restcamp@swkmun.com.na
www.swakopmund-restcamp.com

Characterless but very affordable self-catering accommodation with more than 200 units squeezed onto a flat site close to the sea and town centre. **$–$$**

Secret Garden Guesthouse
36 Bismarck St
Tel: 064 404037
Email: sgg@iway.na
www.natron.net/tour/secretgarden

Quiet, comfortable, very central and affordable owner-managed guesthouse. Good value. **$**

Mile 14 Caravan Park
Bookings through Namibia Wildlife Resorts (see page 261)

Basic site, popular with anglers during the December school holidays, when a shop/kiosk stocks basic supplies. Otherwise, facilities are limited to toilets and hot showers. **$**

Walvis Bay

Lagoon Lodge
2 Kovambo Nujoma Drive
Tel: 064 200850
Fax: 064 200851
Email: french@lagoonlodge.com.na
www.lagoonlodge.com.na

Within walking distance of the town centre alongside the lagoon, this welcoming owner-managed lodge is probably the most comfortable option in Walvis Bay. It consists of just six individually decorated rooms centred around a swimming pool, most of which have private

balconies overlooking the lagoon. **$$**

Walvis Bay Protea Hotel
Corner Sam Nujoma & 10th Rd
Tel: 064 209560
Fax: 064 209565
Email: info@proteawalvis.com.na
www.proteahotels.com

Part of a highly regarded South African midrange hotel chain, this is a clean, functional and very central hotel with good facilities and reasonable rates. **$$**

Courtyard Hotel Garni
3rd Road
PO Box 3493
Tel: 064 213600
Fax: 064 213620
Email: courtyrd@iafrica.com.na

Near the lagoon. All rooms have en-suite facilities. A small indoor pool and sauna. Nice hotel. **$-$**

Kleines Nest B&B
76 Esplanade
Tel: 064 203203
Fax: 064 206907
Email: kleinnest@iway.na
www.natron.net/tour/kleines-nest

Welcoming owner-managed six-room lodge overlooking the lagoon. Massage and aromatherapy. **$**

Hotel Atlantic
Sam Nujoma Avenue
PO Box 46
Tel: 064 202811
Fax: 064 205063

Unexceptional centrally located hotel likely to be refurbished in the near future. **$**

Hotel Langholm
24 Second Street West
PO Box 2631
Tel: 064 209230
Fax: 064 209430
Email: desk@langholmhotel.com
www.langholmhotel.com

A nice, small hotel near the harbour and lagoon. Comfortable rooms. **$**

Esplanade Park Cottages
Tel: 064 206145
Fax: 064 215510
info@wbresorts.com.na
www.wbresorts.com.na

Adequate self-catering bungalows at the lagoon. **$**

Langstrand Campsite and Caravan Park
Tel: 064 2013267

Pleasant campsite at Langstrand (Long Beach), about 10 km (6 miles) out of town along the road towards Swakopmund.

(see page 261)

Namib-Naukluft and Environs

Kulala Desert Lodge
PO Box 6850, Windhoek
Tel: 061 274500
Fax: 061 239455
Email: info@nts.com.na
www.wilderness-safaris.com

This exclusive 12-room camp has a beautiful setting on the Tsauchab River in a 320 sq. km (124 sq. miles) concession abutting the national park some 50 km (31 miles) from Sussusvlei. Good view of the dunes to the west. Within the same concession, and also managed by Wilderness Safaris, are the even more exclusive and pricey Kulala Wilderness Camp and Little Kulala Camp. All are noteworthy for their excellent food, balloon excursions, and guided drives to Sossusvlei and surrounds. **$$–$$**

Sossusvlei Wilderness Camp
PO Box 6850, Windhoek
Tel: 061 274500
Fax: 061 239455
Email: info@nts.com.na
www.wilderness-safaris.com

Built on a small hill offering superb views across the arid plains, this exclusive lodge, set in an private wilderness area 30 km (19 miles) from Sesriem, consists of nine thatched chalets with en-suite bathrooms and private plunge pools. Beautiful scenery. **$$$$**

Wolwedans Collection
Tel: 061 230616
Fax: 061 220102
Email: reservations@wolwedans.com.na
www.wolwedans.com

This trio of superlative small lodges is set amid the dunes of the NamibRand Nature Reserve, a large private conservancy bordering Namib-Naukluft to the south of Sesriem. Consisting of 16 units in total, the three lodges all offer an exclusive wilderness experience and a wide selection of activities in the desert. **$$$$**

Sossusvlei Lodge
Tel: 063 293223
Fax: 063 293231
Email: reservations@sossusvleilodge.com
www.sossusvleilodge.com
With a prime location at the Sesriem entrance gate, this is the closest lodge to Sossusvlei and its 45 en-suite tented rooms are spacious and stylishly decorated. Facilities include a floodlit waterhole and swimming pool, as well as balloon trips and guided drives to Sossusvlei. **$–$$$**

Desert Homestead
Tel: 061 249116
Fax: 061 247818
Email: sossus@iafrica.com.na
www.deserthomestead-namibia.com
Recently relocated and rebuilt on a private concession alongside the C19 about 30 km (19 miles) from Sesriem, this smart owner-managed lodge consists of 20 thatched en-suite

chalets with private verandas facing the sunset. In addition to good food and a swimming pool, the lodge offers popular horseback excursions into the dunes, as well as sundowner drives and guided excursions to Sossusvlei.

Namib Naukluft Lodge
PO Box 22028, Windhoek
Tel: 061 372100
Fax: 061 215356
Email: trixim@afex.com.na
www.namib-naukluft
Set on a 250 sq km (97 sq miles) private reserve abutting the eponymous national park, this lodge, which line between Sesriem and Solitaire consists of 16 modern rooms with private verandas. Day trips to Sossusvlei are offered, and it's well placed for day hikes in the Naukluft Mountains. **$$$**

Zebra River Lodge
Private Bag 11742, Windhoek
Tel: 063 293265
Fax: 063 293266
Email: marianne.rob@zebrariver.com
www.zebrariver.com
Set in the rugged Tsaris Mountains, this small owner-managed lodge is popular with hikers for the several trails that run through the vast property (home to a wide variety of game) and its proximity to the Naukluft Mountains. It's also a useful base for road (or plane) excursions to Sossusvlei. Homely atmosphere and good en-suite accommodation set around a sparkling swimming pool. **$$$**

Solitaire Country Lodge
PO Box 6597, Windhoek
Tel: 061 374750
Fax: 061 256598
Email: afrideca@mweb.com.na
www.namibialodges.com

Situated 83 km (52 miles) from Sesriem, this new hotel dominates the blink-and-you'll-miss-it pit stop of Solitaire on the long dusty road towards Lüderitz. It has 25 en-suite rooms centred on a refreshing swimming pool area, and is a good base for day trips into the Naukluft Mountains and Speetshoogte Pass. Camping sites available. **$$**

Sesriem Campsite
Bookings through Namibia Wildlife Resorts (see page 261)
Twenty campsites set in a grove of shady camelthorn trees at the main park entrance gate, close to the Sesriem Canyon and 63 km (39 miles) from Sossusvlei. There's a reasonably well stocked shop, fuel station, and ablution block, and meals are available at the adjacent Sossusvlei Lodge. **$**

SOUTHERN NAMIBIA

REHOBOTH

Lake Oanob Campsite
PO Box 3381
Tel: 062 522370
Fax: 062 524112
Email: oanobresort@iway.na
www.oanob.com.na
Set on the lakeshore 7 km (4 miles) west of Rehoboth, this is a comfortable and attractively situated resort with good facilities (restaurant, game-viewing hides, internet café) and a variety of rooms and self-catering units as well as camping and caravan sites. **$$**

Reho Spa Recreation Resort
Bookings through Namibia Wildlife Resorts (see page 261)
Built around the hot springs in the town centre, this pleasant and underutilised resort offers accommo-dation in 20 chalets, as we as camping and caravan sites, a restaurant, and a thermal swimming pool. **$**

Mariental and Environs

Intu Africa Kalahari Game Reserve
Tel: 061 240529
Fax: 061 226535
Email: intu@iafrica.com.na
www.thirstlandadventures.namibia.com.na
This 200 sq. km (77 sq miles) private reserve to the northeast of Mariental supports a fair variety of desert wildlife, and is also home to one of the few remaining Bushman communities in southern Namibia. Three lodges are studded around the reserve, all offering good en-suite accommodation and game drives, while the two more upmarket lodges also have a swimming pool. **$$–$$$$**

Bagatelle Kalahari Game Ranch
Tel: 063 240982
Fax: 063 241252
Email: reservations@resdes.com.na
www.bagatelle-kalahari-gameranch.com
This recently opened private ranch, about 45

minutes drive northeast of Mariental, stocks a wide variety of game, including cheetah, giraffe, oryx and various smaller antelope. The stilted dunetop accommodation has plenty of character, great views and good facilities. **$$$**

Auob Lodge
PO Box 6597, Windhoek
Tel: 061 374750
Fax: 061 256598
Email: afrideca@mweb.com.na
www.namibialodges.com
Situated to the east of Mariental near Gochas, about 150 km (93 miles) from the border with the Kgalagadi Transfrontier Park, this three-star lodge consists of 26 spacious rooms with a view on the Kalahari dunes. **$–$$**

Kalahari Anib Lodge
PO Box 800, Mariental
Tel: 061 230066
Fax: 061 251863
Email: info@gondwana-desert-collection.com
www.gondwana-desert-collection.com
Situated on the C20 some 30 km (19 miles) northeast

of Mariental, this lodge consists of 35 comfortable en-suite rooms surrounded by beautiful gardens and the red dunes of the Kalahari. **$–$$**

Hardap Recreation Resort:
Bookings through Namibia Wildlife Resorts (see page 261)
Situated 25 km (15½ miles) from town overlooking the Hardap Dam, this resort has bungalows, camping sites, shop, restaurant, filling station and swimming pool. **$–$$**

Mariental Hotel
Marie Brandt Street
PO Box 619
Tel: 063 242466
Fax: 063 242493
Cell: 081 127 0816
Email: hoofmot@mar.nam.lia.net
A good country hotel. All rooms with en-suite bathrooms, air-conditioning and direct-dial telephones. **$**

Keetmanshoop

Canyon Hotel
Warnbader Road
PO Box 950
Tel: 063 223361

Fax: 063 223714
Email: info@canyon-namibia.com
www.canyon-namibia.com
This fortress-like three-star monolith on the southern outskirts is ostensibly the most upmarket in town, a status undermined by the rather outmoded décor and mildly depressing atmosphere of neglect. Still, it has a big swimming pool, 70 decent en-suite rooms with air-conditioning, and a good restaurant. **$$**

Central Lodge
5th Avenue
Tel: 063 250586
Fax: 063 224984
Email: clodge@iway.com
www.central-lodge.com
Centrally located on the site of the former Hansa Hotel (built 1910), this is probably the most popular lodge in town, and very good value. All 19 en-suite rooms have air-con and Satellite TV, and theirs is a swimming pool and good à la carte restaurant with a budget-friendly wine list. **$**

Bird's Mansions Hotel
6th Avenue
Tel: 063 221711
Fax: 063 221730
Email: birdsmansions@iway.na
www.birdsaccommodation.com
Situated a block up from the Central Hotel, this is similarly good value, consisting of 22 en-suite rooms with satellite TV and air-con, and a central lapa with swimming pool and beer garden. **$**

Fish River Environs
Cañon Lodge
PO Box 80205
Windhoek
Tel: 061 230066
Fax: 061 251863
Email: nature.i@mweb.com.na
www.namibiaweb.com/canyon
Situated in Gondwana Canyon Park, a privately managed extension of the Fish River Canyon National Park, this superb lodge straddles a range of rocky hills some 20 km (12 miles) from the main viewpoint over the canyon. The 30 en-suite bungalows blend attractively into the granite environment; facilities include horseback trips, a

swimming pool and a beautifully positioned restaurant serving home-style cooking in the old German farmhouse. **$$$**

Ai-Ais Recreation Resort
Bookings through Namibia Wildlife Resorts (*see page 261*)
This rather rundown resort at the southern end of the canyon has accommodation in so-called luxury flats, as well as huts, camping sites, shop, restaurant, filling station, mineral spa and swimming pool. **$–$$**

Hobas Resort
Bookings through Namibia Wildlife Resorts (*see page 261*)
Situated at the northern entrance gate to the park, close to the best viewpoints and starting point of the Fish River Canyon hiking tail, this campsite has a shop and swimming pool. **$**

Helmeringhausen

Dabis Guest farm
PO Box 15, Helmeringhausen
Tel: 06362 ask for 6820
Situated about 30 minutes drive north of town, this welcoming guest farm has been in the same German family for four generations, and will be of great interest to anybody who wants to learn about sheep ranching techniques in this arid part of the world. Delicious barbecued lamb chops are something of a speciality. A good stopover between Lüderitz/Fish River and Sesriem. **$$$**

Hotel Helmeringhausen
PO Box 21
Tel: 063 283083
Email: hhhotel@natron.net
This small country hotel, built in the 1930s and strong on period character, lies at the heart of the tiny eponymous junction village. **$**

Grünau

Grünau Country House
PO Box 2
Tel: 063 262001
Fax: 063 262009
Email: grunauch@iway.na
www.grunauch.iway.na
This country hotel is the top

lodge in this small junction town near the South African border. **$**

Karasburg

Kalkfontein Hotel
Kalkfontein Street
PO Box 338
Tel: 063 270172
Fax: 063 270457
Email: kalkfont@iway.na
Situated on the southern slopes of the Karas Mountains, the 17 en-suite rooms here are on the basic side, but comfortable enough. **$**

Maltahöhe

Namseb Restcamp
PO Box 76
Tel: 063 293166
Fax: 063 293157
Email: eden@mweb.com.na
Situated a short distance outside town, this pleasant lodge offers accommodation in spacious bungalows made of natural stone. Amenities include a swimming pool, a good restaurant, and guided game drives. **$–$$**

Hammerstein Restcamp
PO Box 250
Maltahöhe
Tel: 063 693111
Fax: 063 693112
Email: hammerst@hammerstein.com.na
www.hammerstein.com.na
Situated on the C19 between Maltahöhe and Sesriem, this midrange camp with a swimming pool lies in a boulder-strewn farm that hosts some good rock art and a variety of desert wildlife. Situated within day tripping distance of Sossusvlei. **$$**

Aus

Klein-Aus Vista
PO Box 25
Tel: 063 258116
Fax: 063 258021
Email: ausvista@namibhorses.com
Situated 3 km (1.9 miles) from Aus on the B4 to Lüderitz, an area regularly frequented by wild desert horses, this welcoming set-up consists of the 14-

room Desert Horse Inn, the more exclusive hillside Eagle's Nest Lodge, as well as a small campsite. **$–$$$**

Lüderitz

The Nest Hotel
Diaz St
PO Box 690
Tel: 063 204000
Fax: 063 204001
Email: nesthotel@natron.net
www.natron.net/tour/nest-hotel
A good new three-star hotel on a private beach southwest of the town centre. All rooms have a sea view. Restaurant offers good meals. **$$–$$$**

Sea View Hotel zum Sperrgebiet
Woerman Street
PO Box 373
Tel: 063 203411
Fax: 063 203 414
Email: michaels@namibnet.com
www.seaview-luderitz.com
A comfortable modern three-star hotel with 22 rooms, and an indoor pool and sauna. Has a very good restaurant. **$$**

Bayview Hotel
Diaz Street
PO Box 387
Tel: 063 202288
Fax: 063 202402
Email: Bayview@ldz.namib.com
Friendly and unpretentious centrally-located hotel with rooms built around a courtyard swimming pool. **$**

Kapps Hotel
Tel: 202345
Email: pink@mweb.com.na
This central hotel, the oldest in town, is due to celebrate its centenary in 2007, and has plenty of character, though the en-suite rooms are a little rundown. Good value. **$**

E ATING OUT

RECOMMENDED RESTAURANTS, CAFES & BARS

Local Cuisine

Like most African capitals, Windhoek boasts a cosmopolitan variety of culinary treats, and it is undoubtedly the best place for eating out in Namibia. As many as a hundred different restaurants, coffee shops and fast food outlets are dotted around the city, including good representatives of German, French, Italian, Portuguese, Chinese, Indian and even Argentine cuisine, as well as a smattering of places specialising in local, West African and even Ethiopian food – not to mention various South African or global chains such as Debonairs Pizzeria, Kentucky Fried Chicken and Nando's. In other words, there is something to suit all tastes – at prices that seem very reasonable by international standards (main courses generally fall below US$10 in all but the most swish eateries) and generally with a good choice of local beers and South African wines as accompaniment.

A far smaller but otherwise comparable selection of restaurants is to be found in the three main port towns: Lüderitz, Walvis Bay and especially the more resort-like Swakopmund. Seafood is the speciality here, though good meat dishes are also available. Elsewhere, urban centres tend to boast just one or two steakhouse-type establishments catering to undemanding carnivorous local palates. In reality, however, few tourist will spend much time in small-town Namibia: more likely they will spend most of their nights in isolated lodges, rest camps and guest farms, which typically offer high quality (but of necessity limited) 3–4 course set menus (or buffets) for around US$20 per head.

Restaurants in Game Parks & Reserves

The following state-owned game parks/reserves have restaurants: Ai-Ais, Daan Viljoen, Etosha: Halali, Namutoni and Okaukuejo, Gross Barmen, Waterberg, Skeleton Coast Park (Terrace Bay) and Hardap. Meal times are fairly restricted, so check them carefully.

RESTAURANT LISTINGS

WINDHOEK

Abyssinia Restaurant
3 Lossen Street
Tel: 061 254891/2
The place to try Ethiopian cuisine, which consists of various spicy stews (including a good vegetarian range) eaten with a doughy, sour pancake-shaped staple called injera. **$$$**
Restaurant Africa
Alte Feste Museum, Robert Mugabe Avenue
Tel: 061 247178
Serves a good selection of traditional African cuisine - including crunchy pan-fried mopane worms! **$$**

Café Schneider
Levinson Arcade
Tel: 061 226304
Informal street-café setting in which to enjoy coffee, breakfast or lunch. **$**
Central Café
Levinson Arcade
Tel: 061 222659
Street-café setting, ideal for breakfast, lunch and coffee. **$**
Dunes Restaurant
Kalahari Sands Hotel
Gustav Voigts Centre
Independence Avenue
Tel: 061 280011
Buffet meals with seating on terrace, overlooking Independence Avenue. **$$$**

El Cubano
48 Tal Street
Tel: 081 291 7192
Décor reminiscent of rural Havana, a great range of traditional Cuban and Creole dishes, central location, open until 2am Mon–Sat. **$$$$**
El Gaucho Argentine Grill
Sam Nujoma Drive
Tel: 061 255503
A carnivore's delight, this serves generous portions of steak and other meat dishes. **$$$**
Fürstenhof Hotel
Frans Indongo Street
Tel: 061 237380
Formal atmosphere; cuisine

includes French, German and Namibian game dishes.
$$$
Gourmet Restaurant
Kaiserkrone Centre,
off Post Street Mall
Tel: 061 232360
Longstanding purveyor of fine German-style 'Schmecker' cuisine. **$$$$**
Grand Canyon Spur
251 Independence Avenue
Tel: 061 231003
Lively atmosphere, serves American-style burger dishes. **$$**
Jenny's Place
78 Sam Nujoma Drive,
Klein Windhoek

Tel: 061 236792
Fax: 061 225408
Relaxed garden setting,
open 7 days a week for
coffee and cake and light
meals. **$**
Joe's Beerhouse
160 Nelson Mandela Drive
Tel: 061 232457
Open for lunch and dinner in
rustic setting - a good place
for a sundowner. Well-known
for its venison and meat
dishes. Booking for evening
meals usually essential at
weekends. **$–$$**
La Marmite
383 Independence Avenue

Tel: 061 240306
Centrally located and
relaxed restaurant
specialising in West African
dishes. **$$**
Luigi & The Fish
320 Sam Nujoma Drive
Tel: 061 263999
Highly regarded seafood
and pasta dishes.
Mugg & Bean
Town Square, Post Office Mall
Tel: 061 248898
Snacks, hot meals, all day
breakfast, and fresh coffee
overlooking bustling Post
Street Mall. **$**

O Portuga
Nelson Mandela Drive
Tel: 061 272900
Angolan-style Portuguese
cuisine including top-notch
seafood at reasonable
prices, reasonably centrally
located and long opening
hours (12 noon to 11pm
seven days a week). **$$**
Pizza Palace
Eros Shopping Centre
Tel: 061 239997
Affordable pizzas to eat in
or take-away. **$**
Sardinia Pizzeria & Eiscafe
47 Independence Avenue
Tel: 061 225600

Informal setting with good,
reasonably priced Italian
food. **$$**
Taal Indian Restaurant
416 Independence Avenue
Tel: 061 221958
Popular and central
restaurant serving a varied
menu of meat and
vegetarian Indian dishes.
**Yangtze Chinese
Restaurant**
351 Sam Nujoma Drive
Tel: 061 234779
Reasonably priced Chinese
fare with a very affordable
wine list. **$$**

GROOTFONTEIN, TSUMEB, OUTJO & OMARURU

Grootfontein
Le Club
Hidipo Hamutenya Street
Tel: 067 242414
Popular restaurant serving
good value breakfast, lunch
and dinner in an informal
setting. **$**

Tsumeb
Minen Hotel
Post Street
Tel: 067 221071
Fax: 067 221750
www.minenhotel.com
Email: minenmweb.com.na
Good meals served in a
garden setting. **$–$$**

Outjo
Etosha Garten Hotel
Otavi Street
Tel: 067 313130

Fax: 067 313419
The Grasdak Restaurant at
this riverside hotel serves
good value homely food. **$**
Outjo Bäkkerei
Sam Nujoma Drive
Popular lunch stop serving
tasty sandwiches and
burgers, as well as great
range of breads, pies and
confectionaries. **$**

Omaruru
Staebe Hotel
Scheepers Drive
Tel: 064 570035
Fax: 064 570455
Serves German cuisine.
$–$$

KEETMANSHOOP & LÜDERITZ

Keetmanshoop
Central Lodge
5th Avenue
Tel: 063 250586
Good, affordable à la
carte restaurant with a
budget-friendly wine list.
$$
**Lara's Restaurant,
Pub and Grill**
Warmbader Road
Tel: 063 222233
Popular drinking hole
serving good pub grub, as
well as steak, game and
other grills. **$$**
Uschi's Coffee Shop
Warmbader Road

Tel: 062 222445
Inexpensive, friendly local
institution serving good
coffee, sandwiches,
snack, pizzas and light
meals. **$**

Lüderitz
**Rotzi's Seafood
Restaurant**
Hafen Rd
Lüderitz
Tel: 063 202818
Now relocated to the new
Harbour Square Mall, with
a balcony overlooking the
harbour, this serves good
quaklity seafood as well

as various meat and
chicken dishes. Well-
priced wine list.
$$$
Barrel's Bar & Restaurant
Berg St
Lüderitz
Tel: 063 202458
Pleasant drinking hole,
set in a pre-WWI building,
the hearty dishes of the
day come with a buffet
salad and an unusually
generous serving of
veggies. Very reasonably
priced. **$$**
Diaz Coffee Shop
Bismarck Drive

Lüderitz
Tel: 063 203147
Good central location
to stop in for a light
lunch, a filling sandwich
or freshly brewed coffee.
$

PRICE CATEGORIES
Price categories are for a
meal for one including one
glass of house wine:
$ = under US$10
$$ = US$11–20
$$$ = US$21–30
$$$$ = more than US$30

SWAKOPMUND

Café Anton
Hotel Schweizerhaus
Bismarck Street
Tel: 064 402419
Open for breakfast and lunch, but best known as a coffee stop. Great sea views. **$–$$**

Hansa Hotel
3 Hendrik Witbooi Street
Tel: 064 414200
This classy century-old hotel boasts a well-established and highly regarded restaurant with an unusually formal atmosphere and fine choice of Continental dishes with the emphasis on seafood. **$$$$$**

Hotel Swakopmund and Entertainment Centre
2 Theo-Ben Gurabib Street
Tel: 064 400777
Fax: 064 400801
Buffet dinners include a variety of seafood and meat dishes. **$$–$$$**

Kücki's Pub
Moltke Street
Tel: 064 402407
Lively German style bar with very good food and friendly service. Bookings often essential. **$–$$**

Mandarin Garden Chinese Restaurant
Brücken Street
Tel: 064 402081
Decent but overpriced Chinese food. **$$$$**

Strand Hotel
Beach Front
Tel: 064 400315
Well-known for its fresh seafood cuisine. **$–$$**

The Lighthouse Pub and Restaurant
Pool Terrace, off Promenade St
Tel: 064 400894
Good views of the ocean makes the balcony here an ideal spot for a sundowner. The steakhouse-style food is also very good, and reasonably priced. Booking for indoor tables essential at weekends. **$–$$**

The Tug
Strand Road
Tel: 064 402356
Fresh seafood and beautiful ocean views in a permanently grounded tug overlooking the main beachfront. Good seafood. Booking essential. **$$–$$**

Erich's Restaurant
21 Daniel Tjongarero Street
Tel: 064 405141
Wide choice of seafood. Advance reservation recommended. **$$–$$**

PRICE CATEGORIES

Price categories are for a meal for one including one glass of house wine:
$ = under US$10
$$ = US$11–20
$$$ = US$21–30
$$$$ = more than US$30

WALVIS BAY

Crazy Mama's
Sam Nujoma St,
opposite Atlantic Hotel
Tel: 064 207364
Relaxed atmosphere and central location. There's a wide choice but the pizzas are especially good. **$$**

Raft Restaurant
Esplanade Lagoon
Tel: 064 204877
Fax: 064 202220
Under the same management as Swakopmund's Tug, this is as stylish seafood joint offering excellent views of the lagoon. Booking is essential. **$$$$**

Castle Park Restaurant
Sam Nujoma Drive
One of the few places to eat in the city centre on Sundays, this solid and reasonably priced steakhouse is notable for the surreally tasteless hunting lodge décor – capped by a stuffed baboon with bared fangs hovering over the corner of one of the tables. **$$**

A CTIVITIES

THE ARTS, FESTIVALS, NIGHTLIFE, SHOPPING AND SPORTS

THE ARTS

Art Galleries

The National Art Gallery of Namibia (www.nagn.org.na) on Robert Mugabe Street houses the most important permanent collection of local artwork, ranging from colonial era landscapes to contemporary work reflecting the modern political and social situation. Entrance is free on weekdays but a small entrance fee is payable over weekends and public holidays. Namibian works of art can be bought at several private art galleries in Windhoek and Swakopmund.

Galleries in the capital include: Artelier Kendzia, 14 Volans Street, tel: 061 225991, and the Wilderness Gallery, 19 Bülow Street, tel/fax: 061 238207. Swakopmund has a reputation as an artist's haunt and there are a surprising number of art galleries, including: Die Muschel, Hendrik Witbooi Street, tel: 064 402874; Gallerie Rapmund, Bismarck Street, tel: 064 402035; Hobby Horse, The Arcade, Hendrik Witbooi Street, tel: 064 402875.

Theatre

The National Theatre of Namibia

A variety of plays and other theatrical entertainment are staged throughout the year by the **National Theatre of Namibia** (NTN). Many of these are local productions, but international companies touring South Africa sometimes include Namibia on their itinerary. The theatre, which accommodates 470 people, is situated on the corner of Robert Mugabe Avenue and John Meinert Street. The reservations office is

open Mon–Fri, 9am–noon and 2–4pm, tel: 061 237966.

NTN's **Alte Brauerei Warehouse Theatre** in Tal Street is used mainly for drama productions and cabaret shows. As the name implies, the theatre is housed in what used to be Windhoek's brewery – hence the informal atmosphere.

Namibia School of the Arts

Several drama productions are also staged by the University of Namibia's **School of the Arts**. The School sees itself as instrumental in exploring a Namibian indigenous theatre and although its emphasis is mainly on experimental theatre and workshops, classical dramas are also staged. When in Windhoek phone the Department of Performing Arts (tel: 061 225841) for information on programmes. The entrance fee includes a small snack and a glass of wine, beer or fruit juice.

Productions by other performing arts groups are occasionally staged. Watch the press for details.

Other Entertainment

There are several choir groups in Windhoek, one of the most popular being the 30-member **Cantare Audire**. Founded in 1972, the choir won the mixed choir category at the International Eisteddfod in Wales in 1985. Cantare Audire has also toured Germany, Austria and the United States where it performed with the Mormon Tabernacle Choir. Performances are also given from time to time by Namibia's National Youth Choir.

The **College for the Arts** in Peter Müller Street has an active programme of cultural events ranging from art exhibitions to performances

by the Chamber Orchestra which consists of lecturing staff and students. Check the notice board outside the College and the press for details. Regular performances are also given by the 40-member Namibian National Symphony Orchestra.

FESTIVALS

One of Namibia's most colourful and spectacular annual events, the **Maharero Day** celebrations of the Red Flag Herero, takes place at Okahandja on the nearest weekend to 26 August. The day's activities begin on the outskirts of the town with drilling by various units of uniformed men organised along military lines. Poems in praise of their heroes' deeds and their forefathers are intermittently chanted by the men while the women ululate. Mid-morning sees the procession of men, mounted horsemen and women in their Victorian dresses begin to make its way to the graveyard of their great leaders to pay ombimbi (respect) to their ancestors.

The **Mbanderu**, or Green Flag Hereros, pay homage to their ancestral leaders on the weekend before or on 11 June each year, again in Okahandja. On this occasion the women all wear green Victorian dresses.

Another traditional Herero cultural event takes place on the weekend before 10 October when followers of the Herero chief **Zeraua**, also known as the White Flag Hereros, converge on Omaruru.

Although not comparable with the famous carnivals of Germany or Rio de Janeiro, the most important cultural event in the capital is undoubtedly WIKA – the **Windhoek Karneval**. It usually takes place around the end of April or early May, beginning with the Prinzenball on the Friday evening. Particularly popular are the Büttenabende (performances of music and sketches), one of which is held in English. Another of the week's highlights is the Maskenball which takes place on the Friday evening before the Kehraus, which marks the end of the carnival. There is also a ladies' night, a Jugend-Karneval (youth carnival) and a Kinder Karneval or kiddies' carnival.

Swakopmund has its annual carnival, KUSKA – **Kuste Karneval** or Coast Carnival– in August/September, while Otjiwarongo and Tsumeb also have an annual carnival. An Oktoberfest is also held in Windhoek, although on a far smaller scale than the one in Munich.

Film/Cinema

Cinemas in Windhoek (call 061 248980/9267 or 061 248980 for more information) and Swakopmund (tel: 064 400777) have daily screenings, including Sundays.

Windhoek also has an annual film festival, classical film festival and childrens' film festival, presented each year by the National Theatre of Namibia (NTN). These are well advertised in the local press.

NIGHTLIFE

If you're looking for swinging nightlife, you are likely to be disappointed. Very few hotels have night clubs or discos, and there is generally very little entertainment for guests. Windhoek has a few night clubs but they are not in the centre of town. Consult the newspapers and ask your hotel staff if you're keen to find out where the action is.

SHOPPING

Where to Buy

Much of the informal sector is aimed at the tourist market. In Windhoek, souvenir hunters will find rich pickings at the Post Street Mall open air market, and at the street

market on the corner of Peter Müller Street and Independence Avenue. Most curio, book and jewellery shops have the following business hours: Mon–Fri 8.30am–5pm, Sat 8am–1pm.

Supermarkets usually remain open until 6pm in the evening, while the larger ones also open for a few hours on Saturday afternoon and Sundays. Bear in mind that many shops close for lunch between 1pm and 2.30pm or 3pm, especially in the smaller towns.

What to Buy

ARTS & CRAFTS

You'll find a wide variety of curios ranging from genuine crafts made by the indigenous people of Namibia and other neighbouring countries to the usual mass-produced articles in curio shops.

Windhoek

Namibia Crafts Centre, Tal Street in the Old Breweries Building, tel: 061 242222; www.catgem.com/namibiacrafts.
African Curiotique, Gustav Voigts Centre, Independence Avenue, tel: 061 236191.
Bushman Art, 187 Independence Avenue, tel: 061 228828/229131; www.bushmanart.com.
Rogl Souvenirs, Independence Avenue tel: 061 225481.
Penduka Project Centre in Katutura is worthwhile visiting. tel: 061 257210; email: penduka@namib.com.

Swakopmund

Okaporo Curio, Sam Nujoma Avenue, tel: 064 405795.

Outjo

The Tourist Shop, Etosha Street, tel: 067 313176.

CLOTHING

Compared to European prices leather goods are very reasonable. Namibia is world-renowned for its karakul lamb pelts also known as Swakara (south-west African Karakul). The new-born lambs are skinned rather than shorn; the more expensive 'broadtail' karakul is taken from foetal lambs. Swakara coats, jackets and other garments, as well as furs, are produced in Windhoek. Leather goods manufactured from buffalo hide and ostrich skins are also available, but since Namibia's ostrich industry is still in its infancy, ostrich skin products are usually imported from South Africa.

BELOW: every year, the Red Flag Herero commemorate their fallen ancestors in this Okahandja festival

JEWELLERY

Hand-crafted Namibian jewellery is in demand. Jewellery from Zambia, Zimbabwe and Lesotho with its unmistakably African character is also a good buy and easy to find.

Windhoek

Adrian and Jack, Levinson Arcade, Independence Avenue, PO Box 1772, tel: 061 225502.
Canto Jewellers, Levinson Arcade, PO Box 1723, tel: 061 222894; email: andreas@mweb.com.na.
Herle & Herma, Sanlam Centre, Independence Avenue, PO Box 3837, tel: 061 224578; email: anherrle@iafrica.com.na.
Horst Knop Jeweller, Kaiserkrone Centre, Post Street Mall, PO Box 327, tel: 061 228657; fax: 061 249123.
W Meyer Jewellers, 264 Independence Avenue, PO Box 832, tel: 061 236100.

Swakopmund

African Art Jewellers, Hendrik Withooi Street, PO Box 1479, tel: 064 405566.

GEMSTONES

A browse around the gemshops in Namibia is worthwhile. Be warned, though: some of the gemstones which are sold locally are actually imported from South America.

Windhoek

African Gemstone Exchange, Wernhil Park, Upper Level, tel: 061 227735.
Rocks and Gems, SWABOU Building, Ground Floor, Independence Avenue, tel: 061 235560.
The House of Gems, 131 Stübel Street, tel: 061 225202.
The Jewel of Namibia, 197 Mandume Ndemufayo Street, Windhoek, tel: 061 240327.

Swakopmund

Desert Gems, 2 Hendrik Witbooi Street, tel: 064 402400.
Stonetique, 27 Dr Libertine Amuthila Street, tel: 064 405403.
The Tourmaline Shop, NDC Centre, Knobloch Street, tel: 064 462810.

If you're travelling between Swakopmund and Okahandja, the **Henckert Tourist Centre** in the main street of Karibib (tel: 064 550700) is also worth a visit.

ANTIQUES

Windhoek

Bushman Art, Independence Avenue, tel: 061 228828.

CARPETS AND RUGS

Namibia is renown for its outstanding handwoven karakul carpets.

Windhoek Environs

Ibenstein Weavers near Dordabis, tel: 062 573524
Dorka Weavers east of Windhoek, tel: 061 573581
Der Webervogel, Independence Avenue, Kalahari Sands Building, tel: 061 272586; www.webervogel.com.na

Swakopmund

Karakulia Crafts Centre, Knoblauch Street, tel: 064 461415; fax 064 461041; www.karakulia.com.na

BOOKS

Windhoek

Book Cellar, Fidel Castro Street, tel: 061 231615.
Book Den, Frans Indongo Gardens, tel: 061 239976.
Central News Agency (CNA), Gustav Voigts Centre, tel: 061 225625 and Wernhil Park, tel: 061 240369.

Swakopmund

Swakopmunder Buchhandlung, Sam Nujoma Drive, tel: 064 402613
CNA, Hendrik Witbooi Street, tel: 064 404488.

SAFARI / CAMPING EQUIPMENT

Windhoek

Cymot City, Mandune Ndemufayo Avenue, tel: 061 234131
Le Trip, Wernhil Park, tel: 061 233499.
Holtz Safariland, Gustav Voigts Centre, tel: 061 235941
Trappers Trading Co., Wernhil Park, tel: 061 223136.
Camping kit can be hired at:
Africa Safari Kit Hire
29 Gloudina Street, Ludwigsdorf, Windhoek, tel: 081 128 3025
www.askhire.com
Camping Hire Namibia
78 Malcolm Spence Street Olympia, Windhoek (or PO Box 80029), tel: 061 252995
www.orusovo.com/camphire
(See also Camping Car Rental, page 260)

Swakopmund

Safariland-Holtz, Sam Nujoma Drive, tel: 064 462387.

SAFARIS

The following local companies can arrange safaris. Others are available

through the Namibian Tourist Board. (For Tour Operators abroad see page 286; for City Tours see page 260).
Namib Wilderness Safaris
Tel: 061 274500 /239455
PO Box 6850, Windhoek
Tel: 061 225178
www.wilderness-safaris.com
Namibia Tours & Safaris
Tel: 064 406038
www.namibia-tours-safaris.com
Southern Cross Safaris
PO Box 941, Windhoek
Tel/fax: 061 251553
www.southern-cross-safaris.com
Pack Safaris
PO Box 29, Windhoek
Tel: 061 231603
www.packsafari.com
KaokoHimba Safaris
PO Box 11580, Windhoek
Tel/fax: 061 222378
www.natron.net/tour/kaoko/himbae
Small group guided travel to the Kaokoveld.
Trans Namibia Tours
P.O. Box 6746, Windhoek
Tel: 061 371100/37
www.trans-namibia-tours.com
Abenteuer Africa Safaris
PO Box 1490, Swakopmund
Tel: 064 404030
www.abenteuerafrika.com
Desert Adventure Safaris
Tel: 064-403274
Bismarck Str. 38 (or PO Box 2915) Swakopmund
www.das.com.na
Rhino tracking in association with Save the Rhino Trust, and specialist tours.

SPORTS

Hiking

Thanks to Namibia's aridity, the opportunities for backpacking and trail hiking are, understandably, limited. Nevertheless there are some fine self-catering routes, guided wilderness trails and day walks.
Situated in the desolate landscape of southern Namibia, the **Fish River Canyon Backpacking Trail** is rated as one of the five top routes in southern Africa. The 85-km (53-mile) route demands a high level of fitness and since there are no facilities whatever, backpackers must be totally self-sufficient. Groups must consist of a minimum of three people. The extreme summer temperatures and the danger of floods rule out any possibility of backpacking during the summer months and the route is open only between 1 May and 30 September.
The spectacular **Naukluft Hiking**

Trail on the edge of the Namib Desert traverses undulating plains and deep ravines, affording hikers breathtaking vistas. Hikers have an option of a four-day route covering approximately 58 km (36 miles) or an eight-day circular route covering 120 km (75 miles).

The steep ascents encountered on each day's hike and the rocky terrain underfoot are physically demanding and the trail is not recommended for beginners or the unfit. On account of the excessive summer temperatures, hiking is permitted between 1 March and 31 October only. Groups must consist of a minimum of three people and are limited to a maximum of 12. Accommodation is either in renovated farmhouses or basic stone huts without any facilities. Hikers must, therefore, supply their own equipment, including a lightweight stove since it is not permitted to light fires on the trail.

In addition to the two do-it-yourself trails managed by the Directorate of Resource Management, outdoor enthusiasts also have a choice of two guided wilderness trails. The first, the three-day **Ugab River Wilderness Trail** in the Skeleton Coast Park, gives hikers the opportunity to explore the Namib Desert on foot. Only water and firewood are supplied and hikers

must provide their own food and equipment, including backpacks and sleeping bags. Nights are spent under the clear night sky. Trails lasting four-days are conducted every second and fourth Tuesday of the month throughout the year.

The other is the **Waterberg Guided Wilderness Trail** which concentrates on the area's geology, wildlife and history. Game tracks are followed in pursuit of the rare game species inhabiting the park – white and black rhino, sable, roan and numerous other game species. Trails are conducted from a base camp into the wilderness area of the park and are tailored to suit the fitness and interests of the group. The trail camp comprises rustic huts equipped with beds and foam mattresses, cold water washing facilities and a central fireplace. Hikers need to supply their own sleeping bags, food and personal items only, since backpacks, water bottles, all cooking and eating utensils and a basic first aid kit are provided. Trails commence on the third and fourth Thursday of every month between April and November, ending early on Sunday afternoon.

All the above-mentioned trails must be pre-booked in Windhoek at **Namibia Wildlife Resorts** (*see below*) (Note: Hikers on the Fish River

Canyon Backpacking Trail, the Naukluft Hiking Trail and the Ugab River Guided Wilderness Trail must submit a medical certificate of fitness before commencing the trail.)

Those with neither the time nor the fitness for overnight hikes have a choice of several day walks. Routes include the **Waterkloof** and **Olive trails** in the Naukluft section of the Namib-Naukluft Park, the **Wag-'n-Bietjie** and **Rooibos** Trails in the Daan Viljoen Game Park and an option of two routes in the Hardap Game Reserve. There is also a short trail at Halali rest camp in the Etosha National Park, as well as several walks in the vicinity of the Bernabe de la Bat rest camp at the Waterberg Plateau Park.

For more information on any of these trails and hikes, contact: **Namibia Wildlife Resorts Ministry of Environment and Tourism (MET)** Private Bag 13378, Windhoek. Tel: 061 2857200 Fax: 061 224900 Email: reservations@nwr.com.na www.nwr.com.na or **Wanderers Club** Post Street, Windhoek PO Box 2226 Tel: 061 242069 Fax: 061 241340

BELOW: Sossusvlei scenery

Camping

Namibia offers different types of camping opportunities, from camping in the outback (self catering!) as in Kaokoland and Bushmanland, to camping at special sites and rest camps such as those in the national parks, where ablution facilities and supplies are available. *For equipment see page 277.*

Climbing

Namibia has many superb areas for mountaineering, including the Spitzkoppe, Brandberg and Erongo mountains. The Brandberg range is the most challenging: due to the extremely rugged terrain, scarcity of water and extremes of temperatures, inexperienced or unfit climbers should under no circumstances attempt extended excursions here. Careful planning is required and an ascent of Konigstein, the highest point in Namibia (2,579 metres/8,461 ft), is best accomplished with a guide who knows the area (tel: 061 234610; fax: 061 239616). Those who do succeed in overcoming these obstacles will be rewarded with magnificent views and beautiful rock paintings.

For more information, contact the **Mountain Club of Namibia** in Windhoek, tel: 061 232506; email: ehaber@polytechnic.edu.na

Bird watching

The northeastern part of the country is the best area for birding. To date, some 417 species have been recorded for the Eastern Kavango, along with 430 species for East Caprivi. The Popa Falls rest camp and the nearby Mahango Game Reserve (both of which are accessible by car) are especially popular birding localities, particularly during the summer months. Also worth visiting is the Kaudom Game Reserve, which is accessible by four-wheel-drive vehicle only.

Another good area for birding is the Etosha National Park which has recorded some 340 species. Following good summer rains the pan attracts large numbers of waterbirds, but during dry years you are unlikely to spot more than 100 species.

The Walvis Bay wetland, which is used by up to 43,000 Palaearctic migrants, is one of Africa's ten most important wetlands. It also supports 63, 60 and 42 percent of the southern African populations of chestnut-banded plovers and lesser and greater flamingos respectively. North of Walvis Bay, the gravel plains

near the coast are the habitat of 80 percent of the world's breeding population of Damara terns, while Gray's lark inhabits the gravel flats between Lüderitz and southwestern Angola.

The **Namibia Bird Club** organises regular talks and outings. For more information, PO Box 67 Windhoek, tel: 061 225372.

Fishing

The coast of Namibia has long been regarded as one of the most rewarding angling areas along the southern African coastline and from mid-January to the end of March rows of sunburnt anglers are a familiar sight along the coast. But the day's bag can often be disappointing if you're not familiar with local conditions.

The **Swakopmund Restcamp** is a popular base with anglers, as are several overnight campsites north of Swakopmund. Some basic campsites are maintained by **Namibia Wildlife Resorts** (*see page 278*) at Mile 14 (22 km north of Swakopmund), Jakkalsputz (37 miles/60 km north of Swakopmund), Mile 72 (115 km north of Swakopmund) and Mile 108 (175 km north of Swakopmund) in the National West Coast Recreation Area.

Facilities in the **Skeleton Coast Park** are limited to basic campsites at Torra Bay, which are open during the December/January period only, and fully inclusive bungalow accommodation at Terrace Bay. The most commonly caught species of fish are kabeljou (cob), steenbras, and blacktail, but galjoen is the most sought after. Barbel is commonly caught and although often discarded is particularly tasty when smoked.

What you end up with on your hook will largely depend on the bait you use. Red bait is considered a good all-purpose bait, as are fresh pilchards (unless you're after galjoen which favours white mussels and red bait). Steenbras are particularly partial to shrimps and white mussels, while kabeljou will readily take white mussels.

A permit is required to catch some species and anglers must adhere to the minimum sizes and bait collection limits. It is also important to note that it is illegal to be in possession of more than 25 galjoen at a time. For full inofrmation contact the **Ministry of Fisheries and Marine Resources** (tel: 064 405744).

A number of ski-boat owners offer deep-sea angling trips from Swakopmund. Information on these trips can be obtained from the **Namib I**

office on Sam Nujoma Drive; (tel: 064 404287/403129; www.namibi.org.na) or see www.swakop.com.

The inland dams of Namibia are well-stocked with fresh-water species. Hardap, the mecca of freshwater anglers, is stocked with carp, yellowfish, barbel, Orange River mudfish and moggel. The Von Bach Dam just outside Okahandja, is stocked with carp, kurper and black bass, while barbel and kurper can be caught in the Otjivero Dam near Gobabis. Of the five species of fish occurring in the Fish River, the exceptionally large barbel found in the pools below the weir at the **Ai-Ais Resort** are particularly sought after.

Small- and large-mouthed yellow fish, carp and blue kurper also abound in the Fish River. Licenses for freshwater angling in Namibia are obtainable at the Ai-Ais Resort, Hardap, Von Bach Recreation Resort and at Popa Falls restcamp or from the tourist information office. The minimum size limits for the most commonly caught species are as follows: kurper, 8 inches (20 cm); carp and bass, 10 inches (25 cm); yellowfish, 12 inches (30 cm) and barbel, 14 inches (35 cm). Anglers may not catch and retain more than 10 of each of these species, but there is no limit on the number of mudfish and moggel.

"Pap" (maize meal porridge), maize pips and worms are considered the best bait for carp and kurper, while artificial bait and worms are readily taken by bass. You are likely to achieve the best results with chicken liver, worms and fish heads or intestines if you're after barbel.

The Zambezi River in northeastern Namibia offers excellent opportunities for tiger fishing which is usually most rewarding between August and December. Other species you could catch include greenhead and three-spot bream, squaker, barbel and nembwe. Boats and fishing tackle can be hired at Katima Mulilo or, alternatively, you can join a Kalizo fishing safari. Anglers have a choice of weekend, week-long or tailor-made fishing safaris which are conducted from Kalizo's permanent fishing camp on the banks of the Zambezi River, 23 miles (37 km) from Katima Mulilo. Reservations can be made with **Kalizo**, PO Box 1854, Ngweze, tel: 066 252802/3; email: kalizo@mighty.co.za; www.kalizolodge.com.

Hunting

Namibia offers many opportunities for this sport. Animals that may be hunted in Namibia are the Oryx, Kudu, Springbok and Warthog. All other animals may only be hunted after you have obtained the relevant permit.

For more information contact the **Namibia Professional Hunters Association** (NAPHA), Windhoek, tel: 061 234455; www.natron.net/napha.

Golf

The Windhoek Country Club and **Rossmund Golf Club** in Swakopmund have 18-hole golf courses in good condition. Walvis Bay, Henties Bay and Tsumeb also offer the opportunity to play golf.

Horse and Camel Riding

The Namib Desert Ride (400 km / 250 miles) starts in the Khomas Hochland, west of Windhoek, at Farm Hilton. It ends at Swakopmund. More information can be obtained from **Reit Safari Horse Trails** (PO Box 20706, Windhoek; tel: 061 250764, fax: 061 256300; www.reitsafari.com). In Swakopmund, **Okakambe Trails** (tel: 064 402799; www.okakambe.iway.na) can be contacted for horse riding at the coast.

Alternatively, you can opt for a camel ride - call 064 400363.

Further information is also available from:
The Namibia Equestrian Foundation PO Box 5445, Windhoek
Tel: 061 238886.

River Rafting

River rafting can only be done in the extreme south (Orange River) and north (parts of the Kunene River). **Kunene River Lodge** (PO Box 643, Ondangwa; tel/fax: 065 274300; www.kuneneriverlodge.com). Offers river rafting as part of their services. **Felix Unite** (5th Floor, Hill House, 43 Somerset Road, Green Point, Cape Town, South Africa, 8001; tel: 0027 21 6701300; email: namholiday@felix.co.za; www.felixunite.com). Can arrange rafting on the Orange River. **Inshore Safaris** (Walvis Bay, tel 064 202609, fax: 064 202198; email: info@inshore.com.na; www.inshore.com.na) Offer boat trips, dune sports and sea kayaking.

4 x 4 Adventures

Namibia offers a wide range of 4x4 trails, including **The Isabis Trail**, west

of Windhoek (Tel/fax: 061 228839); **The Windhoek-Okahandja Trail**, north of Windhoek (tel: 061 257157); **The Uri Desert Run** (PO Box 83, Koes, tel: 0632532 – ask for 2021); and the **Naukluft Four Wheel Drive Trail** (tel: 061 256446).

Dune Boarding and Quad-biking

The coastal dunes and environment offers dune boarding and quad-biking for the adventurous visitor.
Contact:
Abenteuer Afrika, tel: 064 404030, www.abenteuerafrika.com; or
Dare Devil Adventures, Swakopmund tel/fax: 064 209532; email: daredadv@iafrica.com.na

Ballooning

You can't beat viewing the Namib from a hot-air balloon for sheer thrills. Flights are only undertaken if the weather is suitable and a minimum of two passengers is taken per flight. Contact **Camp Mwisho** on NamibRand Nature Reserve (tel: 061 230616) for more information.
Other contacts include:
Namib Sky Adventure Safaris PO Box 5197, Windhoek
Tel: 063 293233
www.balloon-safaris.com

African Adventure Balloons Swakopmund Adventure Centre

PO Box 2567, Swakopmund Tel/fax: 064 403455 www.namplaces.com/aab; Can arrange skydiving as well as quad-biking and sandboarding adventures.

Scuba Diving

Only experienced divers should attempt to dive Namibia's extraordinary subterranean lakes such as Dragon's Breath and Otjikoto Lake. For more information, contact the **Namibian Underwater Federation** (NUF), PO Box 40003, Windhoek; tel: 061 238320; fax: 061 221417; email: theo@schoemans.com.na

Sky Diving

Windhoek and Swakopmund have ideal conditions for skydiving and paragliding. More information can be obtained at tourist offices. You can also contact the **Swakopmund Adventure Centre**, Roon Strasse, Swakopmund, tel: 064 406096, email: swakopadventure@yahoo.com.

Stargazing

Namibia is one of the best locations for stargazing in the world, thanks to its non-polluted skies. There's an observatory in the Auas Mountains, south of Windhoek; tel: 061 238982 for more information.

BELOW: hot-air ballooning

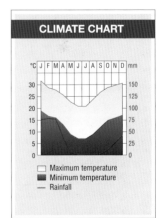

A – Z

A HANDY SUMMARY OF PRACTICAL INFORMATION, ARRANGED ALPHABETICALLY

A irports

International flights land at **Hosea Kutako International Airport** (www.airports.com.na), 45 km (28 miles) east of Windhoek. This is also the arrival and departure point for most scheduled regional and domestic flights to and from the capital. **Eros Airport** (5 km/3 miles) from the city centre serves domestic and some regional charter routes.

B udgeting for your Trip

Assuming that you have pre-booked accommodation and transport, day-to-day expenses in Namibia are low by international standards. The exchange rates are currently as follows: US$1 = N$6.5; GBP/£1 = N$11; and €1 = N$7.5. Some typical prices follow:
Car rental: from around N$250 per day (small sedan) up to N$800 (4x4).
Campsite: private sites around N$100 for two people; national

park sites charge per party, up to N$250.
Accommodation: N$300–500 (small town guesthouse); N$800–1200 (city or town hotel, or guest farm) to upwards of N$2,000 for a very smart lodge.
Petrol: N$5.50 per litre.
Restaurant meal: N$50 (à la carte main course) to 150 (set menu at lodge) excluding drinks.
Soft drink or beer: N$7–12 (pricier at some lodges).
Wine (medium quality bottle): N$35–60 white, N$50–100 red.
Airport transfer: N$100–150.
Bread loaf: N$3–4.

Business Hours

Government offices: Mon–Fri 8am–1pm and 2–5pm. Cashier's office: 8am–1pm.
Banking hours: Mon–Fri 9am–3.30pm (in Windhoek), 9am–1pm and 2–3.30pm (country towns); Sat 8.30–11am.
Shopping hours: Mon–Fri 8 or 8.30am–5 or 5.30pm, Sat 8 or 8.30am–1pm. Supermarkets are

generally open until 7pm, Saturday afternoon between 4pm–7pm, Sun 10am–1pm and 4pm–7pm.
Post offices: Mon–Fri 8.30am–4.30pm (closed 1–2pm in country towns); Sat 8.30am–noon.
Namibia Wildlife Resorts Office: Mon–Fri only, 8am–1pm and 2–5pm (reservations and cashier's office: 8am–1pm and 2–3pm).

CLIMATE CHART

Maximum temperature
Minimum temperature
Rainfall

Climate

On average, Namibians enjoy around 300 days of sunshine a year. During winter (May–September), the days are generally cloudless with clear blue skies, but in summer large masses of cloud frequently build up during the late afternoon.

The cooler **winter** months are also the best time to visit the interior. During these months, average daily maximum temperatures fluctuate between 22–27°C (71–80°F) in the south, between 20–26°C (68–80°F) in the central region, and 25–30°C (86°F) in the north. Evenings are cold, ranging between 5–10°C (42–49°F) in the south, 6–12°C (43–53°F) in the central areas and 6–10°C (42–50°F) in the north. Frost, quite severe at times, can be expected over large areas of the country, although by 11am the temperature has usually risen to 20°C (68°F). Due to the absence of rain during winter, the air is very dry.

During **summer**, average maximum temperatures in the interior generally exceed 30°C (86°F), with temperatures in excess of 35°C (95°F) not uncommon (under these conditions, a mid-afternoon siesta is advisable!). Summer temperatures are usually a few degrees lower in the central highlands, and the moderating influence of the Atlantic Ocean makes the coast a popular destination at this time – despite the fog, which often lingers from late-afternoon to mid-morning.

With an average rainfall of 270 mm (10.7 inches), Namibia can be classified as a largely arid country. More than 80 percent of Namibia's rain is recorded between November and March and occurs as thunderstorms. Rainfall increases markedly from the coast, where less than 15 mm (0.6 inches) per annum is recorded, to the interior (Windhoek has 375 mm/14.8 inches) and from less than 50 mm (10 inches) in the south to more than 500 mm (19.7 inches) in the north and northeast.

The rainfall is, however, very unpredictable, and the evaporation rate extremely high. Fortunately, the rain cools the air sufficiently to avoid the mugginess usually associated with tropical summers.

Crime and Safety

Overall, Namibia is a safe country in which to travel, but in larger towns it is advisable to take care with valuables like wallets, jewellery, and photographic equipment. Never leave a vehicle unattended with valuables inside. Vehicle theft is worsening in

Namibia and care must be taken. Common sense and precautions should ensure that your holiday is not spoiled.

Customs Regulations

Unused personal effects, sporting and recreational equipment, unexposed film, cameras and accessories may be temporarily imported duty-free.

Among items which must be declared, but will be admitted duty-free, are: 400 cigarettes, 50 cigars and 250g cigarette or pipe tobacco; 2 litres wine and 1 litre spirits; 50ml perfume and gifts with a total value not exceeding N$500.

Refundable deposits may be required for the import of radios, tape-recorders, portable television sets, musical instruments, etc. The import of agricultural or horticultural produce, or pets, is not permitted.

Disabled Travellers

Namibia is not yet very well geared up for people with disabilities, but is busy improving the situation. Prospective travellers should inquire from Namibian tour operators about their special needs.

Electricity

Electricity: 220 Volts. The supply is reliable in towns but many bush lodges use solar or generator-driven power, which may only operate during specific hours.

Embassies & Consulates

British High Commission
116 Robert Mugabe Avenue
PO Box 22202, Windhoek
Tel: 061 274800
Fax: 061 228895
Email: consular.windhoek@fco.gov.uk
www.britishhighcommission.gov.uk
Embassy of the United States of America
14 Lossen Street
Private Bag 12029, Windhoek
Tel: 061 221601
after hours tel: 081 127 4384
Fax: 061 229792
www.usembassy.namib.com
The Consulate of Canada
Suite 1118, Sanlam Centre,
Independance Avenue, Windhoek
Tel: 061 251254
Fax: 061 251 686
Email: canada@mweb.com.na
New Zealand Consulate
23 Bodin Street, Pioneers Park,
Academiam, Windhoek
Tel: 061 225 228

Fax: 061 220 346
Email ethomas@iway.na
Netherlands Embassy
2 Crohn Street
PO Box 564, Windhoek
Tel: 061 223733
Fax: 061 223732
High Commission of the Republic of South Africa
c/o Jan Jonker/Nelson Mandela RSA House, Windhoek
Tel: 061 5017111
Fax: 061 224140
High Commission of the Republic of Zimbabwe
c/o Independence Avenue/Grimm Street
PO Box 23056, Windhoek
Tel: 061 228134
Fax: 061 226859
Nationals of the following countries should contact their nearest consulate in South Africa:
Ireland (Pretoria, South Africa, tel: +27-12-342-5062)
Australia (Pretoria, South Africa, tel: +27-12 423 6000)

Emergencies

In the case a medical emergency, dial **211111** or **1199** to reach an operator who will contact an ambulance. The police countrywide emergency number is **10111**. Pharmacies can be found all over the country in major towns.

Entry Requirements
Visas and Passports

All visitors to the country need a passport valid for at least six months after the intended date of departure. Visas are also required, unless you're a national of a country with which Namibia has a reciprocal visa waiver arrangement. These countries are: all EU states (except Greece), Angola, Botswana, Canada, Iceland, Japan, Mozambique, Norway, Sweden, Finland, South Africa, Switzerland, Russia, Tanzania, the US and Zambia.

Entry permission is usually granted for one month, though this will probably be extended to cover up to three months on request. On arrival, immigration officials may ask to see your return ticket (or proof that you have the means to buy one), and you might also need to provide proof that you can support yourself financially during your stay in Namibia. This sort of request is increasingly uncommon, however, and in both instances a credit card should suffice as proof. Entry regulations are subject to change, so it is essential to consult the nearest Namibian Embassy or High Commission, or your travel agent, for the most up-to-date information before you travel.

All visitors planning to remain in Namibia longer than 3 months should apply for an extension well in advance to the Ministry of Home Affairs, Private Bag 13200, Windhoek, tel: 61 2929111. If you're already in the country, you can call personally at the ministry's office in the Cohen Building, on the corner of Kasino Street and Independence Avenue, open Mon–Fri between 8am–1pm.

Etiquette

Visitors should show respect to the local people by exercising sensitivity, tolerance and common sense. A few "don'ts" might be helpful:
• **Don't** photograph anyone without their consent, not even in the heart of the bush.
• **Don't** make a show of your wealth anywhere. The obvious temptation is to relieve you of it in one way or another.
• **Don't** break the law, of course. For tourists, the main hazards are illegal deals with foreign exchange, the traffic regulations, and the ordinances against prostitution, sexual offences and drug taking.

G ay & Lesbian Travellers

Namibian law expressly forbids discrimination on the grounds of sexual orientation and Namibia's high court ruled in 1999 that gay couples have the same rights as heterosexual couples. However, male homosexuality is illegal, based on the common law offence of committing "an unnatural sex crime". The last case was tried in the late 80s. It is not clear whether lesbian acts are an offence. Up until fairly recently, President Sam Nujoma, plus other Ministers and Deputy Ministers openly attacked homosexuals. The Rainbow Project have challenged these attacks and provide support for homosexuals in Namibia.

Contacts: **The Rainbow Project**: PO Box 26122, Windhoek, tel: 061 250 582; email: trp@iafrica.com.na. **Sister Namibia** (women's human rights organization); PO Box 40092, Windhoek, tel: 061 230 618 /061 236 371; email: sister@iafrica.com.na

H ealth & Medical Care

Health Hazards

The only mandatory health requirement for Namibia is a **yellow fever** inoculation. Prospective visitors should, however, make inquiries when booking their holidays

as the situation could change.

Malaria is endemic in the northern areas of the country, including the Etosha National Park, so prophylactics are essential. Take pills as prescribed two weeks before arrival, during the stay and for two weeks after departure. Other preventive measures include using an insect repellent, wearing long-sleeved shirts and trousers in the evening and sleeping under a mosquito net.

No preventive medication is available against **bilharzia** (schistosomiasis) which occurs in the Kavango and Caprivi. Visitors are advised to avoid drinking from and washing or swimming in standing or slow-flowing water with mariginal or submerged vegetation, since the snail hosts usually prefer these environments. If you notice blood in your urine or stool after about six weeks, consult a doctor immediately.

Cases of **tick-bite fever** are occasionally reported, but you are unlikely to suffer any adverse effects if the tick is removed within an hour. This is usually best accomplished by covering it with vaseline or whatever greasy substance is available and pulling the tick gently away from the skin. The bite should be disinfected well. If the bite becomes infected a doctor should be consulted immediately. The symptoms of tick-bit fever – including aching limbs, headache, fever and swollen glands, and – usually manifest themselves within seven to 14 days after the bite. It is advisable to seek medical advice as the disease is easily cured with antibiotics.

Aids (HIV) In common with much of sub-Saharan Africa, Namibia has a high rate of HIV infection and the risks associated with unprotected casual sex barely need stating. Should you require a blood transfusion arise, however, you can be reassured that all blood is screened for the HIV virus and hepatitis B by the Namibian Blood Transfusion Service.

High standards of **hygiene** are maintained at commercial establishments throughout the country and a meal in a restaurant is generally quite safe. However, at informal markets hygiene standards leave much to be desired and meat and fish sold there should be avoided.

Tap water in Namibia the water is potable and safe. Sometimes the taste is not that pleasant, but it's still safe to drink. It is not advisable to drink water directly from dams and rivers. Namibia is a very arid country and water is a very scarce resource and should not be wasted.

Medical Insurance

Visitors are strongly advised to obtain medical insurance in their countries of origin prior to their departure since there is no national health welfare scheme in Namibia.

Emergency Services

Emergency services throughout the country are provided by Aeromed Namibia (tel: 061 249777 or 081 124444) and MedRescue Namibia (tel: 061 230505; fax: 061 248113; email: mri@iafrica.com.na). Ambulance services are also provided by private hospitals and state hospitals. In the case a medical emergency, dial **211111** or **1199** to reach an operator who will contact an ambulance.

Medical practitioners

Medical practitioners in Windhoek are listed under "Medical" in the Namibia telephone directory, but elsewhere they are listed under their surname – usually quite easy to spot. Although there are a number of doctors in Windhoek, getting an appointment can be problematic. The Kalahari Sands and the Safari hotels in Windhoek both have a doctor on call, while a fully-trained nurse is available at Mokuti Lodge.

Pharmacies can be found all over the country in major towns.

Hospitals

There are well equipped hospitals and clinics in Windhoek and every other major town. Windhoek has four hospitals. The privately-owned **Mediclinic Windhoek** (tel: 061 222687) caters for private patients and is equipped to deal with all categories of medical care, including surgery, orthopaedics, paediatrics and intensive care. Patients are usually admitted on the recommendation of their doctor, but in the event of an emergency patients will be admitted. The **Roman Catholic Hospital** (tel: 061 237237) in the centre of town also caters for private patients, while the **Windhoek State Hospital** (tel: 061 222886) has all the necessary facilities for specialised medical care. **Rhino Park Private Hospital** (tel: 061 225434) is the latest addition to affordable medical services.

Elsewhere in the country, there are state-run hospitals in several towns, as well as a Medi-Clinic hospital in Otjiwarongo (tel: 067 303735); Swakopmund hospital (tel: 064 405731) and a Roman Catholic hospital at Usakos (tel: 064 530013).

Internet

Browsing and email facilities are available at most city hotels of any quality, but generally not in more remote game lodges and guest farms. You'll find fast and affordable internet cafés scattered around the larger towns, though the connection can be slow and pricey in smaller towns. Depending on your route through Namibia, you might want to warn business associates (or anxious relatives) that it is quite possible you will spend periods of up to a week without an opportunity to check email.

Maps

The best available is a free map compiled by the tourist board and distibuted at most local and overseas tourist information offices. It is very accurate when it comes to road conditions and distances, and is regularly updated. Good commercial maps are published by Map Studio (a subsidiary of Struik/New Holland) and by Freytag & Berndt and should be available at Stanfords in the UK.

Ordinance survey maps (1: 250 000 and 1: 50 000) can be bought at the Surveyor General's Office on Robert Mugabe Avenue in Windhoek

All roads in Namibia are numbered and clearly signed en route. (*See page 259, 'Out and About' under Getting Around*).

Media

Radio and Television

The Namibian Broadcasting Corporation (NBC) is a statutory body governed by an independent board which is appointed by the Minister of Information and Broadcasting. The NBC has seven radio services broadcasting in a total of nine languages on the FM, SW and MW bands. The National Service broadcasts in English 5–6.05pm and 9pm–6am, while the German Language Service is on the air 10.05am–5pm and 6.05–9pm.

A single-channel English-medium television service is transmitted to the main population centres in Namibia, with a 30-minute news bulletin throughout the week at 8pm, and a handful of programmes in other languages. Most city hotels (but generally not lodges in game reserves) subscribe to the South African satellite service DSTV, a package that includes several international news and sports channels.

Newspapers

Considering its small population, Namibia has a surprising number of newspapers. The emphasis is primarily on local news and, since the Constitution guarantees a free press, newspapers are often extremely critical of government policies and actions.

Three English newspapers are published in Namibia: *The Namibian* (Mon–Fri), the *Windhoek Observer* (Saturday only), and *New Era*, a government-owned newspaper published weekly by the Ministry of Information and Broadcasting and distributed countrywide. *The Namibia Economist* is a weekly business newspaper. *Die Republikein* caters for Afrikaans readers from Mon–Fri. One local German newspaper is published: *Allgemeine Zeitung* (Mon–Fri).

Since all local newspapers are printed in Windhoek, it usually takes a day or two (or even longer) before they are available elsewhere in the country. *The Namib Times* is published twice weekly in Walvis Bay and focuses primarily on news from Swakopmund and Walvis Bay. South African morning and Sunday newspapers, on the other hand, are usually obtainable in Windhoek later the same day. German newspapers available a few days after publication from the Windhoeker Buchhandlung in Independence Avenue (opposite the municipal offices) are *Frankfurter Allgemeine*, *Die Welt* and *Süddeutche Zeitung*.

A wide selection of international magazines, paperbacks and coffee table books are available from bookshops in Windhoek, Walvis Bay, Swakopmund and Lüderitz, while South African magazines are available at corner shops (known locally as cafés) and supermarkets throughout the country.

Money

The Namibian dollar (N$), divided into 100 cents, was introduced in September 1993 as a replacement for the South African rand (ZAR). However, the N$ remains pegged to the ZAR, which is also an accepted currency in Namibia and directly convertible with the Namibian dollar (approximately one-for-one). There are no restrictions on the amount of foreign currency visitors may bring into Namibia.

Most currencies are easily exchanged for Namibian dollars at banks (and, more expensively, in some hotels), with the US dollar, British pound sterling, and the euro being the most widely accepted. All towns of any substance will have at least one bank offering foreign exchange facilities. Depending on your route, however, the long distances between towns means that you may go several days at a stretch without an opportunity to change money, so plan accordingly, bearing in mind that car fuel (petrol or diesel) must always be paid for with N$ or

BELOW: Himba woman and child in the dunes.

ZAR cash throughout the country.

There are a few Bureaux de Change at Windhoek's Hosea Kutako International Airport. You should change any remaining Namibian dollars before departure, as they cannot be exchanged at any European banks, and only at very few South African banks.

Travellers' cheques and credit cards bearing the Visa or MasterCard insignia are widely accepted, but most other credit cards (including American Express) are of limited use. In most towns you can draw local currency (usually to a daily maximum of N$1,000) from at least one 24-hour ATM (auto-teller), but be wary of scams involving 'helpful' locals, especially if you draw money outside of normal banking hours in Windhoek.

For exchange rates, *see page 281, 'Budgeting for your trip'*.

P hotography

Because of the bright sunlight and glare, the best light for photography is in the early mornings and late afternoons. The vertical shadows and harsh light between around 9am and 4pm tend to produce ugly, bleached results.

If you are using film, a rating of ISO 100 will usually give good results for daytime photography. A higher ISO rating is sometimes recommended for wildlife photography, as the faster shutter speed will reduce the risk of camera shake, but (especially if you are using slide film) it is advisable to stick to less grainy 50–100 ISO film, and to use a beanbag or tripod to keep the camera steady.

If you'll be spending a lot of the time in game reserves, carry plenty of film – it's easy to go through a few rolls in one productive game drive. Instead of travelling mile after mile looking for animals, you are more likely to be successful if you wait for them at a waterhole. Pack a picnic basket and take something to read when nothing much is happening.

To protect photographic equipment against sand and fine dust, keep your equipment stowed in your camera bag when not in use. A filter is useful not only to keep dust and sand off the lens, but will also help to reduce glare. Temperatures can also become unbearably hot inside vehicles and equipment should be well insulated and never left in the sun. To prevent film spoiling it should, ideally, be kept in a cooler-box or, even better, stored in a fridge.

Namibians will usually allow you to take photos of them, but you should always ask their permission first and they will often give their consent only once you have agreed to pay them.

There are few restrictions on photography, but you are not allowed to take snaps of State House, the airport, military installations, police stations or prisons. It is also not advisable to take photographs of uniformed personnel.

Photographic shops in Windhoek and Swakopmund offer a wide variety of equipment, but you should remember to pack a spare camera battery, since these are not always available in a wide range. Several outlets in Windhoek and Swakopmund offer a same-day service for the processing of colour print film and 35mm slide film.

Postal Services

Post is relatively reliable and very inexpensive, but delivery times are slower than most Westerners are used to. Expect mail to or from Europe to take at least ten days and mail to the Americas, Asia or Australia to take considerably longer - in other words, odds are that you will arrive home before any holiday postcards you might have sent!

Public Holidays

Although most businesses are closed on public holidays, many supermarkets in Windhoek and the larger towns do open for a few hours in the morning and late afternoon. Note, too, that when the normal date for a public holiday falls on a Sunday, the Monday is often taken as a public holiday.

Namibia has twelve public holidays:

1 January: New Year's Day
21 March: Independence Day
March/April: Good Friday and Easter Monday
1 May: Workers' Day
4 May: Cassinga Day (commemorates those killed by the South African Defence Force in an attack on a SWAPO refugee camp at Cassinga in Southern Angola in 1978)
May: Ascension Day
25 May: Africa Day (anniversary of the founding of the Organisation of African Unity in 1963)
26 August: Heroes' Day (anniversary of the launch of the liberation struggle in 1966)
10 December: International Human Rights' Day (commemorates those killed resisting a forced removal from Windhoek's Old Location in 1959)
25 December: Christmas Day
26 December: Family Day

R eligious Services

There are churches in every town - lots of them - with Lutheran and Catholic churches particularly well represented. Services are held at most churches every Sunday and on all Christian holidays. Visitors will be made welcome. Other religions are poorly represented.

T elephone

Namibia has developed an excellent communications system for both domestic and international services. Direct dialling is available between most centres in the country, and a full international STD system has been introduced.

The code for overseas calls to Namibia is 264 followed by the area code and the subscriber's number. The '0' preceding the area code in the Namibian directory is omitted. The cheapest rate is from 9pm–7am Mon–Sat and 1pm Sat–7am Mon (bear in mind these discounted rates are only applicable to calls made in Namibia and to South Africa).

Mobile/Cellular phones

MTC is Namibia's main service provider; most major towns are covered, as are the main camps in Etosha National Park, but most rural parts of the country have no reception. The system used in Namibia is the GSM900 network and visitors from countries using this system can operate their cellular phones here without problems.

It's also possible to hire cellular phones in Namibia. If you want to stay in regular touch with home, or to have the facility to phone ahead to lodges and hotels, then it's worth thinking about buying a local SIM card (giving you a local number) to insert in your own phone for the duration of your stay. This takes a minute to set up, and once you have paid the starting fee of around US$15, you can send text messages very cheaply (around US$1 for four international messages). Telegrams can be sent from any post office during office hours.

Time Zones

GMT + 1hour April through August (winter) or +2 hours September through March (summer).

Tipping

The rules that you probably use at home should also apply in Namibia. For instance, it is customary to add around 10 percent to a restaurant bill unless a service charge is included (or you feel that the service was inadequate).

It is also customary to tip most service personnel including hotel porters and other attendants – though be warned that most lodgings in Namibia (even some very upmarket ones) will not offer to help guests porter their luggage to their rooms.

Tourist Information

The Namibia Tourist Board

(www.namibiatourism.com.na) is well organised and produces a wide range of useful booklets. The head office in Windhoek is represented by a kiosk on Independence Avenue next to Zoo Park, or can be contacted at tel: 061 290 6000. There are also branches in most of the larger towns in Namibia, as well as information offices in Cape Town (tel: +27 21 419 3190), Frankfurt (tel: +49 69 133 7360, email: info@namibia-tourism.com) and London (tel: +44 207 636 2924, email: info@namibiatourism.co.uk).

Tour operators

Expert Travel

Tel: +44 20 8232 9777
www.experttravel.com
The UK's leading Namibia specialist operator, twice voted 'Top Tour Operator' by readers of the travel magazine *Wanderlust*.

Rainbow Tours

Tel: +44 20 7226 1004
www.rainbowtours.co.uk
Highly regarded London-based southern Africa specialist with a strong emphasis on responsible tourism.

Naturetrek

Tel: +44 01962 733051
www.naturetrek.co.uk

Taga Safaris

P O Box 3208 Parklands,
Johannesburg, Gauteng, 2121,
South Africa
Tel: +27 11 465 5678 /467 2280
www.tagasafaris.co.za

What to Bring

Besides a camera and binoculars for viewing game, other equipment is not necessary, unless you intend to engage in some particular activity such as golf or fishing.

Film is expensive in Namibia and 35mm slide film is often not available in smaller towns, so the best advice is to bring your own. A day pack will be useful if you're keen on rambling, while a money belt (preferably one that can easily be concealed under your clothing) is handy to keep documents and cash safely on your person.

A sleeping bag is essential if you've booked for a guided wilderness trail and, in most instances, for safaris where tented accommodation is provided. A wide range of camping equipment ranging from teaspoons to tents can be hired on a daily basis (*see page 277*). This service is particularly useful since state-owned rest camps and resorts, with the exception of the luxury flats at Ai-Ais, do not supply eating or cooking utensils.

Toiletries, make-up, sunblock and insect repellent are available locally but most are imported and comparatively expensive. It is best to bring your own. Also bring enough personal prescription medicines to last throughout your stay in Namibia.

Points for electric shavers are available at major tourist hotels and most state-owned rest camps and resorts. It is nevertheless advisable to bring battery-operated or disposable razors, especially if visiting the more remote areas.

What to Wear

Dress is generally casual in Namibia and there are few restrictions on what to wear. Men are not expected to wear a jacket, collar and tie in restaurants and cocktail bars in the evening, but on the other hand, shorts, T-shirts and jeans are not allowed in the restaurants and bars of the more upmarket hotels. For a night out at the theatre, smart-casual clothes are perfectly acceptable.

Pack for a warm climate; loose-fitting cotton clothing is the most comfortable and practical. However, thanks to the cool and often windy conditions prevailing along the coast, as well as the early morning and afternoon fog which rolls off the sea, some warm clothing (a windbreaker, for example) is essential throughout the year.

In summer, lightweight dresses or skirts, shorts and short-sleeved shirts/blouses are ideal for day-time wear, while long-sleeved shirts and trousers help keep mosquitoes at bay at night. Equip yourself with a wide-brimmed sunhat or a hat with a neck flap and make sure you have a raincoat for late afternoon thunderstorms.

In winter, light to medium-weight clothing is suitable for daytime use. The variation in day and night temperatures, however, makes warm clothing essential, especially during the early mornings and late afternoons and in the central

highlands. Trousers, long-sleeved woollen shirts/blouses and a warm woollen jersey will come in handy. If you plan to explore some of Namibia's attractions on foot, take a pair of well-worn, comfortable and sturdy walking shoes with leather uppers and rubber soles.

Public nudity is not acceptable at all and is a punishable offence, bathers are expected to wear a swimming costume on the beach and at swimming pools.

If you're going on a safari, it won't be necessary to bring along everything you think you might need – several shops in Windhoek, in particular, specialise in safari clothing and outdoor wear.

Websites

www.namibiatourism.com.na – official site of the Namibian Tourist Board.
www.wheretostayonline.com – extensive accommodation listings for all around the country.
www.holidaytravel.com.na – regularly updated general travel information
www.natron.net – good source of accommodation, car rental and other contacts.
www.expertafrica.com – the UK's leading Namibia specialist tour operator.
www.namibiagetaways.com – extensive accommodation information
www.nwr.com.na – online booking for all state-owned accommodation in national parks and other reserves, including Etosha

Women Travellers

Women travellers, especially those on a guided tour, have very little to fear from Namibia on a gender-specific level. Indeed, a great many women travel there on their own without hassle. Culturally, the country is rather conservative, but in a way that is more likely to be reassuring to single women travellers than to make them feel threatened.

It would, however, pay to dress down more than you might at home, especially in urban areas, where revealing clothes may be perceived to make a statement that is not intended from your side. Some single women also like to wear a wedding ring (and to invent plausible details of a temporarily absent husband) when they travel. Otherwise, apply the same commonsense rules you might do at home - avoid travelling alone or walking in the cities after dark, nip any unwanted male attention in the bud etc.

FURTHER READING

Bird Watching

Sasol Birds of Southern Africa, by Ian. Sinclair and Phil Hockey (1997). Cape Town: Struik Publishing.
Birds of Southern Africa, by Kenneth Newman (1983). Goodwood, Cape: National Book Printers.
Roberts Birds of Southern Africa, by P. Hockey. W Dean, P. Ryan *et al* (7th edition, 2005). Cape Town: John Voelcker Bird Fund.
Southern African Birds: A Photographic Guide, by I. Sinclair & I. Davidson (1995). Cape Town: Struik Publishing.

Plants and Trees

Trees of Southern Africa by Keith Coates Palgrave (1983) Cape Town: Struik Publishing.
Grasses of South West Africa/Namibia, by M.A.N. Muller (1984). Windhoek: Directorate of Agriculture and Forestry.
Damaraland Flora – Spitzkoppe, Brandberg, Twyfelfontein, by P Craven and C. Marais (1993). Windhoek: Gamsberg.
Namib Flora – Swakopmund to the Giant Welwitschia via Goanikontes, by P. Craven & C. Marais (1986). Windhoek: Gamsberg.
Trees and Shrubs of the Etosha National Park, by C. Berry (undated). Windhoek: SWA Directorate of Nature Conservation.
Waterberg Flora – Footpaths in and around the Camp, by P. Craven & C. Marais (1989). Windhoek: Gamsberg.
Damaraland Flora by Patricia Craven & Christine Marais (1993). Windhoek: Gamsberg Macmillan Publishers.

Geology

Rocks and Minerals of Southern Africa by E.K. Macintosh. (1983) Cape Town: Struik Publishing.

People and Culture

Few People, Many Tongues by J.F. Maho (1998) Windhoek: Gamsberg Macmillan Publishers.
Peoples Of Namibia by J.S. Malan (1995) Pretoria: Henkos Publishers.

Mammals and Reptiles

Animals of Etosha, by J. Du Preez (undated). Windhoek: Shell Oil Namibia.
Snakes and other Reptiles of Southern Africa by Bill Branch. (1994) Cape Town: Struik Publishers.
Smither's Mammals of Southern Africa, edited by Peter Apps. (1996) Goodwood: Southern Book Publishers.
Kingdon Field Guide to African Mammals, by Jonathan Kingdon (1997) San Diego: Academic Press.

History and Politics

Samuel Maharero by Gerhard Pool (1991) Windhoek: Gamsberg Macmillan Publishers.
Popular Resistance and the Roots of Nationalism in Namibia by Tony Emmett (1999) Cape Town: Creda Communications.
SWA/Namibia: The Politics of Continuity and Change, by A. Du Pisani (1985), Johannesburg: Jonathan Ball.

Miscellaneous

Touring Sesriem and Sossusvlei, by P & M Bridgeford (1997) Walvis Bay: Typoprint.
Stargazing For the Novice, by Franz Conradie (1996) Pretoria: Kransberg Communication.
The Sheltering Desert by Henno Martin reprint (1999) A.D. Donker Publishers.
The Namib – Natural History of an Ancient Desert, by M.K. Seely (1987). Windhoek: Shell Oil Namibia.
Skeleton Coast, by A. Schoeman (1996). Johannesburg: Southern Publishers.

Other Insight Guides

Among Insight Guides' 500-plus books and maps covering the world, the following titles highlight destinations in this region:
Insight Guide: South Africa paints a complete portrait of this exciting destination, with insightful reporting and vibrant photography.
Insight Guide: East African Wildlife covers the flora and fauna of all the nature reserves; essential reading to complete the African safari experience.
Insight Guide: Kenya is full of information on the country's history, peoples and wildlife parks, with superb photography capturing the very essense of Africa.

In addition, **African Safari**, part of the Discovery Travel Adventures series produced by Insight Guides in association with Discovery Channel, is a sumptuously illustrated yet practical guide to animal watching in 12 African countries, including Namibia.

Feedback

We do our best to ensure the information in our books is as accurate and up-to-date as possible. The books are updated on a regular basis, using local contacts, who painstakingly add, amend and correct as required. However, some mistakes and omissions are inevitable and we are ultimately reliant on our readers to put us in the picture.

We would welcome your feedback on any details related to your experiences using the book "on the road". Maybe we recommended a hotel that you liked (or another that you didn't), or you'd like to tell us about a new attraction or any other details about the country itself. The more details you can give us (particularly with regard to addresses, e-mails and telephone numbers), the better.

We will acknowledge all contributions, and we'll offer an Insight Guide to the best letters received.

Please write to us at:
Insight Guides
PO Box 7910
London SE1 1WE
United Kingdom
Or send an e-mail to:
insight@apaguide.co.uk

ART & PHOTO CREDITS

Karl Ammann 126
Art Wolfe 5B, 186T
Daryl Balfour/Gallo Images front flap top, 117, 195, 254
Anthony Bannister/Gallo Images back flap top, 8/9, 18, 20, 22, 23, 77, 83, 101, 120, 121, 136, 141, 144/145, 146/147, 180, 182T, 185, 204T, 209, 209T, 211, 229
Anthony Bannister/NHPA 255T
Des & Jen Bartlett/Oxford Scientific Films 128/129
Heinrich van den Berg 97
Hu Berry 194
Bodo Bondzio back flap bottom, 6/7, 25, 26/27, 28, 60/61, 69, 91, 93, 106/107, 103, 143, 148/149, 154/155, 162, 164, 166/167, 175, 192T, 195T, 198T, 214, 228T, 232T, 237, 239, 241, 248, 281
Zdenka Bondzio 160, 215
Hilton Brader-Barrit 159
Gerald Cubitt front flap bottom, back cover left and spine, 2/3, 12/13, 21, 57, 65, 66, 70, 102, 104, 110, 124, 139, 140, 165, 168, 172, 177, 184, 187, 188/189, 196, 202, 220, 221, 228, 230, 231, 232, 233, 246/247, 257, 256
Steve Davey/La Belle Aurore 240T
Mark Deeble & Victoria Stone/OSF 111
Nigel Dennis/NHPA 206T, 231T
Mark Downey/Lucid Images 96, 257T, 275
Clemens Emmler/Laif/Camera Press London 253
Michael Fogden/OSF 112, 134
Willie Giess 191, 224/225
Kerstin Geier/Gallo Images 4B, 24, 39, 42, 76, 79, 205, 208, 210, 219
Johannes Haape/Südwest-Archiv 29, 30, 31, 35, 37, 38
Clem Haagner/Gallo Images 114, 122, 133L, 135, 193, 196T
Mark Hannaford/Ffotograff 242, 243
Mark Hannaford/John Warburton-Lee 244, 245

Roger de la Harpe/Gallo Images back cover centre, 4/5, 138, 239T, 255
Martin Harvey/Gallo Images 2B, 197, 207
Martin Harvey/NHPA 176T
Heiner Heine 73, 87, 127, 156, 157
Daniel Heuclin/NHPA 242T
Steve Hilton-Barber 82
Gerald Hinde/Gallo Images 14
Carol Hughes 10/11
Hein von Horsten/Gallo Images 98, 131, 212/213
Gavriel Jecan/Art Wolfe 236
B. Jones 150, 203
Julian Love/John Warburton-Lee 173, 259
Jason Laure 40, 43, 161, 163T, 221T
Francesc Muntada 219T
Alberto Nardi/NHPA 226
Panos Pictures 185T, 217T, 253T
Nigel Pavitt/John Warburton-Lee 223
Pixtal/Superstock 272
Tony Pupkewitz back cover right, 50, 51, 52, 53, 63, 68, 75, 84, 88/89, 90, 125, 276, 181, 186
Tony Pupkewitz/Rapho 19, 41, 48/49, 54, 62
Rapho 74
Johan le Roux/Gallo Images 115
Joan Ryder/Gallo Images 113
Paul van Schalkwyk 16/17, 56, 80, 86, 99, 100, 183, 199, 249
Amy Schoemann 64, 108/109, 118/119, 142, 169, 176, 217, 218, 227
B. Seely 94/95
Laura Stanton/Gallo Images 130, 198
Guy Stubbs/Independent Contributors/africanpictures.net 261B, 264, 273
Peter Tarr 34, 116, 123, 133R, 190
Steve Thomas/Panos Pictures 47
Guy Tillim/South Light 67
Trip/Eric Smith 105, 174T
Trip/M Pepperell 160T
Trip/T Bognar 172T
Günay Ulutuncok 44, 45, 46, 55, 72,

78, 163, 206, 261T
Paul van Schalkwyk 258
Ariadne van Zandbergen 1, 274, 278, 284
Dieter Vogel 36, 85, 174
Paul Weinberg/South Light 81
Marcus Wilson-Smith 178/179, 222
Winfried Wisniewski/Aamy 252
Susanna Wyatt/John Warburton-Lee 280

PICTURE SPREADS

Pages 32/33 *Top row, left to right:* Thomas Dressler/Gallo Images, Anthony Bannister/Gallo Images, Ariadne van Zandbergen. *Centre row:* E.R. Degginger, Anthony Bannister/Gallo Images. *Bottom row:* Gerald Cubitt, Anthony Bannister/Gallo Images, Jim Frazier & Mantis Wildlife Films/Oxford Scientific Films.
Pages 200/201 *Top row, left to right:* Oriol Alamany, Gerald Cubitt, Gerald Cubitt. *Centre row:* Terry Carew/Gallo Images, Michael Leach/Oxford Scientific Films. *Bottom row:* Peter Johnson/Corbis, Clem Haagner/Gallo Images
Pages 234/235 *Top row, left to right:* Art Wolfe, Roger de la Harpe/Gallo Images, Roger de la Harpe/Gallo Images, Panos Pictures. *Centre row:* Clem Haagner/Gallo Images, Gerald Cubitt. *Bottom row:* Michael Fogden/Oxford Scientific Films, Warwick Tarboton/Gallo Images, Beverly Joubert/Gallo Images.

Map Production:
Polyglott Kartographie and Laura Morris
© 2006 Apa Publications GmbH & Co.
Verlag KG (Singapore branch)

INSIGHT GUIDE
NAMIBIA

Art Director **Klaus Geisler**
Picture Research **Hilary Genin, Susannah Stone**
Cartographic Editor **Zoë Goodwin**
Production **Linton Donaldson**

INDEX

Numbers in italics refer to photographs

Looking for the best fly-drives, fly-in safaris and small-group trips to Namibia?

Then contact our serious, straight-talking Namibia team for fresh ideas and expert advice.

We are passionate about Namibia. Most of us have lived and worked there; all of us travel there regularly to keep on top of the latest developments – revisiting places that we know and discovering the best of what's new.

Let our first-hand experience guide you to make the best decisions about your own trip. None of our team work on commission; we aim simply to give you honest, independent advice.

See our websites for trip ideas and to order our comprehensive brochures. Then call us and we'll help you make the most of your trip.

www.expertafrica.com
www.wildaboutafrica.com

EXPERT AFRICA

Tel: +44 (0) 20 8232 9777
Fax: +44 (0) 20 8758 4718

Email: info@expertafrica.com

INSIGHT GUIDES

The classic series that puts you in the picture

Alaska	Dominican Rep. & Haiti	Los Angeles	Russia
Amazon Wildlife	Dublin	Madeira	St Petersburg
American Southwest	East African Wildlife	Madrid	San Francisco
Amsterdam	Eastern Europe	Malaysia	Sardinia
Argentina	Ecuador	Mallorca & Ibiza	Scandinavia
Arizona & Grand Canyon	Edinburgh	Malta	Scotland
Asia's Best Hotels & Resorts	Egypt	Mauritius Réunion	Seattle
Asia, East	England	& Seychelles	Shanghai
Asia, Southeast	Finland	Mediterranean Cruises	Sicily
Australia	Florence	Melbourne	Singapore
Austria	Florida	Mexico	South Africa
Bahamas	France	Miami	South America
Bali & Lombok	France, Southwest	Montreal	Spain
Baltic States	French Riviera	Morocco	Spain, Northern
Bangkok	Gambia & Senegal	Moscow	Spain, Southern
Barbados	Germany	Namibia	Sri Lanka
Barcelona	Glasgow	Nepal	Sweden
Beijing	Gran Canaria	Netherlands	Switzerland
Belgium	Great Britain	New England	Sydney
Belize	Great Gardens of Britain	New Mexico	Syria & Lebanon
Berlin	& Ireland	New Orleans	Taipei
Bermuda	Great Railway Journeys	New York City	Taiwan
Boston	of Europe	New York State	Tanzania & Zanzibar
Brazil	Great River Cruises:	New Zealand	Tenerife
Brittany	Europe & the Nile	Nile	Texas
Bruges, Ghent & Antwerp	Greece	Normandy	Thailand
Brussels	Greek Islands	North American &	Tokyo
Buenos Aires	Guatemala, Belize	Alaskan Cruises	Toronto
Burgundy	& Yucatán	Norway	Trinidad & Tobago
Burma (Myanmar)	Hawaii	Oman & The UAE	Tunisia
Cairo	Hong Kong	Oxford	Turkey
California	Hungary	Pacific Northwest	Tuscany
California, Southern	Iceland	Pakistan	Umbria
Canada	India	Paris	USA: The New South
Cape Town	India, South	Peru	USA: On The Road
Caribbean	Indonesia	Philadelphia	USA: Western States
Caribbean Cruises	Ireland	Philippines	US National Parks: West
Channel Islands	Israel	Poland	Utah
Chicago	Istanbul	Portugal	Venezuela
Chile	Italy	Prague	Venice
China	Italy, Northern	Provence	Vienna
Colorado	Italy, Southern	Puerto Rico	Vietnam
Continental Europe	Jamaica	Rajasthan	Wales
Corsica	Japan	Rio de Janeiro	Walt Disney World/Orlando
Costa Rica	Jerusalem	Rome	Washington, DC
Crete	Jordan		
Croatia	Kenya		
Cuba	Korea		
Cyprus	Laos & Cambodia		
Czech & Slovak Republic	Las Vegas		
Delhi, Jaipur & Agra	Lisbon		
Denmark	London		